Church Monastery
Cathedral

Herbert Whone has studied church symbolism and architecture for many years, and is author of a number of books. He is fascinated by the symbolism of church architecture, and has worked as a guide at Fountains Abbey and written a book about it.

Herbert Whone

Church Monastery Cathedral

An Illustrated Guide to Christian Symbolism

Drawings by Denys Baker
Based on sketches by the author

ELEMENT BOOKS

First published in 1977
Revised edition published in Great Britain in 1990 by
Element Books Limited
Longmead, Shaftesbury, Dorset

Cover Photograph: Michael Holford
Cover Design by Max Fairbrother
Typeset by Poole Typesetting (Wessex) Ltd, Bournemouth, Dorset
Printed and bound in Great Britain by Dotesios Ltd, Trowbridge, Wiltshire

British Library Cataloguing in Publication Data
Whone, Herbert
    Church monastery cathedral.–Rev. ed.
    1. Christian church. Symbolism
    I. Title
    246.55

ISBN 1-85230-179-1

Introduction

It occurred to me some years ago that though there is an increasing interest in ancient monuments, people visiting them do so rather aimlessly. Guide books to our churches, monasteries, and cathedrals, are often available, it is true, but the terms in them are not generally understood. The result is that though there is plenty to see, there is little conscious looking. I found my own children, for instance, constantly asking me the meanings of words and where this or that was to be found in the church. Because of this, and because of my own long-standing fascination with churches and in the subject of symbolism, I undertook to make a glossary of any word that one would be likely to find in a guide book, so that sight-seeing should be more intelligible and more enjoyable for a wide cross-section of people.

As the work took shape I saw that a particular thing had to be taken in its fullest sense. First, there was the simple etymology, the fascination of language – the interest of knowing, for instance, that 'canopy' is derived from the shape of a gnat's eye. Then there was the symbolism of a given thing, often inherent in its name, as with the word 'nave', for instance where the essential meaning is from Latin *navis*, indicating the ship or ark which is a vehicle for the spirit riding upon the waters of life. There were too the historical facts about a thing, interesting in their own right, simply because the existence of a thing now is determined by its roots in the past. And lastly there were purely architectural words needing explanation, and here I realised that it would be pointless to make an academically exhaustive research, since there are many excellent reference books in that field. The aim has been throughout to stimulate interest in the religious buildings and their contents, which are being held by ordinary people in increasing veneration, with special reference to familiar words which may have been too long taken for granted.

I have a special interest in symbolism, as the reader will discern, for, especially in dealing with something so fundamental as religion, the outer is inevitably an expression of the inner. The external temple, certainly, is the church, but the real temple is man's own inner temporal being. And there is a deep relationship between the two. We see, for instance, that oil and wax (see under'Christ' and 'candle' respectively) are constantly used in the church for providing light, and that the property of both is to make for smooth inter-action of parts, whether it be a human being or a machine. Oil is used as a lubricant externally and internally and is clearly a harmonising agent. But a thing exists on three planes, an obvious physical one, a psychological one, and a spiritual one. Oil is an actual physical embodiment of something on the middle of these planes we call love, and which on the highest plane is normally beyond our comprehension. This is especially significant since Christ's central message is one of love: indeed when a man is truly able to love his neighbour, he has finished his work on earth. The point is that such a symbol does not arbitrarily find its way into the church. Oil and wax give the light of true understanding which is from the heart; they are not abstractions merely *representing* love – they have assumed the property of love. In the same way trees and plants have assumed in their external form, inner qualities. In fact all things are merely signatures of inner properties, and such correspondences lie in the principle of the microcosm and the macrocosm, the small world and the great world, which says that man is related in every part of his being to the natural world. Thus, a symbol already lives within him, and to know its nature, he must first recognise it as part of himself.

Again in the symbol of the cross we have a simple crossing of two lines, an archetypal image of all duality – of conflict. Man's cross is his dual nature. The prison of the body is at variance with the freedom of the spirit; on the psychological level, these opposing pulls give rise to great suffering and conflict (a cross state). On the highest conceivable level there is the fundamental duality which Absolute power has made within itself, for once the act of creation has been initiated, it has divided itself into *creator* and *created*. Is there any wonder that the church building came to embody the cross, for it operates on all levels – it is the root of life. It can be seen therefore, that a symbol may be taken on many different levels – it deals indirectly with truth, as with the parables in the New Testament, and I make no claim to cover all possibilities of interpretation, merely to provide what I consider to be an essential key. I am indebted to the long and varied tradition of the inner teachings, to men who throughout the ages have seen the outer as a mere cloak on the inner, and by whose help I have been enabled to arrive at my own structure of understanding.

One thing which recurs constantly in this symbolism is a strange dialectic, for opposites live within each other. Everywhere, evil can be seen to contain the seeds of good and conversely, good has only grown out of what has been considered evil. If the reader turns to the heading 'church' he will see that the ring or circle, though essentially a symbol of eternity is also a symbol of limitation. If he turns to the heading 'cross' he will see that the transfixing is only one aspect, the negative aspect of it, and that freedom lies in that very point, the still point of the cross that most resembles death. If he turns to the heading 'five wounds', he will find that the number five is the key to man's evolution – that though there is a devilish aspect in it, there is also the potentially developed man in *control* of his five senses. The reader will find such paradoxes everywhere, as again in the word Lucifer which though being the name of the Prince of Darkness also means 'bringer of light'. This sort of paradox extends equally to Satan, Sun and Moon, Alpha and Omega, and elsewhere. Man's purpose on earth, given his condensed physical body and his hard egotism, is to re-find his will, to relate the spirit to the body so that he is no longer disturbed by such apparent dualities.

The return journey is the 'work'. The enemy is always the external form; man's inner awareness tends to seep outwards to what his eyes see so that he registers facts about a thing rather than seeking to understand what it really *is*. As soon as an image is erected, representing some aspect of Divinity, the danger is that the image rather than the power itself is worshipped. Man is so fascinated by the outer form that Christ's simple message of inner change and love was subject to the same fate. When it became dogmatised, Church-men were so spell-bound by words and by their own infallibility that they were prepared to kill in defence of them. What has this to do

with religion? Nevertheless, despite this, the church building contains the secrets of spiritual truths, and the medieval period was the apogee of their perfect embodiment,
just as the violin reached its perfected form in the 17th
century. Function and form in both cases became one, and
flowered from a germ of inner meaning. The message of the
cross is fundamentally one of pain leading to love and true
knowledge: the movement is from water to spirit, from foot
to head in the church. It is a pity that so much meaning
has been lost sight of, that now there is so much arbitrariness in the form of Non-conformist churches and their
contents. The Reformation wiped away excesses in iconography and worship of idols in order to recover the inner
man, but it also wiped away a tradition of symbolism
which is hard to recollect when we step into our ancient
monuments. It is this I have attempted to recover in this
glossary.

I also believe that there is a limit to the rational philolo-
gist's explanations of the word origins: there are basic
roots it is true, and these are stated first throughout the
book, but there is also an intuitive wisdom that gives away
secrets so to speak, through words and though they may
differ in time and place, the result is that many words
related by sound or spelling or anagram, are above man's
reason – they come like the elements of a magical musical
performance, undefinably and from a different level. Such
a state holds, I believe, in such words as 'Son', 'altar',
'Devil', 'bell', 'tree' and so on. For the etymological find-
ings, however, I am indebted largely to H. C. Wyld's
Universal Dictionary of the English Language.

For architectural and historical data I would like to
acknowledge my indebtedness to various sources, esp-
cially *Glossary of Architecture*, J. H. Parker, *History of
Architecture*, Bannister Fletcher, *English Architecture*,
T. D. Atkinson, *Monumental History of the British Church*,
J. Romilly Allen, *English Church Craftsmanship*, Fred
Crossley, and *English Monasteries*, Samuel Fox. I have
also referred to *Sacred and Legendary Art*, Jameson, *Symbolism in Christian Art*, F. E. Hulme, and *Brewer's Dictionary of Phrase and Fable*. As I wrote the book, I found
myself tending to be generous in the scope of the words
considered, so that some may not appear to have much to
do with either the outside or the inside of the visible
church, nor even a museum attached to it. Such are 'sacra-

ment' and 'ascension'. Where this occurs I felt that inclusion would add to the general understanding of the Church and the church building. Ideally perhaps, the whole would have been better written free from the restriction of the form of a glossary, but I decided finally that this was the only satisfactory way of presenting the material. My aim, as I have said, has been to stimulate interest on many levels, and in different people, and I can not hope to have the approval of all. But if the improvement in the once half-hearted wanderings of my own family, and the renewed interest of some of my friends are anything to go by, my aim will have been fulfilled.

Harrogate, 1976

HERBERT WHONE

Author's Note to Second Impression

I welcome the re-issue of this book, written fifteen years ago. Since then, however, having given more attention to monasticism – in fact, having compiled a book on Fountains Abbey* – I have felt it necessary to make some additions to the original. In a general way, too, I have needed to clarify some ideas and change words here and there, for the simple reason that clarification is a process continually at work in thinking human beings, authors not excluded.

The same objects hold in the book: they are the general one of provoking thought about terms and objects taken for granted, and the more specific one of getting behind the external forms to the inner meanings.

Harrogate, 1990

HERBERT WHONE

*Fountains Abbey (photographs, literature and documents), Smith Settle, Otley Mills, Otley, W. Yorks.

Note on Symbolism

The following entries deal with symbolism, and the reader may benefit from reading them separately so as to establish a core of inner meaning:

Adam and Eve	Evangelist	Organ
Alpha and Omega	Fish	Pall
Altar	Five wounds	Passion
Amen	Font	Pillar
Apocalypse	Freemason	Right and Left
Ascension	Garden of Eden	Rood
Ass	Glory	Rose
Baptistery	Halo	Rose-window
Bell	Icon	Sacrament
Blessing	Jesse tree	Satan
Book	Key	Sacrarium
Candle	Lamb	Serpent
Chalice	Last Judgement	Spire
Christ	Last Supper	Stoup
Church	Lectern	Sun and Moon
Crucifixion	Lily	Swan
Cock	Lucifer	Swastika
Colour	Lion	Temple
Column	Magi	Tomb
Cross	Man	Transept
Crozier	Mandorla	Trinity
Devil	Mason	Trumpet
Disciple	Mass	Tympanum
Doom	Maze	Unicorn
Dove	Monogram	West end
Dragon	Nativity	Wine
Eagle	Nave	Virgin Mary
East end	Noah	Yew

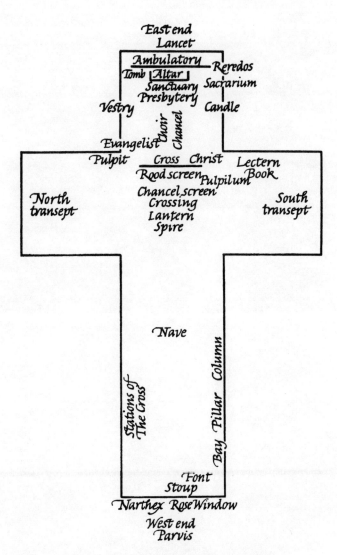

The church as a journey from West to East

A

ABACUS

Latin, from Greek *abakos*, originally a square board covered with sand upon which figures could be traced. Architecturally, it denotes a stone, originally of similar shape, forming the topmost division of the capital of a classical column, and having the distinguishing features of a particular order.

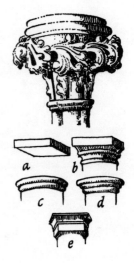

In church architecture, Saxon, Norman, and subsequent styles have a distinctive form of abacus which often indicates age since it may be the only moulded part of the column. The diagrams give a general indication of the changes. Saxon (a) is generally flat and square: Norman (b) was at first square but later had a chamfered top and moulding: Early English (c) was generally circular and at times octagonal: Decorated (d) was either circular or octagonal, or polygonal: Perpendicular (e) was generally polygonal.

ABBEY

Low Latin *abbatio*, 'abbey'. Greek through Syriac *abba*, 'father'. The abbey is the group of buildings, or it is the group of men or women inhabiting those buildings, and named after the 'father' or head of the establishment, as a priory is named after the prior (q.v.) An abbot is equally head of a monastery as of an abbey, though 'abbey' suggests the communal life rather than the isolation of monastic life.

ABBOT

Ecclesiastical Latin *abbas*, 'abbot, Syriac *abba* 'father'. Thus the meaning of the father or head of an abbey or monastery.

1

ACANTHUS

Latin, from Greek *akanthos*, from *akis*, 'thorn'. A type of thorn tree, the leaves of which were used as a model for decorating the capitals of Corinthian columns. The stylised form of the leaf is found wherever the classical influence prevails. (See 'Corinthian'.)

ADAM AND EVE

Adam is from Hebrew *Adama*, 'red' or 'red earth', referring to man's physical existence, and to the blood which is life to his body, and Eve is from Hebrew *Chavva*, 'mother of life'. The names are self-explanatory in the myth.

Representations of Adam and Eve show them as in the Genesis story, naked beneath the Tree of Knowledge, the serpent beguiling Eve, and Eve handing Adam an apple from that tree. The myth refers to the fall of Adam (that is, Man as a race of androgynous spiritual beings) to a life on the level of the senses with its attendant sexual split. The original bi-sexuality is suggested in the name itself, for in this interpretation 'Adam' can be seen to be composed of male and female elements, 'da' and 'ma'. The statement in Genesis is that Adam disobeyed God and ate of the Tree of Knowledge – he chose to experience the sensory world. The serpent symbolises the pride that lies at the root of his wilful separation from the Will of God, and the forked tongue symbolises the duality inherent in the earth life to which he has fallen. Both are naked, in the sense that the fall exposes Man to himself – to what he has done.

The serpent (his self-will) causes his female side, Intuition, or all-knowing Wisdom, to be led into temptation, into time, where it becomes a separate physical being. The inertias of the physical world and the need to re-find his soul in the woman, now dominate his life: in representations of the story, this is indicated by Eve being shown on Adam's left side. (See 'right and left').

The apple, which when cut in two reveals a five-pointed star denoting the five senses, as does the symbol of the fig-leaf in the myth, is the world itself, dependent upon physical generation; it is the fruit of the tree of error, and lodges between his head (the true source of power) and his fallen feelings and lower energies, in the form of the 'Adam's apple'. There is a hard lump here scarcely noticeable in woman – the price of eating is division and a blockage to

section of an

apple

2

his power. Eve has fulfilled her function – life is perpetuated through propagation, and man has to rediscover his will, through material experience, and by constant reference to Eve as his externalised soul. He can do this only by seeing through the illusion proffered by the serpent, his pride, his ego that has lead him into error, and by giving back supremacy to his female side, pure Wisdom, so that once again he may be made whole – male-female. A woman, who is the container of ineffable mysteries, has conversely to redeem man's loss and to forgive and embrace his vulnerability to her negative face. Her aim equally is to be made whole. (See 'virgin'.)

AGNUS DEI

Latin, literally 'the Lamb of God', referring to Christ in his sacrificial role, and giving rise to the image of a lamb bearing a flag with a cross upon it. More specifically it denotes a small cake of wax stamped with this image and given to the faithful, a papal device of distributing the Paschal candle on the First Sunday after Easter. (See under 'lamb' for its symbolic aspects.)

AISLE

Latin *ala*, 'wing'. (The interposed 's' is due to the diminutive of *ala, ascella*.) The aisles in a church are the side divisions parallel to the nave, and separated from it by the pillars. The image of the two wings at the side of the bird is an obvious one, and the connection is perhaps better seen in the modern French *aile*, 'wing'.

Often aisles were built on either side of the nave in a church of simple design to give more space. When a single aisle was added it was on the north side because of the custom of burial on the south side.

ALABASTER

Greek *alabastros*, from the name of a town Alabastron in Egypt where the material was found and used. This stone, soft, white and semi-transparent, was mined and worked in Britain at Chellerston and Tutbury in the Nottingham area during the 14th century and became fashionable in the making of tombs and panels, finely carved and coloured with religious subjects. Reredos and retables (see under their respective headings) were also carved of alabaster with figures derived from the mystery plays of the period. The material was easily destructible and suffered much at the suppression of the monasteries.

ALB

Latin *albus*, 'white': and also seen in Old High German in *albiz*, 'swan', or 'white bird'. The alb is the whole girdled vestment worn by the priest during the celebration of the mass, white in colour as a symbol of the purity of heart necessary in the communicant.

ALMONRY

Old English *aelmysse*, through Latin, through Greek *eleēmosunē*, meaning 'mercy, pity'. The almonry is the room in a monastic establishment used for the dispensing of food to the poor on certain days. It was a haven for those in distress and its presence kept alive the image of the connection between religion and charity. The room was located near the church or near the gate-house. The official dispenser of the alms was the 'almoner'.

ALMS-BOX

Old English *aelmysse*, through Latin and Greek (see 'almonry'). Alms-boxes, large oak boxes used for receiving offerings for the needy, are preserved in different parts of churches and cathedrals. (See 'chest'.)

ALPHA AND OMEGA

A and Ω are the capitals of the first and last letters in the Greek alphabet: they are constantly found in Church iconography with the meaning of the 'beginning and the end', as is also the Latin form *Initium et Finis*. They signify the beginning and end of the cosmic creative process in Revelation:

I am Alpha and Omega, the beginning and the ending, saith the Lord, which is, and which was, and which is to come, the Almighty.

The glyph A signifies the power of God as an initiating creative force, and can be seen either as a plough, the dividing compass, or the triangle of the Trinity raying downwards. In Ω lies the potential fulfilment of the teleological process. The word *omega* (o-mega) is literally the

4

great 'o', sounded as in English 'tone', to distinguish it from the small *omikron* (o-mikron), the short 'o' as in 'box'.

The small 'o', *omikron*, clearly suggests finite encapsulation both in its form and its sound, whereas the great 'o', with its open ends and continuity in its sound, suggests the ultimate freedom from all limitation.

The miniscule form of omega, ω, often replaces the capital but is associated more with the Eastern Church. Its three co-joined arms suggest the final unifying in Man of the three aspects of the Trinity.

Aω

ALTAR

Low Latin *altar, altare*, 'altar' – originally a block of stone or wood upon which sacrifices by burning were offered.

The word was retained to denote the Christian altar, where there was a change of ritual if not of essential function. The ancient sacrifice of animals, representing the death of their psychological counterparts in man, gave way finally to a re-enactment of Christ's sacrificial death. Not only was this death an act of redemption on mankind's behalf, but it also pointed to the need for each man to make his own sacrifice, to renounce his lower self, his animal nature. In the format of the medieval church, Christ's sacrifice is indicated at the crossing, the area before the entry to the chancel where in pre-Reformation times the rood stood on the rood-loft (q.v.) or beam. This crucifix showed Christ suffering as man, and in those times dominated the approach to the eastern end of the church.

Properly a communicant is not ready for entry behind the chancel without some stage in the path of sacrifice having been realised, for the altar is the place where the actual fruit of Christ's sacrifice, his 'body' and 'blood' are made available. Here, the sacrifice of Christ and the final surrender of a man's self-will to the Higher Will in him meet in one act. ('Sacrifice' is from Latin *sacer*, 'holy' and *facere*, 'to make'. 'Holy' and 'whole' come from the same Gothic root and in both words the meaning of healing is implied.)

Words connected with altar all suggest growth through change Latin *altus* means 'high', so 'altar' is literally a raised structure; but it originally meant 'fully grown'. The English word 'alter', from Latin *alterare*, 'to change', which is from Latin *alter*, 'the other of two', suggests that sacrifice is in fact a point of decision – in terms of the altar, a final break from the bonds of self.

In the early Christian church, altars were erected over places where relics of saints were kept, and when stone altars came to be used, the relics of saints were enclosed in them. The idea was thus committed to form that a tomb is really the place of a new life: it is for this reason that the form of the altar is adopted in the tombs commonly found in graveyards of churches. Life has been yielded up, but the tomb or the altar is the place of transformation. Stone altars, common before the Reformation, gave way to the Holy Table, wooden and moveable if necessary, for the celebration of the Mass. Only a few original stone altars remain in this country. (See 'mensa'.)

ALTAR RAILS

There were no altar rails in England before the Reformation. The altar was at that time fenced off at the instruction of Laud to prevent its profanation. This was not a convenience for the communicants as now; in fact kneeling only became customary in the 13th century and before that there was an unbroken tradition of standing.

AMBULATORY

Latin *ambulare*, 'to walk'. A covered way in which to walk, as in a cloister, but especially denoting the area round the back of the high altar which is used as a processional way.

AMEN

Hebrew *amen*, 'so be it' or 'it is established', where the original Hebrew root means 'strength, stability'. As a termination to prayer currently and anciently used in Christianity, amen is a 'word of power', the key to which lies in the letters 'A' 'M' 'N'. The Hindu version is AUM, but in both cases what is indicated is a fundamental division in the Godhead: male – Father, initiator of action, in the letter A; and female – Mother, receptive substance, in the letter M. The same elements are seen in the English word 'am': 'I am' indicates the living spirit in a substantial vehicle.

The link holding the opposites together is in the letter N. With A as an open unconditioned sound, M by contrast,

6

is vibrational activity trapped within substance. There would be total closure in M were it not for the escape route sound takes through the nose, that is through the third letter N. N is implicit in M and has the meaning of 'no-saying' to confinement, through the issuing forth of life and its manifold forms. Thus, whilst on the mundane level, it is a sound of negation, being locked in the head, on a higher level it completes the Trinity, which expresses the whole nature of existence.

The same principle is found in ancient Egypt, where the name of the supreme creator is Amen or Amon. Here the root of the word means 'invisible' with reference to the secret power behind all manifestation. In the English language, the anagram 'name' shows that all things are within man's comprehension, and his own name MAN indicates that all things lie in his being.

ANDREW'S CROSS or CROSS DECUSSATA

The cross with the arms intersecting diagonally is especially associated with St. Andrew. In the form of the Greek letter chi, X, used in the monogram of Christ, it had already been in existence for thousands of years, representing the spinning movement of the universe. It's connection with Andrew may be through the derivation of the name itself – Greek *andros*, 'man' – in so far as man is integral to the whole scheme of creation from the first move or turn. On another level, the story is that St. Andrew requested to be crucified on a cross of a form other than that associated with Christ, out of humility.

The cross is also called the 'cross decussata', from the Latin name for the numeral ten (X), from *decem*, 'ten'. Here the cross signifies all opposites embraced, for ten is the number of ordinal perfection, seen in the number 10, male and female, spirit and matter in one: the line of initiative and circle of receptivity are to be found everywhere in mythology and life.

Heraldically, such a cross is a 'saltire cross', from Latin *saltarum*, 'stile', and *saltatorium*, 'stirrup', both from *saltare*, 'to leap'. The term is applied generally when two diagonal bands (called bends) cross on a shield.

ANGEL

Latin *angelus*, from Greek *angelos*, 'a messenger': cognate with a Sanskrit word *angiras* meaning 'divine being'.

The function of the divine beings known as angels is that of messenger between God and man: in one sense they are superior to man since they are not bound by the finite world, and in another sense man is above the angels because his possibility is a growing towards his own divine nature, whereas angels are limited to their specific role.

According to early tradition (established by Dionysus the Pseudo Areopagite), there are nine orders of angels mediating between God and man – nine because of the squaring of the Trinity, representing the unfolding of man's powers in the three worlds, mind, heart and body, which can also be seen as spirit, soul and body.

For man this division denotes a spirit which is free, a body bound to earth laws, and a unique soul, which is the linking factor. In this life of the soul is a constant searching for relationship between spirit and body. There is a constant relationship between spirit and body, and a searching in his heart for values.

Correspondingly the angels have three major groupings, CHERUBIM, SERAPHIM and THRONES, relating to spirit; DOMINIONS, AUTHORITIES and POWERS relating to the soul; and PRINCIPALITIES, ARCHANGELS and ANGELS, relating to the level of the earth.

In art, Cherubims (divine knowledge) – Hebrew 'those grasped or held fast' – are depicted with heads full of eyes and two wings; Seraphims (divine love) – Hebrew 'those burning' – have the whole body and six wings, two above the face, two over the feet and two for flying. They are nearest to God and are aflame with love; Thrones (divine authority) – Greek *thronos* 'seat, throne' – have double wings and are portrayed supporting the throne of the Almighty and have heads fashioned according to the symbolical animals of the four fixed signs of the zodiac, which are also the symbols of the four Evangelists (q.v.). Thrones are also depicted as wheels without wings. All these, Cherubim, Seraphim and Thrones, have eyes both before and behind.

In the second group there is little attempt at defining exact function and portrayal in art. They are not easily represented because they stand for the Holy Spirit and the heart, but when they are, they have green vestments and hold a stave and a seal called the 'Seal of God'.

In the third group, Principalities control the laws governing the evolution of the earth; Archangels (Michael – judgement, Gabriel – mercy, Raphael – healing, and Uriel – prophecy are the chief ones) serve man as a whole; and Angels guide and protect men on the individual level. This third group is shown in art holding worldly weapons, musical instruments or tools of crafts, affirming their work of relating man to God on the earth level.

APOCALYPSE or REVELATION

Greek *apokaluptein*, 'to uncover, disclose', Latin *revelare*, from *re* and *velum* (veil), thus 'un-veiling'. The Apocalypse of John the Divine differs from the work of the four Evangelists whose aim was to establish the message of Christ on earth in such a way that it could be understood by men on all levels. Here on the contrary, by the uncovering of the veils of normal space-time awareness, John was granted a vision of spiritual realities so complex in symbolism as to protect them from profanation by literal understanding. Many of the archetypal images in the vision are found in iconography, especially the seven spirits before the throne, the Lamb, twenty-four elders, the dragon with the seven horns, the seven trumpets and the New Jerusalem.

In essence, the uncovering or unveiling is the story of the individual soul's spiritual awakening, the opening of seals of power within, leading to a complete perfecting and self-realisation. That the process is a complete one is signified by the frequent use of the number 7 – e.g., seven seals, seven thunders, seven churches, in addition to the ones already given. The individual soul, as in the ancient initiation ceremonies, is the hero (in this instance in the guise of the lamb or the rider of the white horse), victor over all the enemies within him, and these enemies are all the animal qualities epitomised in the 'dragon' and the 'beast' which have evolved through the aeons of time and oppose his inner growth. As in all myth, fairy-story and dream, in the astral world and in ceremonies of initiation, all the images and characters depicted are parts of the hero's own being. Inversion of power is a common theme: the Lamb has become the beast; the bride, the harlot; and the New Jerusalem, Babylon. The process of regeneration is one of reversal and re-righting.

The four beasts around the throne are the same beasts associated with the Evangelists (q.v.). The four horsemen are controllers or reins of the types of energy related to those beasts and their respective elements. The white horse signifies equilibrated power. The seven churches symbolise the seven-fold division in the vast pattern of man's history, and, equally, subtle centres of power along the spine (*chakras*) found in ancient Yogic systems; in both these senses, the churches can be seen as seven seals that one by one have to be unlocked. Such a complex symbolism, full of number puzzles, is like the parables, capable of interpretation on many levels and need special study. (See 'lamb' and 'seven lamps'.)

APOSTLE

Greek *apostolos*, *apo*, 'away', and *stellein*, 'to send' – thus 'one sent forth, a messenger'. In the Christian reference, an apostle is one sent out to spread the message of the Gospel. Christ's twelve chosen disciples were the apostles deputed to do different areas of work in the world after his death, the twelve being associated with the 12 types in the signs of the zodiac. Most suffered martyrdom. In fact, fourteen are customarily credited, twelve being the original disciples, with two additions, Matthias (chosen by lot to fill the place of Judas in the twelve) and Paul. The significance of the number fourteen lies in the fact that the fourteenth letter of the Hebrew alphabet signifies a fish; Christ was known as the Great Fish and much of early Christian symbolism is related to the Piscean era. (See 'fish' and 'piscina'.)

The fourteen disciples were sent into the deep sea of the

10

material world to rescue souls to catch them for Christ. In church and cathedral they are profusely represented and are recognisable by their particular attributes or the circumstances of their martyrdom. The labels or scrolls the apostles carry contain the articles of one version of the Apostles' Creed to which each is said to have made his contribution before disbanding. (This tradition however only arose at the end of the 4th century.) The present form of the Creed was formulated in the 8th century but came directly from even earlier traditions. Paul and Judas are omitted, reverting back to the twelve. It is interesting that in emulation of the twelve disciples with Christ at their head, it became customary, in medieval times, for monasteries, when forming daughter houses, to send out twelve pioneer monks with an abbot at their head. Even as early as the 6th Century, Columba set out with twelve disciples to do his missionary work in Scotland. The following are some of the characterising features of the apostles in iconography: the appropriate article of an early form of the Creed is also given, together with the currently used English version.

ST. PETER: traditionally has white hair and a short white beard, with a broad face. He carries a bunch of keys because Christ gave him 'the keys to the kingdom of heaven'. Sometimes he is seen with a cock because of his denial of Christ, and sometimes with a chain which refers to the story of his imprisonment.
CREDO IN UNUM DEUM PATREM OMNIPOTENTEM CREATOREM COELI ET TERRAE (I believe in one God the Father Almighty, Maker of heaven and earth).

ST. ANDREW: is traditionally aged with white hair and beard. He carries the 'turning' or 'saltire' cross on which he was crucified (see 'Andrew's Cross').
ET IN JESUM CHRISTUM FILIUM EIUS UNICUM, DOMINUM NOSTRUM (And in one Lord Jesus Christ, the only-begotten Son of God).

ST. JAMES (MAJOR): is traditionally in mid-age with short hair and beard. He is the patron saint of pilgrims and is shown with a scallop shell, a pilgrim's staff, and a gourd.
QUI CONCEPTUS EST DE SPIRITU SANCTO NATUS EX MARIA VIRGINE (And was incarnate by the Holy Ghost of the Virgin Mary).

11

ST JOHN: is traditionally young and without beard. John is shown with a cup which has a winged serpent flying out of it, with reference to the story that when John was challenged to drink poison he made the sign of the cross and Satan flew out of the cup in the form of a serpent. John then drank the contents of the cup unharmed. (See the similarity of this story with the role of John, and his usual symbol of the eagle, discussed under 'Evangelists'.)

PASSUS SUB PONTIO PILATE, CRUCIFIXUS, MORTUUS ET SEPULTUS. (And was crucified also for us under Pontius Pilate. He suffered and was buried.)

ST PHILIP: is traditionally young with or without beard. He carries a long staff topped by a cross because he died hanging from a long pillar: sometimes he carries a basket of loaves.

DESCENDIT AD INFERNOS, TERTIA DIE RESURREXIT A MORTUIS (He descended into hell and the third day he rose again according to the Scriptures.)

ST. JAMES (MINOR) OR JAMES (THE LESS): is traditionally in mid-age with short hair and beard and resembling Christ due to the supposed blood relationship between them. Note the important article of the Creed afforded to him.

ASCENDIT AD CAELOS, SEDET AD DEXTERAM DEI PATRIS OMNIPOTENTIS (And ascended into heaven, and sitteth at the right hand of the Father).

ST. THOMAS: is traditionally young and without beard. He carries a builder's rule or sometimes the lance by which he was killed.

INDE VENTURUS EST JUDICARE VIVOS ET MORTUOS (And he shall come again with glory to judge both the quick and the dead).

ST. BARTHOLOMEW: carries a knife because he was flayed by one.

CREDO IN SPIRITUM SANCTUM (I believe in the Holy Ghost).

ST. MATTHEW: is traditionally an old man with a white beard. He is represented with a hatchet by which he was killed and often carries a money-bag indicating his trade as tax-collector. For an account of his role and symbol as evangelist see under 'Evangelist'.

SANCTAM ECCLESIAM CATHOLICAM; SANCTORUM COMMUN-
IONEM (And I believe one Catholic and Apostolic Church).

ST. SIMON: is traditionally old and with white beard. He
carries the saw by which he was sawn to death.
REMISSIONEM PECCATORUM (I acknowledge one Baptism
for the remission of sins).

ST. MATTHIAS: is traditionally old and with white beard.
He carries a battle-axe because he was beheaded by one.
CARNIS RESURRECTIONE (And I look for the Resurrection
of the dead).

ST. THADDEUS (JUDE): is traditionally old with white
beard. He is shown with the club by which he was killed,
and sometimes carries a boat.
ET VITAM AETERNAM (And the life of the world to come).

JUDAS ISCARIOT: is represented with an ill-favoured
countenance. He carries a bag because he was treasurer,
and betrayer of spiritual values for money.

ST. PAUL: traditionally has a high forehead, long oval
face and flowing beard. He carries a scroll denoting his
epistles and a sword, because he was a fighter for the cause
and died by the sword.

APSE

Latin *apsis*, from Greek *apsis*, 'arch' or 'vault'. Thus a
semicircular or often polygonal projection at the eastern
end of a church having a vaulted roof. The apse originated
in the early churches that derived from the basilica, and
remained more of a continental feature. Certain early
English, Saxon and Norman churches have the apsidal
shape at the eastern end – the crypts especially have
retained this form under a changing superstructure. The
eastern ends of English Gothic cathedrals are almost all
square in shape.

ARCADE

Medieval Latin *arcata*, Latin *arcus*, 'bow'. A series of
arches supported on columns, as in a cloister or ambulatory, but the term is more generally used to denote those
found as decoration on the inside or outside of walls, and

filled in with masonry. In the latter sense it is called 'blind arcading'.

ARCHANGELS

Greek *arkhos*, 'leader' and *arkhé*, 'beginning' (for 'angel', see under that heading). There are seven principal angels or archetypal spiritual beings whose habitation, according to Christian dogma, is before the throne of God, but of these only four are customarily singled out. (The significance of the number four is discussed under 'Evangelists'.) Their function is essentially mediation between the higher planes and man in his finite vehicle.

MICHAEL (Hebrew 'who is like unto the Lord') is found in the Bible narrative, and in iconography does battle with forces of evil. He is a patron of Christian warriors and is the defender of causes, so that in effigies of him he is clad in armour. As such he is a popular saint, as the immense number of churches in England and Wales dedicated to him show. On an inner level he could be seen as the real Self delivering the soul from the domination of the pseudo-self. He is also judge of the dead and is often represented with scales in which the soul of a man is weighed for judgement.

GABRIEL (Hebrew 'God is mighty') is the archangel of annunciation. He announces the future birth of John the Baptist to Zacharias, and of Christ to Mary. He is a messenger from higher planes to the earth level of a new inner birth of the spirit. In the Annunciation to the Virgin Mary he is represented as bearing a lily or an iris, the symbol of union between heaven and earth.

RAPHAEL (Hebrew 'healing of the Lord') is the dispenser of divine mercy to the sick, as in the story of Tobit. Raphael forewarned Adam of his situation. He is shown carrying a pilgrim's staff or a fish, a reference to the Tobit story.

URIEL (Hebrew 'flame of God') is an agent of prophecy in that he reveals the Will of God to man. He is seen with an open book or a spear.

ARCHITRAVE

Italian, from Greek *arkhos*, 'leader, chief', and Latin *trabs*, 'a beam'. Thus, chief beam. The lowest part of the entablature (q.v.) in classical architecture resting immediately upon the column.

ARMARIUM

Latin *armarium*, 'cupboard' (*arma*, 'arms, tools, implements'). Thus, a large cupboard in a cloister, or sometimes between the south door and the door of the chapter house, used for keeping books and materials for copying and illuminating. In a monastery, the brother in charge of the library was the 'armarius'.

ASCENSION

Latin *scandere*, 'to climb' – with *ad* we get *ascendere* and with *de, descendere*. The fact that *scandere* is cognate with Greek *skandalon*, meaning 'trap' or 'stumbling block', suggests the condition of any attempted ascent. In iconography, the Ascension is customarily represented by Christ ascending into clouds with only the lower part of the body or the feet showing, and the disciples looking up in awe. The looking up is the reverse image of the adoration of the shepherds looking down to the new-born child on the earth. The two images are the beginning and the end of empirical evidence of Christ on earth.

The Ascension, however, is followed by a final momentous occurrence – the descent of the Holy Spirit upon the apostles, described in Acts as tongues of flame, and so represented in art, showing that the Christ power was not lost by his disappearance from earth, but was a gift to the earth for all time – a special impulse in the evolution of Man.

The three key points of Christ's life, as represented in the Church festivals, may be seen in the three key places in the church building. (See 'crucifixion' and 'church'). The birth (Christmas), at the time of the winter solstice, when death appears to reign and the sun may not appear again, may be seen as being at the foot of the church. It is here that baptism symbolically enacts the eternal possibility of re-birth of the light of the spirit.

The Crucifixion and Resurrection (Easter), the time of the triumph over death, may be seen as being at the crossing, where the rood shows Christ as man, suffering on the cross. The actual point of the crossing, that is the crossing of the forces of time and eternity, is one of anguish, and yet of potential enlightenment. (See 'crossing').

The Ascension (Whitsuntide or Pentecost), coming after a period of deprivation, demonstrates the ultimate release

WHIT
Ascension

EASTER
Resurrection
Crucifixion

CHRISTMAS
Birth

from materiality and affirms an at-oneness with Divine Intelligence: it may be seen as belonging to the sanctuary. It is here, at the altar, that the comm-union of all in Christ is re-enacted. The 'wit' in Whitsuntide, as in 'white', is the pure wit of Higher Intelligence. At this level, the Holy Spirit uses a man as its instrument – he knows what he has to do without intrusion from his lower self. Pre-Christian initiations, or mysteries as they were called, effected such a release and ascent, but it was the birth of Christ that heralded a new era in which each man was to be responsible for his own birth, death, and transfiguration and in which his 'I' consciousness brought about his own release.

The earlier name 'Pentecost' means 'the fiftieth day' – that is, the fiftieth day following the Sabbath after the Jewish Passover: but the term was replaced by Whitsuntide soon after the Norman Conquest.

ASHLAR

Sometimes the word *achelor* is used. A term used to distinguish hewn, dressed or squared stone used on the outer surface of a wall from stone roughly cut at the quarry. it is not certain what the connection is with the suggested derivation through Old French *aisselier* to Latin *axilarius*, diminutive of *axis*, 'board' or 'plank'.

ASS

Old English *assa*, and other Germanic forms, all from Latin *asinus*. The ass figures in Christian iconography by virtue of the fact that Christ rode into Jerusalem on this, the most lowly of animals. It is lowly because it is a beast of burden; and it is also stubborn and characteristically needs goading into action.

The ass symbolically is the burden of the physical world that the spirit has to bear and bend under. The inertias of that burden need to be broken through by the spirit within – the function of the goad. Christ rode on an ass indicating his readiness to take the burden of the errors of the world on his shoulders, and by voluntarily sacrificing his life, to redeem its direction. Man's spirit, once free, is now confined in a lowly material cage: the dark mark of the cross on the back and shoulders of the ass affirms that heavy burden. (See 'Nativity'.)

16

AUGUSTINIANS (or AUSTINS)

A monastic order founded in Chartres, differing little from the Benedictine Order, and so named through following the rule of Augustine, Bishop of Hippo (5th century). They were an order of canons known by the abbreviation Austin Canons, and held something of a half-way position between monks and secular clergy, combining strict vows with work in local parishes. They were untonsured and were known as Black Canons from their black cloak. Their houses, usually priories, were established in Britain from 1105 and include Oxford, Bristol, Carlisle, and are the most numerous after the Benedictines. At the Suppression there were 170 houses.

AUGUSTINIAN (or AUSTIN) FRIARS

One of the four main orders of mendicant friars, founded in Italy in 1250 by Pope Innocent IV. They were in England by the same year. (Not to be confused with the monastic order above.)

AUMBRY OR AMBRY (earlier word ALMARY)

Latin *armarium*, 'cupboard', *arma*, 'tools'. An aumbry is a small enclosed alcove, usually on the north side of the chancel, where the precious vessels of the Eucharist and the reserved sacrament are kept.

AUREOLE

Latin *aura*, 'gold', connected with *aurora*, 'dawn'. Thus, through the image of the radiating light of the sun at dawn, the aurole is the radiating mantle enveloping the body as opposed to the head of a divine being. Mainly due to the needs of sculpture, it often becomes the 'vesica piscis' or 'mandorla', that is the elliptical shape drawn around the figure of the Almighty, Christ or the Virgin, always indicating glorification and apotheosis, and victory over the forces of evil. The generic term 'aureole', however, covers all forms of radiating light, varying according to the posture of the subject: very often it is circular when the figure is seated.

It came to be used more generally for the nimbus, the golden circle or disc of light surrounding the heads of saints, martyrs or any sacred figure. (See 'mandorla', 'glory', 'halo'.)

B

BALDACHIN

Baldachino, the Italian name for Baghdad. Originally, a baldachino was a canopy made of cloth from Baghdad, especially that canopy ritually carried over the Pope. It came to mean a structure of marble or stone on pillars, erected over an altar in a church.

BALUSTER

French *balustre*, 'small pillar', Latin *balaustium*, Greek *balaustion*, 'flower of the wild pomegranate'. The pillar was so named because of the shape of the flower; it is small, circular and swelling in the middle, usually supporting a handrail. Such pillars can occur in Norman churches as columns, but subsequently are only found in the 16th century with the influence of the Renaissance. The later and impure versions of the word are 'banister' and 'balluster'.

BALL-FLOWER

An ornament or moulding in the form of a round flower with three petals forming the cup. It belongs to the Decorated period of English architecture.

BANNER

An emblem of victory. The banner is an allusion to the conversion of Constantine who included his vision of the cross in his own banner. The banner is depicted along with the lamb as a symbol of victory over death. It says in fact, that he who dies to himself, lives. For this reason the banner is carried by Christ when he is depicted rising from the grave, or in his subsequent appearances on earth. Continuing the image of the lamb, John the Baptist is also shown with such a banner sometimes having upon it the words 'Ecce Agnus Dei' ('Behold the Lamb of God').

BAPTISTERY

Greek *baptisterion*, 'bathing place or swimming bath'. *baptein*, 'to dip'. The baptistery is the part of the west end of a church where the font stands for the administering of the sacrament of baptism. The term was adopted by the early Christian Church because its ritual of baptism consisted of total immersion in water – until the year 1552 (the date of the second Prayer Book) children were dipped three times, first on the right side, then on the left and then with their face towards the font. Ritual baptism as such, had long been used by the Jews, and was a symbol of the washing away of error and impurity; in Christianity, it represented both this and 'christening', that is, the rebirth in Christ, or en-Christing, denoted by the wearing of the chrisom (q.v.) by the child. For this reason we use the term 'Christian' name – a new name for a new estate. In the early Church, however, such a name was a mark of a realised spiritual level, as opposed to a mere patriarchal name.

Church rituals naturally underwent modification. Baptism by fire, the fire of the Holy Spirit (pre-figured in Christ's baptism by John the Baptist) was later added. Here, the dove appears, as elsewhere, as a symbol of the pure fire of the Spirit. Thus, the consecrated water in the font represents the potentially purified substance of the human body, and on a higher level the immaculate Cosmic Womb from which all things are born, and which man may re-enter regenerate through the power of the Holy Spirit. This connection between water and fire in the sacrament is reflected in the still current practice of the child holding a lighted taper after baptism. It is connected too with the words of Christ in John's gospel, 'Except a man be born of water and of the Spirit, he cannot enter into the kingdom of God.' We may note, however, that baptism takes place at the West end of the church (materiality) as opposed to the East end (the spirit). For mention of the octagonal shape which figures in both baptistery and font, see under the heading 'font'.

BAROQUE

Portugese *barrocco*, 'an irregularly shaped pearl'. From this association, 'baroque' until the 19th century was a term meaning grotesque in design. Baroque was a style prevalent in roughly the 17th century, though in northern and western Europe it extended through the 18th century, involving the sculptor's use of strong curves and diagonals, and the painter's use of chiaroscuro (light and dark): the whole was intensely realistic. The Baroque leads into the Rococo. There is little true Baroque style in the architecture of Britain. Wren's St. Paul's is not wholly committed to the style and Vanbrugh's work is very individual.

BARREL VAULTING

The most simple kind of vault over a rectangular floor: also called a wagon-vault and also a cylindrical vault. The barrel vault was used classically and is found in Norman architecture. Also in Early English ceilings (basically a pointed arch where there was no stone vaulting), the frame produced the effect of the barrel vault.

BAR TRACERY

See 'tracery' and 'window'.

BASILICA

Greek *basileus*, 'king'. The original meaning was of a king's throne room, but in Roman times it came to mean a hall for the administration of justice. Such a hall was a simple oblong shape with a rounded semi-circular end (apse) where a tribunal sat. In front of the tribunal was an altar for sacrifices. The early Roman Christians adapted their needs to this form, giving an entrance chamber or narthex, a nave and an apse with an altar.

The basilican-form church was introduced into Britain along with the missionary enterprises of St. Augustine, and was largely confined to the south east (for instance St. Pancras at Canterbury), though crypts at Ripon and Hexham (circa 670) are part of what were basilican-type churches. After the 7th century, the form gave way to the indigenous Celtic style – a square presbytery, tall west tower and transepts. A return to the basilican form after the Conquest was short-lived.

BASILISK

Latin *basilicus*, 'a kind of lizard', thus a kind of serpent, Greek *basiliskos*, 'a little king,' *basileus*, 'king'. As a fabulous creature depicted in art it has the body of a cock and a tail made of three serpents. Its glance was said to kill and it could only be conquered by holding a mirror before it, when, frightened at its own image, it burst. In Christian art, the basilisk is an embodiment of evil. Psychologically, evil is disempowered when it is seen face to face.

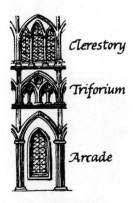

Clerestory

Triforium

Arcade

BAY

French *baie*, 'an opening', from a word *bayer*, 'to gape', now in disuse.

A bay is one of the compartments into which the nave of a church is divided, and the term is also applied to divisions in the roof. In a cathedral the bay is composed of three levels, arcade, triforium and clerestory, one above the other. The function of the arcade is to take the strain from above with the minimum of support, i.e. in the piers; the function of the clerestory is to let in light; the function of the triforium, as with all middle areas, is to balance and link higher and lower levels and form a living architectural whole. With its sloping outer roof over the aisles, it provides space for a gallery, which often runs around the church at that level (see under each heading).

BEAK-HEAD

An ornament in Norman doorways which has the shape of a bird's beak, hooked, and projecting downwards.

BELFRY

Middle English *berfray*, from Old French *berfroi*, from Latin *berfridus*: a Germanic loan word – Middle High German *bercfrid*, 'a watch tower'. This is in turn from two German words: *bergen*, 'to protect' and *frit*, 'a place of security'.

Bells were hung in watch towers as alarms, and the original meaning gradually gave way to a stress on the bells themselves.

BELL

Old English *belle*, related to Dutch *bel*, 'bell'. The Old English word *belen* is 'to bellow'.

The bells of the Middle Ages were a part of life – as timekeepers, for festive occasions, and for informing people of emergencies. Parish churches had two or three bells, but larger churches monasteries and cathedrals had up to eight, or even more. At the Dissolution, bells were disman-

21

tled, and like lead from roofs, melted down for their value as metal.

Bells have always played an important part in Church life; upon their installation they were blessed and often given a holy name. Their function was to banish evil, and equally their repeated sounding was as a prayer drawing the people away from worldly pursuits back to the centre of their being. Also, a bell proclaimed the moment when the host was raised for adoration, and sounded the solemn note of death.

The bell, like the gong, sounds out power, as the heart of God radiates power from the centre of Being to the extremities of creation. Thus the connection between 'bell' and 'being': the bell is strength and beauty in one, and is a very basic symbol.

There is a tradition which says that bells in the Church were first used in Campania, a district in central Italy, thus giving Low Latin *campana*, 'bell', and the word *campanile*, 'bell-tower'.

BENEDICTINES

A monastic Order which originated in the founding of Monte Cassino, circa 520 by St. Benedict. St. Benedict was the first to firmly establish Eastern monasticism in the West. His famous 'Rule' laid down the basic pattern of monastic life, which held for Benedictines and its many reform movements into the Middle Ages, and to the present day.

The basic three-fold vow was one of Poverty, Chastity, and Obedience; and along with this was what St. Benedict called 'Stability', that is, the need to remain a member of a family in one place, as opposed to being an itinerant holy man. An important dictum was 'Orare est laborare: laborare est orare' (to pray is to work: to work is to pray). Work and prayer alternated throughout the day. Prayer was embodied in the 'Opus Dei' (the Work of God), i.e. the reciting of seven Offices each day (see under 'Office'). Manual work included what we now term arts and crafts. But all was to the glory of God.

The Benedictine rule established order into arbitrariness in religious procedure in this country. The older monasteries in Britian such as Westminster, Canterbury, Peterborough and Whitby are all Benedictine. The monks were known as Black Monks from their black habit. At the

22

time of the Suppression there were 276 Benedictine houses.

Latin *biblia*, Greek *biblia*, 'collection of writings' – both from an Egyptian loan word *biblos*, 'the pith of papyrus'. The Latin singular *biblia* signifies the Book of all books, but the Greek word *biblia* is a plural noun signifying the collection of books on paprus rolls upon which the writings were found.

The Bible is in two parts. To people of New Testament times, the Old Testament was referred to as the Holy Scriptures. The Old Testament concerns the covenant made by Moses to which the people of Israel failed to adhere, thus giving their sense of despair. The New Testament tells of a new covenant, redeeming the old, which was brought about by the incarnation of God as man in Jesus Christ.

The Old Testament, written in Hebrew, was essentially in three parts, drawn together circa A.D. 90 along with a fourth book added at a relatively late date. It consisted of: the Pentateuch (literally 'made of five books'), mainly The Law; the Prophets, mainly prophetic material; the Writings, all other books not included in the first two sections; and the fourth part, now called the Apocrypha.

The first Christian writings forming the New Testament are those of St. Paul about the middle of the 1st century with the four Evangelists following later in the century. It was not until the middle of the 2nd century however that there was reference to the Gospels as whole unit. Though Jews of Palestine were bi-lingual, the mother tongue was largely Greek, not Aramaic, and the Gospels were written on papyrus in Greek, the earliest dating from the 3rd and 4th centuries. Only in the 4th century do we find a whole New Testament, and there are only two examples, known as Codex Siniaticus and Codex Vaticanus.

Due to such variable sources, versions made by the Latin Church were becoming more and more numerous and inaccurate, and it was St. Jerome who, late in the 4th century, revised the New Testament and finally translated the whole of the Old Testament into Latin (the Latin language was then the unifying agent of Europe) using original Hebrew manuscripts. This version, the Vulgate, an abbreviation of *vulgato editio*, 'popular edition', from *vulgus*, 'multitude', remained the parent of all Western European bibles for many centuries. In the 8th and 9th centuries translations were made from the Latin in Britain, as in the added word-for-word text in the Lindisfarne Gospels, but these were mostly partial and it was Wycliffe's Bible (14th century), the work of five scholars, that gave the first whole translation into English. In Europe as a whole the theological influence of Luther led to many translations from the Latin and Greek. The versions of Tyndale, Coverdale and the so-called Great, Geneva, and Bishop's (Rheims) Bibles were in this tradition, and led to the Authorised Version, known as the King James Version, in 1611. This was carried out by forty-seven scholars with instructions to use the previous versions of the 16th century where necessary, and in particular, large parts of Tyndale's translation, were used.

However, in considering the translations of the Bible certain facts are worthy of note: that the original text was in Greek uncials or capitals (see 'uncial'); that transmission by manuscript was prone to error and embellishment; that there were no breaks shaping words into sentences, nor was there any division into chapter and verse. (Chapters are found for the first time in the Latin bible printed in Paris in the 13th century, and verses were used first by the Parisian typographer-royal, Stephen, in the 16th century.) These were contributory factors to the difficulty of interpretation – whether a sentence was interrogative or not, for instance – facing the early translators, and the Authorised Version could be said to have had only three major printed versions in Latin or Greek at its disposal: the first printed Bible in Latin in 1462; that in Greek in 1514 by Cardinal Ximenes along with a Latin translation, known as a 'polyglot'; and Erasmus' version of 1516. The Parisian typographer Stephen produced a version almost identical with Ximenes and Erasmus, and Walton's 'polyglot' of London 1600, used Stephen's edition. (See 'book' for the wider issues of the 'Book of Life' and 'Breeches Bible'.)

BISHOP

Old English *biscop*, Old High German *biscof*, Latin *episcopus*, Greek *episkopus*, 'overseer'. (From *epi*, 'over' and *skopos*, 'a watcher'.) Thus one who presides over a particular area being colonised in the early Church. (See 'cathedral'.)

BLACK DEATH

An event often referred to in guide books of religious houses. The disease was at its height in this country in 1348 and 1349. There is little specific evidence as to number of mortalities in the monasteries, but it is estimated that about three-quarters of the Cistercian monks in Europe perished. It is also known that in some of the smaller houses in this country, the inmates died to a man. More than half the population of this country succumbed.

The chaotic economy and scarcity of labour that followed was a contributory factor in the decline of the lay-brother system in monastic life. Another factor, in the North at least, was the plundering of estates run by lay-brothers by Scottish armies in the early 14th century. The latter part of the 14th century was a period of reconstruction during which the quality of the clergy had to regularise itself. The disease recurred to a lesser degree between 1360 and 1379., and in the Great Plague of 1664–5.

BLAZON

Old French *blason*, 'shield' and 'coat of arms', Middle English *blazon*, 'shield', connected with German *blasen*, 'blow' or 'proclaim'. In this sense it is the same proclamation of a man's lineage as is in the word 'herald'. It has come to mean more specifically the accurate description of the arms – to blazon is to paint and inscribe a shield with appropriate arms. Until the 15th century French words were used, then English blazonry used its own adopted words. The order in the science was: first the 'tincture', that is the colour of the 'field' or background, then the main 'charge', that is the object on that field and its tincture, then other lesser charges. Blazonry is based on the sharp contrast between the field and the charges: for instance a gold or silver field (called 'metal') would have a pure red, blue, black or purple charge.

BLESSING

Old English *blédsian*, 'to bless, consecrate', from a German root *blod*, 'blood'. The idea inherent in the word is that of sacrifice through the shedding of blood, and is also seen in the French *blesser*, 'to wound'. Shedding of blood, fusing, and drinking blood are part of many primitive rituals.

Creation implies a diffusing and distributing of power out of a centre, which, in a sense is a sacrifice or self-elected wound on the part of the Creator. Sacrifice finds its ultimate expression in the crucifixion of Christ, for here God assumes manhood and suffers death for the purpose of redeeming mankind's fall. The cosmic drama, it seems, is built on wounding and the shedding of blood – and even, in the eucharist, the symbolic drinking of it.

The blood is mediator between the spiritual and physical levels, being the carrier of the essence of a particular creature. Thus the blood in man carries his tainted nature. It may be, that like the colour red, it signifies pure life force, but it also signifies danger in the rising of the blood in a bestial sense.

The blessing is a supplication via the priest that the receiver should be restored to spiritual health via regenerated blood. It is given on behalf of the Trinity (Father, Son and Holy Ghost – thumb, first finger, and second finger respectively), with special reference to the sacrifice made by Christ – 'Through Jesus Christ our Lord'.

The same power is invoked at the blessing of water for mass and for baptism – that through the mediation of His Sacrifice, the element water may be purged of all uncleanliness.

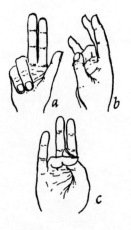

When the hand is seen giving the Benediction with the third finger touching or crossing the thumb, and the others either erect or curved (b and c), the Eastern Orthodox Church is indicated. (The break between East and West occurred technically in 1054 though there was some overlapping.) There are two known suggestions for the emergence of the Eastern form. In the first it is said that the fingers spell out by their shape, and in sequence, the letters IC XC, the first and last letters of the Greek words Ἰησοῦς Χριστός, Jesus Christ. In the second, the erect little finger gives I, the thumb crossing the third finger gives X, and the slightly separated index and second finger gives 'v', the first letters of the words Ἰησοῦς Χριστός νικα, 'Jesus Christ conqueror'.

BOND

A variant of 'bind', found in all Germanic languages, meaning 'to tie up'. In building, the term denotes the way

26

that stones or bricks overlap in the building of a wall. In Flemish bond the 'header' showing its end, and the 'stretcher' showing its side, alternate, whereas in English bond, used between 1560 and 1700, the alternation was by layer.

BOOK

Old English *boc*, 'document', from a Germanic stem meaning 'beech-tree'. Old Norwegian also has *boc*. The word 'book' is derived from the custom of inscribing letters on pieces of beechwood in temperate regions. The 'Book of Books', the Bible, was of course written on parchment scrolls.

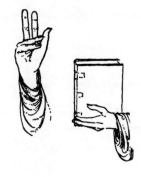

The Latin *liber* 'book' (from which library') also has the meaning of 'inner bark of a tree'. But *liber* also means 'free' – freedom is the essential element in the pattern of the Book of Life. This pattern is a simple one, of three stages – the three acts of a play: the losing of freedom, a dark state out of which a re-awakening takes place, and the re-gaining of freedom after much struggle. Seen on the vast time scale of man's history, as a spirit being he suffered a descent into a physical condition, acquiring in the process a hard ego structure. In that darkness, God's incarnation as man gave the stimulus for the re-awakening of his spiritual centre, his true 'I'. Finally, the new direction began to take root, and fallen energies to be resurrected into spiritual light. (Mankind is just beginning to witness that possibility).

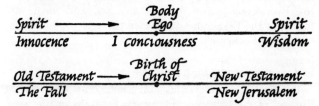

Meantime, each short human life has the same theme: first the innocence of childhood and the descent into total self-immersion, a darkness of spirit; then in the depths of pain and frustration the seed of a new birth; and finally, the journey to the re-gaining of freedom. The Book, the Word of God, tells of this fall and re-birth, so that Birth, Crucifixion, Resurrection and Ascension are to be seen as stages in inner transformation.

BOOK OF HOURS

A prayer book for the laity consisting of prayers for private worship, and reaching popularity in the 15th century. The calendar is illustrated by the Occupations of the Month, and the life of the Virgin is illustrated in eight miniatures according to the canonical hours (q.v.) as follows:

The Annunciation – to Matins
The Visitation – to Lauds
The Nativity – to Prime
The Annunciation to the Shepherds – to Tierce
The Presentation in the Temple – to Nones
The Flight into Egypt or the Massacre of the Innocents – to Vespers
The Coronation of the Virgin or the Flight into Egypt – to Compline

The quality of the work varied because of the enormous numbers made, but some of the finest illuminated manuscripts are among them.

BOSS

French *bosse*, 'lump, knob'. A boss is the projecting ornamental carving found at the intersection point of ribs and ceilings, or at the end of weather-mouldings above doors and windows. In the Norman vaults they are rarely found; in the Early English period ceilings have carved bosses mostly of foliage and occasionally small figures; in the Decorated period foliage, animals, and heads are found; in the Perpendicular period there is an abundance of armorial bearings.

BRASSES or SEPULCHRAL BRASSES

The first brass engravings on tombstones appeared at the end of the 13th century, mostly on slabs in the pavement in the church but sometimes raised as altar tombs. The alloy metal used was called latten and was originally embedded in pitch and fastened by rivets, the incised lines being filled with a resinous substance.

In Britain separate pieces of brass such as the inscription and canopies were inset about the whole stone whereas on the continent the whole engraving was done on one rectangular piece of brass. The images illustrate the many changes in armour of the knights of the period. By 1400, different social classes were adopting brasses as monuments, and from the Lancastrian period (1400–53) about 500 brasses are known to exist. From 1453 to 1485, in the Yorkist period, the engraving deteriorates in quality and from the Tudor period up to 1547, 2,000 brasses remain of varying quality.

Monumental brasses suffered at the Dissolution of the Monasteries and in 1537 when church plate was confiscated, many brasses were removed for melting down. Some brasses were, however, re-engraved by using the reverse side or by simply altering the existing figures: such brasses are known as 'palimpsest' (q.v.). During the reigns of Elizabeth and James I (d. 1625) few brasses were laid down and many were fixed to walls. The deterioration continued in the Caroline period up to 1660.

BREECHES BIBLE (THE GENEVA BIBLE)

A bible often seen in show-cases of churches, and so-called because the word breeches was in this particular bible substituted for the fig-leaf in the story of Adam and Eve in Genesis.

In other respects it was an important landmark in the translation of the Bible into English. Published in Geneva in 1560 by William Whittingham with the aid of two others, it was the first to have ordinary roman type, the first to have chapters divided into verses, and also the first to use italics for words whose purpose was merely to explain and connect in order to clarify meaning, though both of these latter innovations had already been made in other tongues earlier in the 16th century.

BREVIARY

Latin *breviarium*, 'summary', from *brevis*, 'short'. A book, used by priests, containing Divine Office for each day and having special services for Sundays and Saints' Days. It is usually in the form of one book for each season.

BULL

Middle English *bule, bole*, Middle High German *bulle*, from a base meaning 'to swell'. The bull, the fixed earth sign of the zodiac (Taurus) is the symbol of St. Luke in Christian iconography. The idea behind the fixed signs is

that of the establishment of power on the physical plane via the elements. The Evangelists established the message of Christ, each in his own way, corresponding to one of the modes of activity of these fixed signs. The element 'earth' in its 'fixed' state is connected with phallic power and sexual secretion – hence the root 'to swell' and the connection of the bull with the throat. (See 'Adam and Eve'.)

The other three fixed signs of the zodiac and their corresponding animals and Evangelists are: Aquarius (air sign) – man, Matthew; Leo (fire sign) – lion, Mark; Scorpio (water sign) – eagle, John. The eagle 'Aquila' is an extrazodiacal sign substituted symbolically. (See under 'Evangelists'.)

BULL (PAPAL)

From Latin *bulla*, 'seal'. Specifically, a knob or boss of wax used to endorse a Papal edict, but the term is used generally for the edict itself. There is the same meaning of 'swell' as in the previous entry.

BUTTERY

Old French *boterie*, from *boutellerie*, 'the place where bottles are kept'. In a monastery it is the store place for wine and ale, and the place from which they were dispensed. (Thus the modern office of 'butler' as dispenser of drink.)

BUTTRESS AND FLYING BUTTRESS

'Flying'

Old French *bouterez*, from *bouter*, 'thrust, push'. The characteristic of the soaring medieval cathedral is the need to counter-balance the outward thrust of the high vaults. Such a counter-thrust begins with the delicate 'flying' buttress, immediately opposite the vault, which joins an increasingly heavier support descending vertically to the ground. (See 'Gothic'.)

C

CALEFACTORY

Latin *calefacere*, 'make hot', from *caleo*, 'be hot' and *facere*, 'to make'. The term used in a monastic establishment for the room containing the large fireplace used for general heating purposes.

In temperate latitudes, the fire was lit from the beginning of November to Easter. The room is best viewed as common-room where the rule was relaxed and some comfort could be had. Normal domestic activities such as mending clothes, greasing shoes, tonsuring, and the four times per year obligatory bleeding, were carried out here – in the winter time at least. In the summer, the open cloister would be used for many of these needs.

CAMBER

Latin *camera*, 'arch, vault', Greek *kamara*, 'any construction with a vaulted or arched roof': the roots mean 'bent'. Thus in architecture, a slight curve on a surface: it also denotes the slope of a beam in a roof, such as a tie-beam.

CAMERA

Latin *camera*, 'vault, arch', Greek *kamara*, 'any construction with a vaulted roof'. The word also came to be 'chamber' through Old French *chambre*, from the same root.

'Camera' when used in referring to a monastic building, is used in the same sense as 'chamber' – that is the special anteroom or private room of a dignitary.

CANDLE

Latin *candela*, 'tallow-candle', *candere*, 'to glow, burn'. The significance of the candle in Church ritual derives historically from the words in Revelation XI – 'These [referring to two witnesses] are the two olive trees and the two candlesticks standing before the Lord of the earth.' The olive tree and its oil symbolise love (see 'Christ' and 'oil') and the candle with the light it generates in burning, the power of Wisdom to illuminate the human soul: both are simple and powerful symbols of Pure Being. The Biblical 'candle' is a misleading translation, and refers to the common oil and wick lamp, of which the 'candlestick' would be the stand.

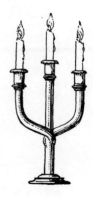

Later, in the monastic period, the Church specified that lighting should be from candles (their present form) made of pure beeswax, especially at the altar. Again we find the idea of purity – animal fat (tallow) was avoided when possible. Purity is in the very nature of the bee: it gathers the purest essence of flowers – honey has always been seen as a symbol of spiritual truth – and all is centred around the Queen bee, the archetype of Being or Wisdom. The candle then, is lit in man's temporal temple or church, as a symbol of the unchangeable and inexhaustible light of Wisdom lying within him.

Seen historically, beeswax was an expensive item. Records show that swarms and wax itself, were often bequested to monastic houses. It is worthy of note that due to inadequate lighting, a monk's repertoire of Psalms was perforce memorised until changes in the 14th century when music was more commonly written and stalls were better lit.

CANON

Latin *canonicus*, 'one subject to rule or canon'. Greek *kanon*, 'straight rod, carpenter's rule'. Greek classical authors were referred to as *kanones* because they were models of perfection in their conformity to rule. Hence all the meanings: a rule set by the Church; or in 'canon law' the whole system of Church law recognised by civil authority before the Reformation. Canon is also applied to a church dignitary in a cathedral. In addition it is used to denote monks in certain monasteries, where they were called Canons Regular (i.e. 'following the rule'). The rule was that of St. Augustine of Hippo which gave the name Augustinian Canons.

CANONICAL HOURS or OFFICES

The word canonical is from the Greek *kanon*, 'a straight rod' and 'a standard of excellence': and further back from *kanna*, 'reed'.

The Canon is thus the system of Church law in Western Europe prior to the Reformation, and the canonical hours are the hours of prayer standardised by the Benedictines and laid down in monastic institutions. Originally the order was: Nocturnes, (or Vigils), Lauds, Prime, Tierce, Sext, Nones, Vespers, Compline. Nocturnes (night) and Lauds (praise at daybreak) however came to be joined into one, Matins or sometimes Matins Lauds (morning), giving seven canonical hours.

MATINS: ecclesiastical Latin *matutinus*, from *Matuta* 'Goddess of Morning' (whence the associated word *maturus*, 'mature') – variable

PRIME: Latin *primus*, 'first', because the first hour of daylight – variable but now fixed at 6 a.m.

TIERCE: Latin *tertius*, 'third', because the third hour of the day – variable but fixed now at 9 a.m.

SEXT: Latin *sextus*, 'sixth', because the sixth hour – variable, but now fixed at 12 noon.

NONES: Latin *nonus*, 'ninth', because the ninth hour – variable, but now fixed at 3 p.m.

VESPERS: Latin *vesper*, 'evening' – variable, but now fixed at 6 p.m.

COMPLINE: Latin *completa*, 'completed'. The last service in the day – variable, now around 9 p.m.

'Variable' is indicated because initially, before being fixed, the times changed according to the period of daylight available – i.e. long periods in summer and short in winter. In summer the celebration of Lauds at an early day-break necessitated the spreading of the subsequent offices, and conversely their contraction in winter. Seven offices had to be fitted into a day whatever its length.

These Offices, seven because of the words in Psalm 119 'seven times a day do I praise thee', consisted mainly of the chanting of the Psalms. It was obligatory for the whole 150 to be sung during the space of a week, which on average, meant four or five hours of services in a day. They were not evenly distributed, as more importance was given to Lauds (Matins), called 'earthly rise', and Vespers called 'earthly rest', which were therefore longer.

The seven points of the day have been related to the crucial times in the Passion of Christ; for instance, condemnation to death (Tierce), Crucifixion (Sext), gives up the Ghost (Nones). In the 'Book of Hours' they are related to the significant phases in the life of the Virgin Mary, and they have also been related to the sequence Christmas, Lent, Easter, and so on. Or they may be equally seen as six periods followed by one, completing the seven days of creation.

The services, not practicable for parochial congregations, were joined at the Reformation to give a morning service and an evensong.

33

Over a pulpit

CANOPY

Latin *canopeum*, from Greek *konopein*, 'gnat'. *Konopein* is a combination of *konos*, 'cone-shaped', and *ops*, 'eye' or 'face' – descriptive of the shape of a gnat's head. A canopy is a cone-like structure of wood or stone erected over a pulpit, font or sedilia in a church, taking its name from such a shape. The constructions vary according to the style of the period, those of the Early English period being simple in form with the Decorated and Perpendicular ones being worked in greater detail.

CAPITAL

Latin *caput*, 'head' (the genitive case is *capitis*), Sanskrit *kapalum*, 'skull'. The head of a column in architecture. In the great English periods – Norman, Early English, etc. – the capital clearly indicates the age of the work. Norman capitals are diverse, Early English are devoid of carving, simple or of bold clear foliage, and in the Decorated period the foliage is much more complex and representational. In

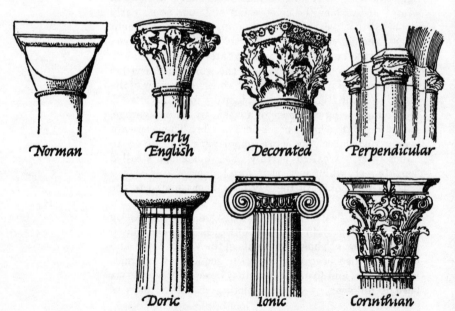

Norman   *Early English*   *Decorated*   *Perpendicular*

Doric   *Ionic*   *Corinthian*

Perpendicular work, capitals are often polygonal and plain with less pronounced mouldings and, when foliage is used, it is stiffer in quality. In classical tradition there are

34

three major forms of capital (see 'column' and 'order') –
Doric, Ionic and Corinthian.

One of the four main orders of mendicant friars (relying
upon alms for support), taking their name from Mount
Carmel in the Holy Land where the order was founded by
St. Berthold the Crusader. They were expelled by the Saracens in the 13th century and came into Europe. In the 15th
century St. Theresa the Spanish mystic founded an aus-
tere discalced branch. ('Discalced' means literally 'de-
shoed' – but in effect meant either barefoot or in sandals.)

CARREL

From French *carré*, 'square', and/or *carreler*, 'to floor or
pave with tiles'. In a monastery the alley of the cloister
against the church wall was the one used as living
quarters by the monks. Such alleys were often divided by
wooden partitions into small rooms or carrels for the
purpose of writing or study. They faced inwards towards
the garth, leaving room for a throughway behind. The
word probably refers to the squared effect made by the
partitions.

As an alternative to carrels, some monasteries simply
had benches against the wall of the church with tables
upon which to study.

CARTHUSIANS

A monastic order founded about 1086 by St. Bruno, and
taking its name from the original monastery at Chartreuse
(Latin *Cartusianus*) near Grenoble, France. The order was
extremely ascetic and its architecture severe. Speech was
forbidden and each monk ate and worked in the solitude of
his own cell around the cloister. At the Suppression there
were eight Carthusian houses in Britain.

CARTOUCHE

Italian *cartiocco*, Latin *carta*, 'leaf of paper or papyrus',
Greek *khartés*, leaf of papyrus'. Following the Egyptian
meaning of an oval shape bearing the title of a king, a
cartouche has come to mean a tablet, enclosing an inscrip-

tion, usually with an ornate frame. They are frequently to be found on tombstones and commemorative plaques.

Greek *kathedra*, 'seat': *kata*, 'down to' and *hedra*, 'seat' – thus 'a seat to sit down on'. A cathedral is a church with a bishop's seat or throne, and thus a symbol of authority within the structure of the Church: the name 'cathedral' became applicable only when an establishment had been endowed with a bishopric. The same seat is found also in the Latin language, for the 'see' of the bishop derives from *sedes*, 'seat'. The throne itself is found in the stalls of the choir, distinguishable by its size and the richness of its carving. The power of the bishop was originally in the nature of head of a family of clergy, but the growth of the chapter, exercising power over property, finance, and most Church affairs, caused his position to become an increasingly honorary one. The loss of the original function is now compensated by the responsibility for a diocese.

Architecturally, the cathedrals and monastic churches of Western Europe were at first similar in design to the Roman basilica where the tribunal presided in the apse with the altar in front of it. The bishop's throne was in the centre of the apse, where the clergy also sat, with the altar and singers to the west of them. Gradually the monk's choir came to be enclosed by screens, and the transepts were moved westwards. Variations of form in time and place were however inevitable. In England, the cathedrals built in the late 11th and 12th Centuries underwent eastern extensions from the 13th Century onwards. This was in order to provide for more altars in the chantry chapels (vide), which were needed for the growing custom of saying masses for the dead. These extensions, often culimated in a Lady Chapel, and gave rise to there being equal areas for the clergy as for the laymen. They also contributed to the dignified length of the English Cathedral. It is interesting to note, that the building of a cathedral was always started from the east end, and progressed westwards. If this is borne in mind whilst looking at the present day building, confusion through the mixing of styles can often be avoided. The first cathedral founded in this country (circa 600) was in the see granted to St. Augustine at Canterbury: that at York was built by Paulinus in 627 –

but of these and other early churches only traces in crypts remain.

Seen from an 'inner' point of view, the early church was a place of teaching, open only to those undergoing initiatory instruction, and as it became open to the people certain inner truths were inevitably lost. Nevertheless, their essential meaning was still held and disguised in the form and contents of the church, especially in the cross which had established itself as the symbol of Christianity. In the medieval period, the cruciform cathedral was taken by the religious zeal of the time and thrown upwards into vertical vaults and spires. The attempt to reach heaven was the cause of drastic changes in architectural techniques: upward thrust needed balancing against downward pressure, insubstantial aspiration against substantial reality, fire against earth. Thus the cathedral became a fine instrument with the two forces reconciled in a third, its perfectly balanced structure. (See 'Gothic'.) The life inside it in medieval times was equally a balance between the priesthood with the mystery of the sanctuary, and the people carrying on everyday activities of craft, festivity, education, and worship, in the nave. The cathedral was, in a sense, the soul of the people.

CATHOLIC

Greek *katholikos*, 'universal'. *Kata* is 'according to' and *holos*, 'entire, whole'. The term originally denoted the Holy Catholic Church, embracing all Christians in one body, and after the Reformation it denoted all those Christians under the jurisdiction of the Pope, as opposed to the Reformed, Protestant Church. The Catholic Church in this sense claims true universality through an unbroken tradition from Christ himself, a universality until recently affirmed by the use of Latin throughout the world.

CELL

Middle English *celle*, meaning the private room of a monk or a nun, from Latin *cella*, 'store-room, granary, mean hut or apartment'. The root meaning is from Old High German 'to conceal, hide', with a possible reference to the hidden dwellings of persecuted monks in the desert.

Cell or *celle* is also used to denote a minor religious house which was dependent upon a greater one. It was often regarded as a place of convalescence, and reputedly suffered some abuse. St. Albans had a cell at Redburn and Finchdale Priory and Lindisfarne both became cells of Durham.

CELLAR or CELLARIUM

Latin *cella*, 'store-room or granary hut', Greek *Kalia*: this is from a root meaning 'to hide or conceal' whence Latin *celare*, 'to hide' and the English 'conceal'. The connection is through the safeguarding of property and food in times of invasion. In a monastery the place for provisions was called the *cellarium* and the monk in charge, the *cellarer*. The role of the cellarer was an important one; he was in a sense the 'mother' of the establishment as opposed to the abbot or father, and much care was taken over his appointment.

CELT

Latin *Celta* and Greek *Keltoi*. The Aryan-speaking race known as Celts included the ancient Gauls, and inhabited a large area of Western Europe. The Bretons, Scottish Gaels, Welsh, Cornish, Irish and Manx all stem from the migrations of this race.

In pagan Europe, before Christ, the bronze work shows a high degree of skill and was typified by the use of spiral curves. There was no attempt at realistic representation and the few specimens of animal forms are conventionalised. With the advent of Christianity into Ireland, bringing an unprecedented flowering of decorative art, there were inevitable modifications. The Irish Celts had an inventiveness and precision which found expression in interlacing circles, key patterns and knot patterns. The spiral ornament of the illuminated manuscripts, as in the Book of Kells and the Irish sculptured crosses of the 7th to 10th centuries, is the greatest achievement of Celtic Christian art. Irish monasticism, spreading to Northumbria, brought a marriage of it and the native style to give such manuscripts as the Lindisfarne Gospel-book. It carried on the tradition of sculpture in Irish-Saxon sculptured stones.

CEMETERY

Latin *cemeterium*, Greek *koimētērion*, 'consecrated ground for burying the dead'; from words meaning 'lying down, sleeping, bed, place to lie'. In medieval life the term implied the graveyard attached to the parish church. It was only after 1852 when acts were passed in the interest of hygiene in towns that cemeteries began to be places separate from parish churches.

The graveyard of the parish church was by tradition on the S. side of the church (that facing the sun), the N. being ground used only for those dying in mortal sin or in some way unworthy of Christian burial. When a single aisle was later added to a church it was usually on the N. side where there were no graves; and when two aisles are added, it is usually the case that the N. was the first one of the two.

CENSER (also called THURIBLE)

Latin *incensum*, 'something burnt'; thus the vessel made of gold, silver or brass which hangs by chains and burns incense during the Church rituals. Thurible is from Latin *thus*, 'frankincense' and Greek *thyos*, 'a sacrifice', suggesting early sacrificial rituals.

In form, the censer ranged from simple spherical to more complex designs, lids in the Romanesque period having towers and battlements, and in the Gothic period, elaborate traceries. The intention was to represent the Heavenly Jerusalem.

CENTAUR

A mythical half-horse, half-man creature, from Greek *Kentauros*, a member of a race of Thessaly. It was the centaur Chiron who, through being teacher of music, medicine and hunting to many heroes, was placed by Jupiter in the heavens, to become the constellation Sagittarius: here he represents essentially the power of the horse plus the wisdom of man, and is represented with bow and arrow (Latin *sagitta*, 'arrow'). In medieval times the centaur was called the Saggitary, and in Norman fonts and carved doorways he is seen with bow and arrow in contest with monsters, denoting the conquest of the flesh by harnassed spiritual power. (See overleaf).

CHALICE

Latin *calix*, Greek *kalyx*, 'cup, outer vessel of a flower or bud'. In the Church ritual the chalice is the cup used to contain the wine in the celebration of the Eucharist. As

On a misericord, Exeter

such it represents the chalice of the Last Supper referred to in the New Testament, and in the original Roman ritual, by the words:

> Take and drink ye all of it. For this is the chalice of my Blood of the new and eternal testament ...

It is also the supposed receptacle of the blood of Christ at the crucifixion, in which association it becomes known as the Holy Grail.

The historical controversy centering around Joseph of Arimathea and the Holy Grail is not within the scope of this book. What is essential is to note that the cup as such is primarily a female image, a container – it is the cup of existence, the waters of existence, of which all must partake. As the chalice or Grail of the Church, it is the means whereby those who partake of its symbolic blood might be re-joined to the whole Body of Man, through the mediation of Christ's sacrifice. The derivation of the word itself (see also 'ciborium') suggests the perfected essence at the heart of the flower.

The drinking of the blood of higher beings, here as in primitive rituals, has always had the purpose of taking in the power of that being. It is the blood which, as mediator between spirit and the physical plane, is a register of the subtle essence of the being it inhabits.

As the chalice is female, so the spear that draws the blood from Christ's side is male; it is the original spear of wounding, the divine act of initiative out of which the world sprung, as it is also the spear of truth and healing which sheds the blood of sacrifice – that is, sacrifice of the illusion created by the world.

40

The actual form of the chalice underwent many modifications. Originally made of a variety of materials, gold and silver were eventually decreed in the 9th century, with the exception of pewter for poorer communities. The original two handles died out during the 10th-12th centuries, and the hemi-spherical bowl only gave way in the 14th century to a more conical form. Many examples of chalices of these times are preserved due to the custom of ecclesiastics having the chalice and paten (q.v.) they had received at their ordination buried with them. From the 14th to the 16th centuries the stem is long, there is a pronounced baluster or 'knop', and the base is hexagonal in shape.

In the middle of the 16th century when elaboration in ornamentation was becoming excessive, came the Reformation which replaced the chalice by the 'Communion Cup' in Britain. The conversion to the new form took time: it resembled more a domestic beaker, being larger and allowing the laity to participate. The spirit of simplicity and a people's religion thus found its way into the sacrament, the focal point of meaning in the Church. (See 'sacrament' and 'mass'.)

1529

Chalice

1570

Communion Cup

CHAMBERLAIN

From Latin *camera* and Greek *kamera*, 'any place with a vault or arched roof', 'a private or enclosed room'. Such a room was the dormitory of the monastery. The officer in charge of it was the chamberlain. He was responsible for the general comforts of the monks, for cleanliness, for annual changing of straw for beds, for water for shaving, for baths (three or four times a year), for tonsuring and for clothing.

CHANCEL

Latin *cancelli*, 'cross-bars' and *cancellare*, 'to enclose by a lattice'. Thus the meaning of the east end of a church containing the choir, clergy and altar, that is, the sacred area separated from the nave by a lattice called a 'chancel screen'. The screen is also known as the 'choir screen', 'pulpitum', or in a parish church 'rood-screen'. The chancel itself is also called the 'choir' and because there are daily choral services performed in the cathedral it is in this sense more applicable here, though the meaning behind the word 'chancel' is thereby lost. 'Sanctuary' and 'presbyter' are also loosely used for the sacred area east of the screen. All these terms are best considered together.

The underlying idea in the chancel is that of cancelling out by enclosure, of the protecting or screening of the holy secrets from profanation by the uninitiated, an aim found in all ancient religions and mystery rites. It existed in the inner sanctuary of the Jewish temple and in the early Christian church as a low wall and columns supporting a beam: both these were places for the guarding and dispensing of sacred mysteries, only due to those errata adequately prepared.

The Eastern Church has retained the emphasis on the mystery of the Mass by not celebrating it in open view, but behind the screen at the entrance to the sanctuary. In the West, such a separation of nave and chancel held until the time of the Reformation when the chancel was opened for the receiving of Communion by the congregation. This entailed destruction of most of the parish church 'rood-screens' and also of the stone images in the cathedral choir screen.

(Note the current imagery of the expression 'to cancel out' by the use of two cross-wise strokes.)

CHANCEL ARCH

The single stone arch at the entrance to the chancel found in the earliest Norman churches and common to all later parish churches in this country. It corresponds in form to the windows, so revealing the age of the church; but it often bears signs of widening and the later superimposition of the rood-screen.

The screen across the arch, from the earliest times, was to preserve the sanctity of the chancel, an aspect of which was the mundane one of protection from the fouling by dogs, which in parish churches were allowed into the nave with their owners. (See under 'chancel').

CHANTRY or CHANTRY CHAPEL

French *chanteur*, Latin *cantare*, 'to sing'. A chantry is the name given to a chapel or altar or any part of a church where priests chanted prayers on behalf of the respected dead, as for instance a founder or benefactor of a particular establishment, and later the landed families and their descendants connected with a parish. In monasteries, the need for more altars for an increasing number of benefactors, was a major factor in extensions made at the Eastern end of the church in the 13th century, and also of later structural modifications in the aisles of the church. Fountains Abbey with its fine Chapel of the Nine Altars, is an example of such an extension. The original function of the priest was to mitigate by prayer the suffering of the soul in purgatory. In this respect a chantry was often a bequest to provide such a privilege for the deceased.

Much importance was attached to the quality and magnificence of the craftsmanship in the stone screens, canopied niches and so on, in such chantries. In cathedrals an abbot, bishop or king would vie to produce the finest work, thus giving rise to many chantry chapels in one building. Equally, in the parish churches the families who were at the same time donors had their tombs built by the finest available craftsmen.

CHAPTER HOUSE

Old French *chapitre* (variant of *chapitle*), Latin *capitulum*, 'head of a column', which in turn is a diminutive of *caput*, 'head'. Thus a chapter is the head or governing body of a cathedral or collegiate church, meeting in the chapter house, a room or building attached to a cathedral for this purpose.

In monasteries, the chapter convened daily after mass. It was a place where internal affairs were regulated – questions concerning discipline, property, the election of officials, and so on. It was also a place of correction where monks confessed their sins before their brethren and were allotted punishment by the abbot. (Periods on bread and water and flogging were the most common forms of punishment). It was also the place where novices, after their period of training, received the habit of the order, and where 'collatio', the reading before compline, the last office of the day, took place.

The first activity when the chapter convened, however, was the reading of a chapter of the Rule of St. Benedict (*capitulum* in Latin also means 'division of a book' i.e. 'chapter'); this gives an equally valid origin of the term 'chapter house'.

In all cases, seating was around the walls. In Cistercian monasteries, chapter houses are rectangular. In English cathedrals, they are mainly polygonal with canopied stalls or a stone bench around the walls and a single column supporting the vault.

CHARGE

Old English, from Old French *chargier*, 'to put a load on'. Thus a connected meaning in heraldry of a figure carried on a shield – a 'bearing'. The object on the field, basic charges, are bands and linear motifs called 'ordinaires'. From the beginning, the horizontal bar had interchangeable names (i.e. 'fesse', 'barre', 'baston'), but the name quickly assumed more specific meanings. Crosses became variegated and fields subdivided, giving a complex vocabulary.

CHASUBLE

Medieval Latin *casubula*, diminutive of *casa*, 'cottage' – thus 'little cottage'. The chasuble is the embroidered and bejewelled covering over a priest's alb or cloak, suggesting a small shelter. Originally tent-like, with a hole for the head, the shape was modified to oval in accordance with Gothic idiom. Front and back have ordinary or Y-shaped crosses. During the celebration of the Eucharist, it is a reminder of the seamless garment of Christ, which signifies the unified power of the spirit. The Y symbolises the directing of spiritual force to the heart in priest and participant.

CHEST

Old English, from Latin *cista*, Greek *kistē*, 'basket'. Many kinds of old chest are found within the church. Some of the earliest remaining, originally referred to as 'trunks' because they were hollowed out trunks of trees, belong to the time of the Crusaders. These stem from the order of Henry II that parish churches should collect offerings towards the relief of the Holy Land: they have slits in the lid.

There were alms-boxes or poor-boxes which continued throughout the centuries, though the earliest were simply hollowed out, vertically standing trunks with lids. Also the church had need of chests for books and vestments and these are partitioned accordingly. Most of the early chests were banded with iron. It was only in the 13th century that chests began to be made from five planks with a sixth as a lid.

44

CHEVET

Old French *chevez*, from Latin *caput*, 'head'. A term used to describe the rounded apse when surrounded by an ambulatory (q.v.) with chapels. It is really a French feature but is found in some cathedrals as at Norwich, Gloucester and Westminster Abbey.

CHEVRON

Old French *chevron*, 'rafter'. The shape of the chevron is of an inverted letter V resembling a pair of rafters. It is used heraldically, and as a Norman moulding, where it is known as a 'zig-zag'.

CHIMNEY

Old French *cheminée*, Latin *caminus*, 'hearth', Greek *kaminos*, 'oven'. This is connected with *kamara*, 'vault'. The chimney was originally the whole structure – the fireplace and flue and projection above the building to take the smoke away. The chimneys in monastic buildings were hollowed out, vault-like spaces in the walls.

CHI-RHO MONOGRAM

(See under 'Monogram'.)

CHOIR or QUIRE

Greek *khoros*, 'dancing in a ring, a festive dance performed in a circle to the honour of the gods'. The choir in a church is the area east of the rood-screen ('chancel-screen' or 'choir screen' in a cathedral) between nave and sanctuary, which houses the choir or body of singers. It is often called the 'chancel'.

As the word indicates, Greek religious dances accompanied by singing were circular, reflecting the rotating solar system and vaster rotating systems in the universe of which man is a part. In the Greek theatre singing and dancing took place in the area below the stage, and this was called the *orkhēstra*, from *orkheisthai*, 'to dance' – whence the English 'orchestra'. Early Christian mystery rites had chanting to circular dances, but as Christianity became externalised, dance and music separated; the term 'choir' lost the implication of the dance, as later in the West the music assumed its independent role in the orchestra.

45

In the monastic churches with their cruciform shape and short Eastern limb, the choir was at the place of the crossing: this also holds with cathedrals with a short Eastern limb such as Peterborough, Gloucester, and Westminster. Generally in cathedrals, the choir extended into the presbytery, the place of mystery protected by the chancel screen, where music was an integral part of ritual. Stalls faced inwards and in the 15th century rose to artistic heights in the beautifully carved canopies and misericords.

In monastic establishments the choir monks (so called sometimes to distinguish them from the illiterate laybrothers whose function, though bound by the same vows, was to work rather than pray) followed largely the Rule of St. Benedict. This required the performing of seven offices each day, and the whole of the 150 psalms each week. This meant approximately four hours of chanting per day, and in early monastic times represented a considerable feat of memory. It was only in the 14th century that with adequate lighting and more uniform and substantial musical notation, music came to be read.

× LA

× SOL

[×FA

  ×MI

×RE

× UT

Many secrets lie in music, but none is more relevant here than the cosmic hierarchy indicated in what has come down to us as the tonic-sol-fa system. As early as the 10th century, the monk-musician Guido d'Arezzo had given the names UT RE MI FA SOL to the currently used hexachord. Ostensibly they were based on the first syllable of the lines of the Hymn to St. John – UT queant laxis: MIra tuorum: SOLve polluti: REsonare fibrus: FAmuli gestorum: LAbu reatum. The inner meaning may be seen in this way: UT signifying divine power in each man, rises through RE, Regina de Coeli, the Moon – MI, Microcosmos, man on earth, image of all things – FA, Fata, fate, the planetary forces – SOL, the sun as life force – LA, Lactea, the Milky Way, the galaxy to which the solar system belongs.[1]

In this cosmic ladder the most significant point is the place of the semitone, the transition from MI to FA. (In the hexachord system, whichever the root note, the semitone was made to fall between MI and FA). This place of tightening symbolised the need for man's spiritual effort to gain mastery over enslaving external forces. For further reference to music, see under *plainsong*.

*(see 'The Hidden Face of Music' Gollancz)

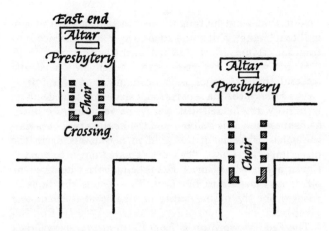

CHRISOM

Greek roots: *khrio*, 'anoint with oil' and *soma*, 'body'. Prior to 1552, baptism entailed a three-fold dipping of the child, who was then dressed by the priest in a white vesture called a chrisom. This was to be delivered back to the priest at the 'churching' of the mother (the ceremony of purification about a month after the birth). The chrisom was intended to symbolise the anointed or en-Christed body. In some effigies in churches, it is clear from the baptismal robe that the child has died within a month after birth.

CHRIST

Greek *khristos*, 'anointed one', *krisma*, 'an unguent'. Similarly, Messiah, our form of the Hebrew *mashiah*, literally means 'anointed one'.

To understand the significance of Christ, we need to look at the ritual of anointing. From the beginning of history, oil has been used in the consecration of kings, places and temples. In the consecration of kings, oil poured over the head effected a transference of the power of the deity in whose name the rite was being performed. What then is the nature of oil? Oil in the body allows the smooth functioning of bones and sinew, as it does the parts of a machine; taken inwardly or used outwardly it is a lubricant and has healing powers. The psychic counterpart of oil is love – it is man's egotism, his hate, which vitiates his relationship with other men and creates a bitter chemistry in his body. Christ's message was one of love in that what he taught was the sacrifice of the self-will to a Higher Will – and such love is accompanied by a fragrant oil and a flow of health in the body.

Words we may associate with 'Christ' are 'crux' and 'crucial', both of which have an implication of a 'crisis'. Greek *krisis* means 'a separation, a decision'. The decision is to do with the self-will, the point at which the bitter selfishness releases its hold and the healing oil operates – the same crisis as in the gold in a crucible or in the direction of an illness. The work of man, then, is to find the Christ in himself, a Christ who is being born whenever the oil of love begins to function. This brings the light of wisdom, for the other quality of oil is that it burns and gives light.

The English word oil is from Latin *oleum*, from Greek *elaion*, 'olive tree', an emblem of divine reconciliation and good will, whilst in Greece a crown of olive was the highest national distinction. Greek *kharis*, 'favour, grace', related to *khrisma*, is found in *eucharist*, thus *eu* 'good' with *kharis*, 'good grace': the Eucharist carries the essential idea of divine reconciliation, a re-membering of the individual soul into the Body of Christ through love.

'Jesus' is a translation of the Hebrew word *Jehoshea*, 'Jah saves', that is, 'God saves'. 'Jesuah' and 'Joshua' are from the same source and the idea of liberator is in Joshua too, for this Old Testament forerunner led the children of Israel into the Promised Land. Thus the combined idea in 'Jesus Christ' of a being, God's chosen human vehicle, destined to save mankind, and that Being's self-anointing in the realising of total love.

CHURCH

Anglo-Saxon *circe*, Western Germanic *kirike*, Greek *kuriakon*, 'church': derived from Greek *kurios*. 'Lord, master'. Thus the meaning of the Church as 'belonging to the Lord'.

Stone circle

But there is also reference in the circe or kirk to the circle, for properly the Church, the Body of God, is the whole of nature, the universe in which one system revolves within another. All belongs to the Lord – all is holy. The earth moves within such a rotating cosmos, and from it the sun appears to progress in circular manner – through the zodiac. Standing stones of the Druids were circular in design, as were temples and Christian rotundas

48

– in fact the Holy Sepulchre itself at Jerusalem, a Constantinian building, was round, and the Knights Templars built most of their churches in that form. Early sacred dances representing man's progression through and subjection to these cosmic energies were also circular. And so also are the spiralling forms of the water-lines and field forces of the earth over which it is likely that most sacred buildings were specifically located. (See 'ley-lines').

Knights Templar Church, London

The idea inherent in the kirk or circe is that in the act of creation, the power of the Lord is locked in such systems: indeed, in the word church (kirk) itself, the letter 'k' at the beginning and end of the word indicates this sonically. For man, locked in such a system, with its laws imposing upon him, the key to freedom is only to be found in the still centre of the circle – the hub of the wheel. In this imagery, Christ is the thirteenth point at the centre of twelve disciples, as is Arthur at the Round Table of Knights. In both instances, the twelve represent permutations of energy (referred to in astrology), and the centre point is where differences are embraced and transcended. Equally, in any closed system, differences abound, so that in the Church itself it is only at the still centre point that the oneness of all sects may be grasped and dispute ended.

The English word 'church' however covers both *kuriakon* and *ekklēsia*, and it is the latter that describes more clearly the structure of the Church as a body of people. To the Greek in pre-Christian times, *ekklēsia* meant an assembly of civilians', really 'those called or summoned out' – (*ek*, 'out' and *kaleo*, 'summon'). The original twelve disciples were the prototypes of all those to be summoned out by Christ to a life of sacrifice: they were, in effect, the original Church.

It was this ancient glyph of the cross which Christianity eventually took over – though it was not until the 5th century that it came to symbolise Christ's death on the cross. The cross, which is essentially the intersection of two forces, with the resultant pinning to a point, represents all aspects of sacrifice: eternity to time, spirit to matter, God to a mortal frame, and for man, a universal to an individual consciousness. Christ's ritual death affirmed the need to reverse this situation; it proclaimed that by the sacrifice of material and egotistic values, the wrong could be redressed – the cross of suffering could become the cross of triumph. It was also a pointer to the

fact that henceforth it was every man's 'I' consciousness, his true Ego, that could effect his *own* release, and contribute to the new direction in the evolution of mankind. In this sense, each man is his own altar, temple or church.

This idea can be carried further by analogy. With his feet touching the ground, vulnerable to the sensual level (the 'heel' in mythology), he can move up from the first moment of awakening by the Holy Spirit (font) to a painful change of heart at the crossing, to a throat voicing new aspiration (the choir) and finally to an ultimate illumination in the head (altar). 'See 'cross', 'right and left', 'baptism', 'east end', 'nave', 'crucifixion'.)

Seen as an organisation, the first gathering of the twelve disciples was in effect the first Body of the Church. When the gift of tongues was made available at Pentecost the Church was alive by virtue of the Holy Spirit, and it was then a question of succession of authority. Early Christians held their gatherings in the houses of converts, but soon there was a need to adapt larger buildings: it was the adapted Roman basilica-type building that was called a *kuriakon*. The Eastern Orthodox Church retained the basilican plan whilst the Western Church moved to its own particular form, that of the Latin cross.

CIBORIUM

A Latin word meaning 'drinking cup' from Greek *kiborion*, the 'fruit of the Egyptian water-lily' or 'a cup made in the form of that fruit'. The term has come to mean the vessel with a lid used for preserving the sacrament (the wafer or piece of bread given to the congregation at the Eucharist as a symbol of the Body of Christ). Originally, in the early church, such a vessel was suspended within a curtained canopy on four columns over an altar, but from the 13th century onwards the canopy fell into disuse and the vessel with a lid, standing on the altar, took its place. It is an interesting point that the chalice (the container of the wine at the Eucharist) also derives from the form of a flower. (See 'chalice'.)

CINQUEFOIL

French, literally 'five-leaves'. A figure of five equal curved sections often used to form a window, especially as an image of the five-petalled rose with its association with the Virgin Mary. (See 'rose'.)

CISTERCIAN

A reform movement within the Benedictine Order, founded in 1098 at Citeaux (Latin *Cistercium*, whence the name) in Burgundy, with the aim of abiding more strictly to the Rule of St. Benedict. As St. Bernard became abbot in 1112, and was regarded as a second founder, Cistercians often carry the name Bernadines.

Through St. Bernard's charismatic influence, the Order spread widely over Europe, whilst in this country, Rievaulx, Furness, Fountains and Kirkstall were among the many orders established in the early 12th century. Due to their white habits (undyed wool) they were known as 'white monks'. The monastic church and buildings followed a pattern of austerity, being devoid of decoration, sculpture or coloured glass.

The Cistercians adopted a system of lay-brothers, that is monks who whilst taking the usual vows, were illiterate and were employed in the necessary crafts, or sent out to distant granges to overlook sheep farms. It was from sheep farming that the Cistercians in England derived their great wealth. Due to many factors, by the 15th century, the ideals had deteriorated, and an Order with ideals of poverty had become wealthy land-owners.

CLERESTORY or CLEARSTORY

Literally 'clear-storey', from French *clair*, 'light' and storey, denoting the upper row of windows in the nave which is above the roof of the aisles, and so named because it allows in the light, whereas the triforium below it is a blind storey blocking out the light. Clerestories are only found in larger churches and cathedrals. (See 'bay'.)

CLERIC

Latin *clericus*, Greek *klērikos*, 'belonging to the clergy'. *Kleros* in Greek means 'inheritance', and the idea among the early Christians was that the Christ power was passed down through those in authority. The 'cleric' or 'clerk' of the medieval times already indicated that writing and learning was vested in the Church. 'Clergy' is an old French modification of this – *clergie*, 'learning'.

CLOISTER

Latin *claustrum*, 'lock'; an 'enclosed place'. Thus in a monastic building the cloister is an open space called the 'garth' or garden, with a covered way or ambulatory enclosing it on all sides. It is also 'locked' in the sense that as the focus of monastic life, and surrounded by dormitory, chapterhouse and refectory, it was the area most protected from intrusion.

The walk along the church wall was in effect the monks' living area and place of study: it usually faced the South, i.e. the heat and light of the sun. For this reason, cloisters in this country are on the south side of the nave, except for topographical building difficulties. This living area was often partitioned into small closets called 'carrels', used for individual study and writing. Initially, the arcading of the cloister had no glazing, but gradually acquired windows as protection against the elements.

Collegiate churches also had cloisters, as at Lincoln, Wells, and Hereford.

CLUNIACS

The Cluniac monastic order was founded in 910 and took its name from its original house at Cluny in Burgundy, France. It was a reform group within the Benedictine order advocating that the ecclesiastical authorities rather than kings should have the power to appoint members of the clergy. Its greatest fame, however, was achieved as a powerful centre of art, especially of sculpture. None of the greatest English monasteries were of this order, though a feature of their architectural design, the double transept, was adopted in many cathedrals. At the time of the Suppression there were twenty houses in Britain.

COCK

Old English *coce*, Low Latin *coccus*, connected with Low Latin *coccum*, 'scarlet berry', after the colour of the comb. The comb is serrated and bears the idea of division, and through its blood-red colour, of sacrifice. The crowing of the cock heralds the day and to the Greeks, the cock was dedicated to Apollo through association with the rising sun (Divine Mind), and to Aeschylus through the idea of health from early rising and early bed-going. But the day is the day of the natural world, of light, which in one sense is an adversary of the spirit (see 'Lucifer'). Thus in announcing the day, there is pride too; the cock begins his lustful activity (a fact expressed in everyday vernacular), and crows on its own dunghill.

The idea of Peter's denial of Christ belongs here: human beings weep bitterly when they realise the error of their pride and its consequence, the fall into a material world. Thus the cock on the weather-vane of the church is a constant reminder of the danger of the denial of the spirit: a coxcomb is a fool in the worldly sense. It suggests here and elsewhere in Christian symbolism the need for watchfulness. In Eastern mythology the cock symbolises lust and pride. Thus there are two faces to the cock – the watchful one, and carnal indulgence which is death to the spirit.

COCKATRICE

Old French *cocatrice*, 'ichneumon', Latin *coctrice* from *calcatric*, 'the tracker'. The Latin *calcare* means 'to track', a description from the Greek of the *ikhneumon*, a small animal that breaks the eggs of crocodiles to destroy them.

The French cocatrice became one of the many medieval mythological beasts, said to be hatched out of a cock's egg by a reptile. Its glance was said to be able to kill. In heraldry, the head, wings and legs were those of a cock, and its body and tail those of a serpent.

The cocatrice also has the name 'basilisk' and is found on finials and outer walls of cathedrals.

COLOUR

Latin *color*, 'colour' – in general – and 'outward appearance' connected with Latin *celare*, 'to hide, keep secret'. Other connections all suggest 'concealing'. Colour in the sense indicated in the word is a disguise on a primary unified light or truth: it is a differentiation which destroys unity, as number begets numbness. Both are part of the *maya* (illusion) of creation.

In Church symbolism, altar coverings, hangings in general, and the chasubles of the priests, change according to the particular festival. In iconography and in more general symbolism, the use of colour is based on a primary triad which corresponds in essence with three aspects of power, the nature of the Persons of the Trinity.

The Father, the energy source of Will, is red (hot); the Son, formative idea world or Word, ordering and limiting that energy, is blue (cold); and the Holy Spirit, mediating force, the flow of life itself, is yellow (neither hot nor cold). On a human level this is reflected in many contexts, but it remains basically: red of action, blue of thought and yellow of mediation and of healing. Each colour has a positive and negative aspect, the divine, as against the fallen, man. Red is pure will, but negatively rage, 'seeing red': blue is perfect logical clarity, but negatively a 'blue funk', the interference of the dualistic mind: yellow is pure love but negatively the colour of cowardice and lack of courage. (Thus the colour of the garments worn by Judas.)

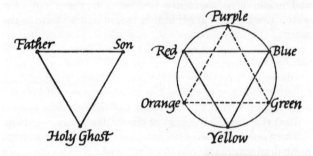

Red then is always energy, a creative or destructive energy. Blue is the colour of the Son, but since the world is conceived not only in mind but also through matter, the womb of matter, the Virgin Mary is also given the colour blue: it is light and clear indicating the purity of her Wisdom. Yellow is the colour of gold, the untarnishable nature of love and indicates the luminous radiance of the divine state.

Secondary colours, those resulting from the admixture of two primary colours, are to do with the relationship of man to God – his striving. Each has to be seen in relation to the two colours of which it is composed and also in relation to its opposite primary colour. (See the diagram.) Green is a colour of development, orange of fruitful love, and purple is the colour of man's possible kingship, his own Self authority. Negatively, without any striving to the divine state, green is stunted growth (green with envy, sickly green), orange is false love and purple is mortality as opposed to eternal kingship.

In the Church, purple is associated with the man Jesus

54

Christ; it represents his kingship, a state reached only through sacrifice. Thus it also symbolises mourning, penitence, and renunciation. Red, the colour of energy, also refers to the blood of sacrifice, as in the blood of martyrs, and to the very first sacrifice, that of the Father in begetting the world. Gold or yellow, because of its associations with the fire of the Holy Spirit, is connected with festivals, as more commonly, is white. White (Christmas, Easter, Ascension) is used to denote rejoicing, because it embraces the whole spectrum of colour in one, thus representing the undifferentiated spirit: and in the same way, black is connected with deprivation and mourning – simply lack of light.

The use of colour in the Church is however not accurately predictable. A general rule laid down at the beginning of the 13th century suggested white for feasts, red for martyrs, black for penitential seasons, and green for others; this remained unclarified until a rubric of greater complexity was laid down in 1570.

COLUMN

Latin *columna*, 'pillar'; related to Latin *columen*, 'height, summit'. A column is a pillar of stone carrying the weight of a superstructure.

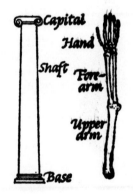

In ancient Greece there were three main types or orders of column, deriving from certain areas and periods, notably Doric, Ionic, and Corinthian. The quality of each column found expression in its total shape and proportion, especially in its capital (q.v.). The transition from one to another historically is an expression of the unfolding of the three-fold nature of the human being.

The Doric column (q.v.) was formed in the masculine image, inspired by the gymnasts of Olympia – it stood for controlled balance of the will. The Ionic column was formed in the elegant feminine image – it expressed the poetic grace and material concepts of the Ionic philosophers. The Corinthian (q.v.) column was modelled on the sharper edges of the Attic philosophy of Plato and Aristotle. Its acanthus leaf represented the flowering of the intellect. This three-fold development is indicated in the balanced format of the three-story building where the Doric is the lowest order, the Ionian the middle, and the Corinthian the highest. It is also an inherent division in the human being which follows the nature of the Trinity of forces, as in willing, feeling, thinking (abdomen, heart, head) or upper arm, forearm and hand, and so on. The column itself is three-fold, consisting of base, shaft, and capital, as the entablature (q.v.) is also composed of three parts. (Compare each order and refer to 'pillar'.)

COMMONWEALTH

A disastrous period for Church history. In 1643 under Cromwell's instigation, all that remained of medieval church art was ruthlessly destroyed. Stained glass windows in churches and cathedrals were wholly destroyed, fine woodwork was burned, and wall-paintings, pictures and stone sculpture either defaced or destroyed.

After the Suppression of the Monasteries under Henry VIII (1536–1539) and the destruction of chantry chapels, altars and icons in the reign of the boy-king Edward VI circa 1549, this was the final death blow to all that remained of the original Roman tradition.

COMMUNION RAIL

Due to the spirit of the Reformation there was much disorder in the state of the churches from the mid-16th century. There was, for example, the controversy over the position of the altar or communion table: the Eucharist was seen either as belonging to the body of the church or as a sacred sacrifice belonging to the chancel end. Prior to the Reformation, 'houseling benches' (q.v.), movable benches, were used for communicants, but Archbishop Laud finally decided the issue during his primacy (1633–41), placing the table at the east end and introducing communion rails, stipulated to be about a yard high. At the same time, among other things, he introduced the Italian credentia or credence table (q.v.).

COMPLINE or COMPLETORIUM

From Latin *completa*, 'completed'; in monastic terms, the completed work of the day. Compline is the last of the seven daily Offices or services, varying in time according to season, country, and specific Order, but between 6 and 9 p.m. The Office has in mind the giving of thanks for the coming rest from labour. Immediately it is over the much respected rule of silence prevails. This is a reminder that all activity returns into the still centre gratituously given

56

in sleep, which is a rehearsal for death, the true life of the spirit.

CONSECRATION CROSS

Latin *consecrare*, 'to dedicate, consecrate' (*con* and *sacer*, 'holy'). From the 12th century onwards, when churches were consecrated, the walls were anointed with oil and marked with a cross. Customarily there were three crosses for each wall, inside and outside, making twenty-four in all. Traces of these crosses, of varied design, are still to be found.

CONVERSI

See under 'lay-brothers'.

COPE

Allied to 'cape', from Medieval Latin *capa*, and originally from Latin *caput*, 'head'. Thus, 'a covering for the head'. Now the word denotes a long cloak worn by clergy on ceremonial occasions.

CORBEL

French *corbel* or *corveau*, Latin *corvus*, 'raven'. A corbel is a block of stone projecting from a wall, suggestive of the projecting beak of the raven. It serves as a support, taking internal structures such as beam or vaulting, and is often beautifully carved. When there are a large number of such corbels in a line below the roof eaves (there are some remarkable examples in Norman churches), such a group is called a 'corbel table'.

CORINTHIAN (COLUMN)

From Corinth, a part of ancient Greece having its own style of architecture, the other two being Doric and

Ionian; it was graceful in proportion, as the Ionic column, having fluted shaft and a capital of carved acanthus leaves. It is said that the architect Cellemachus had a vision of the acanthus motif hanging over the grove of a virgin – a symbolic image of the takeover of the female Ionic phase in Greek history by the phase of the faculty of reason. The scroll form of the acanthus leaf is used in Roman work and continues wherever the classical influence is found. The order is the highest in a three-storey building.

CORNICE

Italian *corona*, 'crown cornice': a horizontal projecting moulding directly under the eaves of a roof, and carved according to the style of the period.

CREDENCE or CREDENCE TABLE

Medieval Latin *credentia*, Latin *credere*, 'to believe, trust'. The small table by the side of the altar on which the bread and wine are placed ready for the Eucharist. The term is a reference to the commital of faith in the act of celebrating the mass. Laud introduced the credence at the beginning of the 17th century.

CRESSET STONE

Old French *craisse*, 'grease', Latin *crassus*, 'thick'. From grease comes the meaning of a vessel for holding burning oil or pitch. A cresset stone is a block of stone with one or more cup-shaped holes, used for containing oil or candles for use in lighting churches in medieval times.

CREST

Old French *creste*, Latin *crista*, 'a cock's comb or tuft on the head of animals'. Thus, a tuft, originally worn on helmets as distinctive identification in battle when the arms on a shield would be lost to sight. In heraldry, a crest is a personal device depicted above the shield.

CROCKETS

A variant of *crochet* which is a diminutive of *croche* or *croc*, a Germanic word meaning 'hook'. Like the musical note, the crotchet, the Gothic architectural device of the same name, is in the form of a hook. Carved projecting hooks decorate the spires, pinnacles and canopies, either stone or wood, of our churches and cathedrals. The varieties of form are innumerable and correspond to the particular period of architecture.

CROSS

The word 'cross' replaced the Old English word *rod*. All forms of the word come from Latin *crux* (genitive *crucis*), 'cross', and this is from an Aryan base *ker*, 'to grow', from which the word 'create' derives.

The symbol of the cross is as old as the history of man. It is an image of one force intersecting another, and is essentially to do with the duality inherent in creation. Thus there are many possible interpretations. First and foremost the cross may be seen as eternity (vertical line) crossed by time (horizontal line). The fact of man's eternal nature being pinned in time is the cause of his frustration, his 'being cross' as we say. There is pain and conflict in the cross. The time line has usurped the eternal one, and he struggles to recover equilibrium. Nevertheless, the vertical line is present in any and all points of the time line, and there is the possibility of this being realised in life.

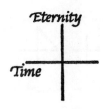

The reality of it is only achieved by sacrifice of the usurping forces, the errors acquired by man in the time process. Christ's death on the cross is a symbol of the sacrifice of all that is illusory in the world. The more a man achieves this, the more time is lived in eternity, the more he is 'in the world but not of it', the more apparent duality is dispelled, and the more the point of the cross becomes a living here-and-now awareness.

Secondly, the cross represents God's descent into time, his taking on a finite nature as an act of reconciliation, a gift of Love. The death on the cross – Truth crucified at the hands of ignorance – is the final act of Love, a means of stamping that image irrevocably upon humanity. The pain of self-crucifixion, it says, leads to Illumination. The idea of the cross as a symbol of reconciliation is even reflected in our everyday practice of using an X to denote a kiss.

Historically, a cross inside a circle antedates one taken out of a circle. When outside, a later stage in man's evolution is signified, as a spiritual unity is lost to an independent physical existence. One of the earliest crosses taken out of the circle was the Egyptian T or Tau cross where the horizontal line is seen simply as a bar imposing a limit

59

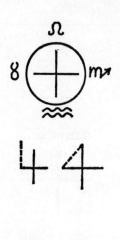

upon the extent of the vertical line, for, as has been said elsewhere, creation means a restriction on power. In the other Egyptian cross, the 'crux ansata', the handled cross or 'ankh' – the abstracted cross has the protective circle above it. As with all crosses, it can be seen as a tree of life or of death – it represents the pinning in time, but it is also the Cross of Life borne by Thoth. It also resembles the glyph of Venus, which, though to do with the higher aspects of love, are also to do with the lower ones of physical generation.

Even the circle is open to dual interpretation, for though because of its nonceasingness it is a symbol of eternity, it is also a ring of limitation holding what is inside it captive. In this sense it represents the limiting power of all the repetitive cycles of nature and time – thus man is fixed in that circle upon his own unique cross. This gives a different view of the cross inside the circle. The individuated point is man on earth at the centre of the four points of the compass, the four fixed signs of the zodiac, the mandala, or any other archetypal glyph rooted in the cross. The cross fixes power onto a point, and this is the meaning behind the number 4, which, in either of its forms represents physicality, power crucified.

Rood   Altar

Despite this ancient symbolism, the earliest images used to represent Christ were the fish, the lamb, and the lion; it was only in the 5th century that the cross was used to convey the central meaning of Christianity. This cross was of two kinds – the Greek cross geometrically perfect, and the Latin cross, formally suited to take the transfixed body of Christ. It was the latter that was adopted later as the plan for the church building.

It is more likely, however, that the cross upon which Christ died was a simple stake or T cross. Moreover, such a stake is symbolically the sacrificial tree, the tree of many mythologies that represents the created world, the proliferation of life and the sacrifice by God of his own power. In Scandinavian mythology and in the Kabala the roots of the tree arise in heaven, a clear image of this truth. It is the tree upon which all men are nailed, and yet it is also the Tree of Life. Here is the dual aspect of the cross again.

We find the same truth in the placing of the crosses in the church building. Before the chancel at the place of the crossing is the tree or cross upon which Christ was crucified – the cross of suffering and death: this is the traditional rood (q.v.) upon the rood-beam which was a key feature of all parish churches up to the time of the Reformation. In this crucifix, finity and duality are shown in a variety of ways; the sun and moon are shown to the right and left of Christ respectively, the Dove is above and the skull below his body, and the thieves at either side are those of the past and the future, the duality in thought that steals the present moment. The other cross or tree is that of Life, properly found on the altar: in this cross, Christ, and potentially the Christ in all men, reigns in glory with the aureole of illumination – it is the result of the sacrifice and renunciation on the first cross, the state of Christus Rex where all is seen as One, and a man is a mere vehicle of Divine energies. Today a plain cross is generally seen on the altar, a partial loss of meaning, but the presence of a crucifix of the first sort, indicates a misunderstanding of the symbolism.

Many types of cross are seen in iconography, most of which stem from heraldry. Surmounting a staff, and carried before them in procession a triple bar signifies a Pope, a double cross signifies an archbishop, and a single cross a bishop (see diagram). A cross elevated on three steps is called a Calvary cross, the steps symbolising the three graces, Faith, Hope and Charity. The cross with its

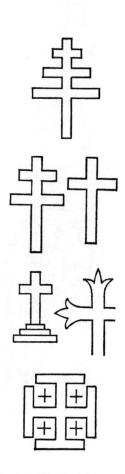

ends in the form of a fleur-de-lis, is called a cross-fleury. The cross with four small ones within its arms is the Jerusalem cross, its total of five crosses symbolising the five wounds of Christ. It was established by the Crusaders, (See 'Maltese cross', 'pattée cross', 'raguly cross', 'St. Andrew's cross' or 'cross decussata', and 'Tau' or 'St. Anthony's cross'.)

CROSSING

The name given to the area between the transepts and before the chancel or rood screen (pulpitum in a cathedral). Above is the central tower or lantern which allows light to fall onto this area. (For the symbolism of the crossing see 'cross', 'transepts', 'church', 'lantern', 'Ascension'.)

CROZIER

Crozier head

Old French *crossier*, 'the one bearing the cross' in the early Church, though later the word came to mean the actual staff itself. The roots of 'crozier' are however Germanic, giving *crucche*, 'crutch or staff' in Middle English. The 'crook' of the shepherd from the same root has the image of drawing sheep into the fold, and reflects the pastoral function of the bishop.

The staff or wand of office, originally a simple wooden walking stick with a curved handle, and always a symbol of authority, was one of the most hallowed possessions of the early Christian saints, capable of transmitting magical powers. In Ireland especially, the staff was guarded zealously as a relic capable of effecting magical cures, and the metal shrines made as protection were of great artistic merit. In England the staff was blessed in the consecration of a bishop as early as the 9th century, and its power is also seen in the legend of the staff of Joseph of Arimathea which bore the Christmas-flowering hawthorn.

Representations of the pastoral staff are seen frequently in monumental effigies in churches, but most of the actual staves the heads of which in the Middle Ages became the vehicles for much beautiful ivory work, were destroyed at the Reformation. It was always held in the left hand so as to allow the right to be free for ritual acts such as blessing.

The symbolism of the 'rod' or 'staff' is connected with the Tree of Life, the vertical force of growth and aspiration whether in nature or in man. In man this force is located around the spinal column, capable of rising in the form of transmuted sex energy. Whether in the Greek *'caduceus'*, or in the Yogic *'kundalini'* the staff of authority has been realised when the power from the earth or sex level has been regenerated to become the flower in the skull.

CRUSADER

With many European versions of the word, from *cruciata* (past participle of *cruciare*, 'to mark with a cross') denoting the cross worn by those fighting for the cause of Christ.

The object of the crusaders was the recovering of the Holy Land from the Saracen invaders. This was successfully accomplished in 1099 by a mainly French force, the first Crusade; but Saladin the Sultan of the Saracens recaptured it in 1187. Later crusades were an attempt to regain the lost ground.

The Third Crusade (1189–93) is significant in Britain since it was led by Richard I (the Lionheart) and included knights from throughout Europe. The seven crusades occurred between the years 1096 and 1270.

The stone effigies of crusaders in churches often have the left leg bent at the knee. This is a mnemonic of the sacrifice of the self-will to the service of Christ, and reflects the image of Christ on the Cross. (See 'right and left'.)

CRUCIFIXION

Latin *crucifixus*, 'one fixed to a cross' (*crux*, 'cross' and *fixus*, past participle of *figere*, 'to fix'). The Crucifixion is the focal point in Church doctrine and iconography. It can be taken on many levels. Upon Creation, all God's power is in a sense, crucified – Eternity by time, Spirit by matter,

Truth by ignorance; and in the final event, the Creator himself is crucified on a mundane cross.

Jesus Christ the man, on the other hand, consciously and voluntarily sacrificed his mortal body, knowing the part this had to play in the cosmic drama. And as that sacrifice was the surrender of the self-will to the Will of the Father, illustrations of the Crucifixion show Christ's head falling to the right (heraldically, that is – left as seen by the spectator). The right side is always that of the Will, the left of the devilish, ego-tainted forces. For the same reason in iconography the left leg of Christ is pinned under the right leg which remains straight – though this occurs regularly only after the 13th century. The spear pierces Christ's right side, for the shed blood is the agency for the regeneration of the earth.

Such a central theme contains much symbolism, and images associated with the historical fact are found everywhere in sculpture, art and furnishings in churches. They include: the stigmata; the crown of thorns; the seamless garment; purple robe; ladder; rope and chain for the deposition of the body; the ewer used by Pilate to wash his hands; hammer and pincers; spear which lanced Christ's side, and chalice containing the blood; the pillar of scourging; two thieves.

Of these the stigmata represent the sacrifice of the sensual life (five senses, five wounds); the seamless garment represents the pure and undivided spirit; the two thieves at right and left represent the duality inherent in time; the purple robe signifies royalty; the spear and chalice represent respectively the masculine principle of initiative and sacrifice, and the world, the female recipient of these – thus of the blood of Christ. The sponge of vinegar on a reed symbolises the very bitterest dreg of suffering upon total renunciation of self-will – the last thing to be tasted by Christ in this world. The reed here is a symbol of great antiquity in mystery rites – it is power that bends without breaking, as with the Spirit under assault.

In iconography there are two crucifixes – Christ suffering and Christ triumphant. (These are discussed under the heading 'cross'.) Historically it is only after the 11th century that Christ is shown naked and dead. Previously he was fully clothed with eyes open and with two feet nailed separately to the cross (see 'icon'). Significant symbolism, established in medieval times, gave way later to the degraded sentimentalism in which inner experience had become a dry shell.

CRYPT

Latin *crypta*, 'a vault', Greek *kruptos*, 'hidden'. The word denotes an underground chamber beneath a church used as a chapel or burial place. The crypt was especially hallowed in early Christianity since the bones of saints and founders were put there and became shrines which could only be viewed from an opening on ground level. (See 'tomb'.) Due to the vulnerability from attack of buildings at ground level, many ancient crypts have been preserved under more recent buildings, e.g. Ripon Cathedral and Hexham Priory (Saxon); York and Gloucester Cathedral (Norman).

CUPOLA

Italian from Low Latin *cupa*, 'cup', Latin *cupola*, a diminutive of *cupa*, 'tub'. Thus, a roof resembling an inverted cup, the outside of which is usually a dome.

CURATE

Low Latin *curatus*, 'one who has the care of souls' (Latin *cura*, 'care'). The word 'cure' is also derived from this root, and thus a curate is a healer of souls. The incumbent or vicar of a parish originally had the name of 'curate', but now the title is reserved for an assistant.

CUSP

Latin *cuspis*,'A point'. One of the points projecting from the underside of an arch, giving a trefoil or multifoil form to the arch. Cusps originated in the later part of the Early English style, when they sometimes terminated in a leaf.

DADO

Italian *dado*, 'cube, pedestal'. The pedestal (small column) between the base and the cornice. Architecturally it has come to mean the lower part of the walls in a room

when decorated differently from the upper, especially by panelling with mouldings resembling a continuous pedestal. It is usually separated from the upper half by a moulding.

DAGGER MOTIF

A common motif in the window tracery of the Decorated style, pointed at the foot and either round or pointed at the head. The inside is cusped. When the motif is curved it is a 'mouchette'. It is common in the complex curves of the 'flamboyant style'. (See 'tracery'.)

DEACON AND DEACONESS

Greek *diakonos*, 'a servant'. The most junior rank in the ordained ministry, below a priest and bishop.

DEAN

Latin *decanus* from *decem*, 'ten'. Originally a monk supervising ten novices, a dean is now a senior priest in charge of a cathedral, or, as a rural dean, a subsection of a diocese.

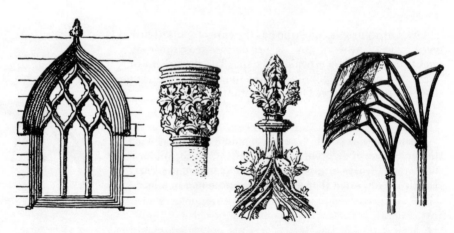

DECORATED PERIOD

A period of English architecture following on from Early English, from 1307–77, broadly equated with the 14th century. It is so called because the simplicity of the early style changes into ornateness. Decoration now predominates. Windows have geometric and flowery tracery

(see 'tracery'), the clearstory is heightened, vaulting has many ribs giving an effect of star shapes, and the ogee arch is used. The names Geometric and Curvilinear used in relation to this period really refer to the tracery in the windows.

DENTIL

Latin *dens*, 'a tooth': thus a decorated classical motif on a moulding.

DEVIL

Middle English *devel*, Latin *diabolus*, Greek *diabolos*, 'slanderer' (Greek *diaballein* is 'to slander, accuse'). In art, the devil is illustrated with a tail, hair, horns and claws, indicating a close affinity with animality, a reference to man's own animality. Though man began as a spirit being, his power, in its descent through the planes, assumed animality. With his will orientated to that debased condition and to egotism, i.e. to all that is opposed to true life, he is a servant of the devil, symbolised in the inverted five pointed star or pentacle (the five senses) as in the diagram. With his will orientated to the Will of God, he may become an upright balanced man who uses rather than abuses his senses. *Live* in reverse is *evil*: *devil* is the embodiment of forces committed to opposing true life.

Even so, the Devil may be seen as Deus Inversus, God inverted, in the sense that the devilish condition is the very means of man's development – thus the connection between *devil* and *develop*. This being so, it is God who can be blamed – he is the goat, the original scapegoat at whom it is possible to point an accusing finger; thus the meaning in the Greek word. If this is not understood, then man, locked in his own debased power, is in Hell. If he acknowledges the purpose in his suffering, and hands what he has arrogated to himself, back to the Source, he is free.

Hell is represented in iconography as a region of chaos, heat, animality, aimless movement, and the acrid fumes of hate – all stirred by the Devil. These are only comprehensible images of psychological agonies experienced in waking life, or more obviously, after death when hell is the sum total of all errors (sins) as re-experienced by a man as he sits in his own judgement.

In medieval carving, on fonts, the struggle between good and evil is often depicted: baptism is the initial move

67

in the regenerating of debased power. In the Roman blessing at baptism is found the idea of exorcising 'every wile of devilish deceit'.

DEXTERA DEI

Literally 'the right hand of God' but referred to simply as 'the hand of God': in iconography the image is of a hand, usually issuing out of a cloud and representing God the Father – the First Person of the Trinity. The symbol of the hand was originally used because of the obvious difficulty of personifying an abstract power. But about the 9th century God the Father began to be represented as the middle figure of three Persons, and by the 16th century, with God shown in pontifical robes, the externalised form had degraded the simple symbol.

The image of the hand was still used in medieval times and is found in many Old Testament scenes, such as the sacrifice of Isaac, Moses and the Burning Bush, Moses receiving the Law, etc., and in many of the principal incidents of Christ's life in the New Testament. It is used whenever God intercedes on behalf of man, speaking to him or blessing him. This intercedence is suggested in the hand reaching downwards and also in the open palm. The hand has, in fact, its own three aspects corresponding to the aspects of the Trinity – the closed fist, the energy of which is as yet unleashed (Father), the fingers, capable of precise shaping of raw material (Son), and the palm of the hand, receptive and open in an attitude of love (Holy Spirit). The Dextera Dei expresses the love in the Father's power. (See 'blessing' and 'right and left'.)

DISCIPLES

Latin *discipulus*, 'a learner, pupil', related to *discere*, 'to learn'. The word disciple is closely connected with the disciplines presented by a teacher. In the New Testament the twelve disciples each represent a part of the whole, as Christ represents the whole. Their unique way of spreading the Christian message corresponds to one of the cosmic energies of the twelve signs of the zodiac. The number 12 is significant as a multiple of 3 and 4: three aspects of absolute power, as in the Trinity, unmanifest, play through the four elements of the manifest world, giving twelve permutations. It is a number of developmental progression represented in the division of the rose window of cathedrals.

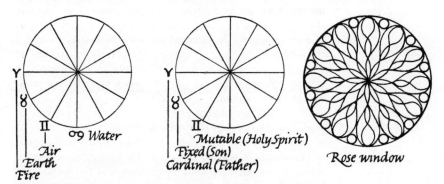

Because each being has a unique energy pattern his personal discipline is to awaken and embrace the others so as to become a whole man. For this reason Christ is properly at the centre of a round table as was King Arthur. Both are the potentially whole man, and the beings around them are the partial man. Whenever the number 12 is seen in mythology, as in the twelve Labours of Hercules, or even in the twelve members of the modern jury, there is the same idea of seeking a whole by synthesising the parts. In hearing and spreading the gospel in their unique ways, the disciples were continuing a fundamental symbolism. (See 'apostles' and 'Last Supper'.)

DOG-TOOTH

The most characteristic ornament on moulding in Early English architecture, known as dog-tooth because it consists of four leaf-forms drawn up to a point resembling the tooth of a dog.

DOMINICANS

One of the four main orders of friars (brothers depending upon alms for their existence) named after St. Dominic, an Augustinian canon, who founded the order in 1205 – they are sometimes known as the O.P. – Order of Preachers, and first came to this country in 1221, founding a house in Oxford. Due to the black mantle over a white habit they also became known as Black Friars.

69

DOOM

Old English *dom*, Old High German *tuom*, judgement, decree': from an Aryan root 'to do' or 'to put'. The 'doom' is the name given to a medieval painting or stage depiction of a scene where the damned are pitchforked by the devil into the mouth of hell – a version of the Last Judgement. It was often found in medieval churches in the form of a tympanum covering the area between the chancel arch and the rood screen.

The idea of judgement obviously indicates the decree of God, but the devil in this role, is given the appearance of his awe-inspiring assistant. This original majestic aspect of the devil, however, gave way to a farcical aspect in which he became the butt of ridicule and the buffoon of the medieval stage. In this guise, all that was base on human nature could be expiated – and the devil became a scapegoat. The later Punch and Judy show is a continuation of the same theme, with Punch the devil being irreverently knocked on the head and ridiculed.

DORIC COLUMN

From *Doris*, one of the partitions of ancient Greece. It is the strongest and most ancient of columns, massive, without base, with a simple capital and shallow fluting. The diameter is approximately 2/11ths of the height. In a three-eyed building, where each storey has a different order, the Doric is always the lowest. The Doric column was formed on a strong masculine image, complementary with the Ionic column which was based on the elegant female form. The Romans, whilst keeping the proportions, introduced a plinth and scalloped flutings.

DORMITORY

Low Latin *dormitorium*, 'sleeping room', *dormire*, 'to sleep'. The sleeping room in a monastery sometimes abbreviated to DORTER.

DORTER

An abbreviation of 'dormitory', the sleeping room in a monastery (See above). The 'rere-dorter' (q.v.) is the room containing closets, behind the sleeping quarters.

70

DOVE

Middle English *dūve*, Gothic *dūbo*, related to Old English *dūfan*, 'to dive', from an Aryan base meaning 'to go down into water'. The dove is a symbol of the Holy Ghost, and as such is found carved on font covers, in representations of the baptism of Christ, the Annunciation to the Virgin Mary, and in the creation of the world. It is a symbol of the reconciliation between God and man, spirit and matter: it is the symbol of God's love for his creation.

In the New Testament, the Spirit of God is said to descend like a dove, and images show the bird diving head first out of heaven onto earth, from eternity into time, following the imagery of the derivation of the word. At the rite of baptism, the descent is into the waters of materiality – a symbolic banishing of all impurity from the human condition. In man's inner life, the fire of the spirit, the white dove, descends only into a prepared vehicle.

In a wider sense of the earth's evolution, the Holy Spirit saves and reconciles man, constantly sowing seeds of new spiritual beginnings in times of degeneracy: for instance the dove brought an olive branch into the ark of Noah, rescuing Truth from the flood of error, an indication of God's reconciliation with man. Or we may see how Truth mysteriously shifts to a new civilisation when an old one decays. In another sense the Latin word for dove is *columba*, and Columbine in the origins of pantomime represents the perfect human soul, companion of Harlequin (the eternal Spirit) and daughter of Pantaloon (the physical level). Here she is clearly a reconciler between the two levels. Strangely the column (Latin *columna*), so integral to the church building, is a support between ground and roof, again reflecting the function of mediation between high and low.

DRAGON

Greek *drakon*, 'a dragon, serpent'. It is literally to do with sight – Greek *derkomai*, 'to see'; thus 'one who sees'. The sight here suggested is that intrinsic to physical world and the attendant time-process. The chief enemy of man's spirit is his involvement in the world of sight, the dragon. It is this that devours his free spirit. This is the same dialectic as is found in 'Lucifer' where the word means 'bringer of light' though he is in effect the 'Prince of

Darkness'. Sight is a great gift, but it usurps man's inner sight: the dragon may bring fire, the source of light, but it burns up all in its path.

The killing of the dragon in Christian art represents the overcoming of forces that hold man in bondage. St. George who kills the dragon is literally 'earth worker', and equally St. Michael (Hebrew, 'he who is like unto God') is shown clad in his armour fighting the same fight of the spirit, as do all children of God. Satan, the embodiment of evil, is shown in the guise of a serpent or dragon.

DRIPSTONE or WEATHER-MOULDING

A stone or projecting moulding which takes away the dripping of water from above a door or window, and is in some instances used decoratively on the inner wall of a building. (See 'hood-moulding'.)

DRUID

Old Celtic *druid – dru* and *wid. Dru* means 'very strong' and *wid*, 'to know': thus 'very wise'. *Wid* is the same root as *wit*, related to Latin *videre*, 'to see' and Old English *wis*, 'wise'. The *dru* part of the word is also related to Greek *drus*, 'oak' or 'tree'.

Druidism is an ancient Celtic system of religion, governed by a priesthood, a repository of learning covering all conceivable subjects within an embracing cosmology. The extant writings, dating from before the advent of Christianity, belie the notion that Britain was a savage place before the coming of the Romans. There are many remarkable similarities in the early canons to the tenets of early Christianity, and it is little wonder that the Druidism of Wales was absorbed so readily into early Christian monasticism.

E

EAGLE

Low Latin *aquila*, 'eagle', Latin *aquilus*, 'dark-skinned', with reference to the colour of the bird. Classically a symbol of victory of higher spiritual forces over lower terrestrial ones, as when it is represented with talons on a serpent. In Christianity the higher spiritual force is the

Logos or Word which had the power to introduce order into chaos – to formulate unformulated power. The eagle with its capacity to see from a great height (birds and air are both symbols of the intellect) surveys all below it. So the Word supervises the manifest world. Thus the connection with St. John whose symbol is the eagle: and in the church the position of the carved eagle on the lectern (q.v.) indicating the capacity of the spirit to soar above the letter of the law.

When depicted fighting with a serpent the conflict indicated is between the Creator's rudimentary Power and his ordering Intelligence; it is a conflict in that Intellect is a limit upon Power, and is responsible for the shaping of the world. It is, in fact, the Son opposing the Father, an opposition referred to in early Christianity. But the end of the opposition is not the killing of the Father by the Son, the serpent by the eagle, but the return of the Son, a reconciliation with the Father and thus the fulfilling of the Word. This is seen in the story of the Prodigal Son and in the pattern of a man's life. Energy and intelligence then work together, and the image becomes one of the eagle and serpent intertwined.

The two-headed eagle of the Eastern Church, looking right and left, affirms the power of the overseeing Logos over the dualities in time and space. The eagle, as the constellation representing St. John and as one of the four creatures associated with the Evangelists, is explained under 'Evangelist'.

EARLY ENGLISH

The period of architecture following upon the Norman, beginning in 1189 and continuing until 1307; it is thus broadly equated with the 13th century. Notable features are – tall lancet windows and pinnacles, and groups of slender shaftes replacing sold Norman pillars: other features are buttresses, foliated capitals and graceful rib and panel vaults. (*See overleaf*).

EAST END

'East' is from a Germanic root *austr*, 'east', which is connected with Latin *Aurora* and Greek *eos*, both meaning 'dawn'.

The orientation of the church with the altar at the east end derives from ancient pagan traditions. Monuments,

Spirit
light
E
|
W
Dark
matter

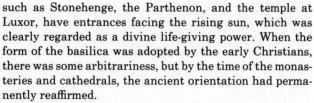

such as Stonehenge, the Parthenon, and the temple at
Luxor, have entrances facing the rising sun, which was
clearly regarded as a divine life-giving power. When the
form of the basilica was adopted by the early Christians,
there was some arbitrariness, but by the time of the monasteries and cathedrals, the ancient orientation had permanently reaffirmed.

The sun was symbolically seen as the Son, that is as
Christ the Son of God, since it was seen to resurrect daily
and annually out of darkness, as Christ rose from the
darkness of the tomb into eternal life. The power of resurrection in all its forms, whether it is seen in the cosmos at
Christmas and Easter, or psychologically in the re-righting of man's fallen energies, is a function of male will, of
the spirit's affirmation of power over matter, life over
death. East is connected with Easter, the festival of the
resurrection of light celebrated at the vernal equinox.
Thus the male lancet window symbolically belongs to the
east end of a church (and where its three divisions are
under one arch, the unity of the Trinity), whilst the rose
window, as female, belongs to the west end. The entry into

74

a church at the west end symbolises man's entry into the material world, and through baptism a return towards the re-birth of the spirit. This is also reflected in the two towers on either side of the west door (the duality of the world), and the single central tower above the crossing (the light-filled unity of the spirit). (See 'pillar' and 'lantern'.)

The East as the source of wisdom and truth is found everywhere in fairy story and myth: there is the same quest for the divine intelligence and life power that derives from the light of the sun. (See 'west end'.)

EFFIGY

French *effigie*, from Latin *effigies*, 'likeness, portrait', which is associated with *effingere*, 'to form, fashion'. Thus the meaning of a figure fashioned to represent a person.

The figures at the feet of effigies have various significances. They may represent any enemy of the spirit, such as a serpent denoting evil, trodden underfoot, as in Eastern symbolism; they may have heraldic meaning or describe the subject by name or vocation; or they may be emblems of qualities, as the lion, strength, and the dog, fidelity.

In a church, effigies traditionally have their foot towards the altar, a reminder that in death all will be raised up to face Christ, the Judge. There was no attempt at realistic portraiture in them until about 1500 and thereafter.

EGG AND DART

A classical decorative motif on a moulding consisting of alternating egg and dart forms.

ELEPHANT

Latin *elephantus*, Greek *elephantos*, genitive of *elephas*. In the period of medieval wood-carving, the elephant, by virtue of its tremendous power, symbolised the majestic power of good over evil. It is found in stall work or bench ends, often with howdah upon its back.

EMBATTLE

Old French *bataillement* and *bastiller*, 'to fortify'. A figure used in heraldry and on Norman moulding resembling the parapet on a tower.

EMBRASURE

Old French *embraser*, 'to set on fire, inflame'. The word in architecture means the splay on the interior wall of a door or window, whereby the opening is wider on the inner than the outer wall. The reason for the use of the word is unknown.

ENCAUSTIC

Greek *enkaustikos*, 'burnt in'. Pavements and floor space in monastic institutions often have tiles where the colour has been fixed by a process of burning in. The effect was to produce something like a Roman mosaic – and the term tesselated (Latin *tesselatus*, 'composed of small stones') sometimes given to such tiles is inaccurate. The arms of founders are often found on the tiles. The art of their manufacture seems to have been the prerogative of the monasteries and cathedrals, for they are not found elsewhere.

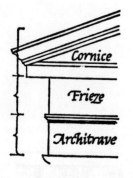

ENTABLATURE

Latin *tabula*, 'a table or board'. The whole of the horizontal superstructure lying upon a column in classical architecture. This is divided into three parts, as there are three major types of column (q.v.) and the column itself is of three parts – base, shaft and capital. The architrave is immediately above the capital, the frieze above that, and above that is the projecting part or cornice.

EPISCOPAL

Latin *episcopus*, 'an overseer', from Greek *episkopos* (*epi*, 'over' and *skopos*, 'a watcher'). This is the word from which 'bishop' derives. The word episcopal signifies anything belonging to or vested in bishops, i.e. jurisdiction.

ESCUTCHEON

Old French *escuchon* (variant of *escucon*) from Latin *scutum*, 'shield'. *Scutum* is related to *cutis*, 'skin or hide' denoting the hide of which a shield is made. Thus the general meaning of a shield shape upon which coats of arms are depicted.

EVANGELISTS

Latin *evangelium*, 'gospel', Greek *evangelion*, 'good tidings, gospel', (*eu*, 'good' and *angelia*, 'message'). The Evangelists are the writers of the four Gospels – Matthew, Mark, Luke and John. They are four in number because four is the number denoting the establishment of power on the material plane, as is seen in the symbolism of the four rivers in the Garden of Eden, the points of the compass, the solidity of the cube and so on. Each of the writers in his own way affirms and announces the incarnation of God as man.

The particular mode of expression of each Evangelist is related to the four elements through which the substantial universe manifests, and because incarnation is a fixing into physical existence, each is related to one of the four fixed signs of the zodiac – air, fire, earth, water.

MATTHEW (Hebrew *Mattatiah*, 'gift of God') is related to Aquarius ♒ (air), because he evaluates as a man, sorting out the whole situation with clarity of memory and formal accuracy – he speaks of the human origins of Christ.

MARK (Latin, derived from *Mars*), is related to Leo ♌ (fire) because his energy is directed to authoritative statement – here is power, the power to draw men out of error, not mere statement.

LUKE (Latin name *Lucius*, from *lux*, 'light' – compare with the use of the word in 'Lucifer' (q.v.)) is related to Taurus ♉ (earth). His version is more intimate, more internal, and more on the material plane.

JOHN (Hebrew *Johanan*, 'God is gracious') is related to Scorpio ♏ (water). He is the odd man out – his is a version of visionary qualities that goes beyond the limits of the other three – in fact to the Higher Intelligence of the Logos.

Thus the Evangelists in Christian art, often found surrounding Christ in a window or at the termination of the limbs of a crucifix, take on the nature of the animals associated with these fixed signs:

Matthew – a man's head
Mark – a lion

77

Luke – a bull
John – an eagle

except that the eagle of St. John has replaced the Scorpion of the zodiac: he has assumed identity with the constellation Aquila, Eagle, which lies outside the zodiac. Why is this? The change is obviously not an arbitrary one. It is because a passionate attachment to the world can become equally a passionate desire for spiritual change – Scorpio is closely connected with both the sting of sexuality and with regeneration. (Such a regeneration is in fact prefi-

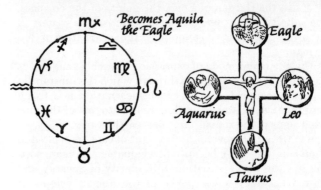

gured in an earlier John, John the Baptist, who declared the possibility of it through baptism.) Consider, too, John the disciple whom Jesus loved for the sheer strength of his devotion. It is such intense devotion, epitomised in the sign Scorpio, that can lead ultimately to a break out from the confining circle of temporality into the eagle eye of simultaneous comprehension on the level of the Logos. It is for this reason that the extra-zodiacal constellation Aquila, the Eagle, has been attributed to John. (See 'eagle' and 'lectern'.)

These four 'beasts' are constantly depicted in iconography from an early date, surrounding Christ in Majesty or embellishing the ends of the arms of the cross, and their placing in the zodiacal sequence accounts for the order of the names as generally spoken – Matthew-Mark and Luke-John being pairs of opposites. Man is the central theme and purpose of creation and is correctly placed first, whilst the break out of the circuit of time is placed last as the ultimate achievement. The placing of the different symbols, however, has been arbitrary, even to the point of losing the natural heavenly sequence. In the version in the diagram the eagle rises above the head of Christ, suggesting the regeneration of man's sexual energies implied in the signs Taurus and Scorpio.

Thus one of the most commonly seen symbols in the church, and one of the least noticed, is seen to convey a wealth of meaning – a key to inner development. The fact that the four Evangelists and their symbols are archetypal spiritual powers is shown in their being represented with the wings of Cherubim: that they are of great antiquity can be seen in the four-fold imagery of the sphinx of ancient Egypt. Here the head is of a man, the claws are of a lion, the body and tail are those of a bull, and the wings are those of an eagle. The higher aspects of these animals give the occult dictum 'know' (man), 'dare' (lion), 'keep silent' (bull) and 'do' (eagle). The imagery is also found in Ezekiel's vision of the creatures supporting the throne of God and in the four creatures of the Apocalpyse. (See Ezekiel I vs 5–10, and Revelation IV vs 6–8).

Whereas in the 5th century Byzantine artists depicted the Evangelists as half-man, half-beast, by the late Middle Ages in the West man and beast were separated, three of them with their respective animals by their sides. Often a scroll is used with each man or beast showing the initial words of each gospel. A representation of all four Evangelists in one animal (as in Ezekiel) is known as a 'tetramorph'. 'See 'man', 'lion', 'bull', and 'eagle'.)

F

FALDSTOOL

Old High German *faldstool, fald*, 'to fold', and *stuol*, 'a chair'. Originally a stool or chair without arms, foldable and portable, for use by a bishop in a church other than his own. The term now applies to the desk to which a stool is attached and from which the litany is read. The litany desk faces away from the congregation, the priest addressing his prayer towards the altar.

FAN VAULTING

See under 'rib vaulting'.

FERETORY

Middle English *fertre*, 'shrine, tomb or bier'. Latin *feretrum*, from Greek *pheretron*, 'bier': all from Greek *pherein*, 'to carry'. Thus, a reliquary or casket containing the relics of a saint designed to be carried in a procession. The term is also applied to that part of a church devoted to such a shrine. (See under 'relic'.)

FIELD (in heraldry)

Old German *felt*, 'field, plain'. In heraldry it is the background of a shield – or of a given quarter of the shield upon which the charge is found. The field could be variegated in two ways – one, by 'powdering' (a scattered pattern of small charges of varying types) and, two, by subdivision with lines, some of which are extensions of the ordinary charges.

FIG-LEAF

Latin *ficus*, 'fig-tree', connected with Latin *fictor*, 'one who fashions or makes images'. The connection between the two words is found in the symbolism of the fig-tree as used in Genesis. The fruit of the fig-tree consists largely of seeds, and the fig-leaf Adam and Eve used to cover themselves in the story denotes the covering or loss of the inner creative power caused through physical generation. The meaning is that from that moment the will of man was lost to the stimulus of the outer world epitomised by the woman. (See 'Adam and Eve'.)

FILLET

Latin *filum*, 'thread'. A small flat strip or band separating different mouldings and found in both classical and Gothic work.

FINIAL

Latin *finis*, 'end'. The upper projecting part of a gable or pinnacle; also the top of the decorated end of a bench or screen. They were especially employed along with the crockets in the Decorated period.

FISH

'Fish' is one of many similar words, from a common Germanic root, of which one is Latin *piscis*, 'fish'. The fish as a symbol is closely connected with Christ. In the early Church he was called Iesous Ichthos (Jesus the Fish) or sometimes 'The Great Fish'. This was because Christ's birth heralded the beginning of the zodiacal era of 2,150 years, the Sign of Pisces (The Fishes). His disciples were known as 'fishers of men' and the early Fathers referred to their charges as *pisciculi*, 'little fishes'; the basin for washing the sacrificial vessels near the altar was a *piscina*, and the Greek word *ichthys* ('ιχθυς), 'fish', is made from the first letters of the words meaning 'Jesus Christ Son of God Saviour'; even the bishop's mitre (q.v.) is in form of a fish's head, and in the New Testament we find the story of the Feeding of the Five Thousand with five loaves and two fishes and the feast on the shore of the Sea of Tiberius after Christ's Resurrection. The fish was a eucharistic symbol in early reproductions of the Last Supper and the elliptical aureole surrounding Christ in Majesty and later in the Middle Ages, the Virgin (q.v.), was called the *vesica piscis*, 'the bladder of the fish'. This is again a reference to the Piscean Age and to the redemption of man in the material 'sea' by the compassion of Christ.

Early oil lamp

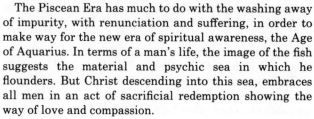

Pisces

The Piscean Era has much to do with the washing away of impurity, with renunciation and suffering, in order to make way for the new era of spiritual awareness, the Age of Aquarius. In terms of a man's life, the image of the fish suggests the material and psychic sea in which he flounders. But Christ descending into this sea, embraces all men in an act of sacrificial redemption showing the way of love and compassion.

FIVE WOUNDS

The five wounds are those made by the nails which fixed Christ to the cross – one through each foot and hand, and one made by the lance in the breast. They are generally seen as a symbol of the necessity of dying to the five senses. (See 'devil'.)

The five wounds, however, can be seen in a dual light. Five is a sacred number in so far as it signifies the fully perfected physical man – an aggregate of all that has precursed him in order to give rise to the perfect vehicle for the new individualised or 'I' consciousness. It is the five-sense apparatus that enables him to relate to the external world, a reflection of which is seen in the five toes and fingers. Negatively however, contingent upon this

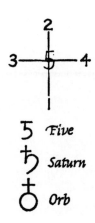

2

3 — 5 — 4

1

5 *Five*

♄ *Saturn*

☦ *Orb*

81

perfect form is a bondage to the senses, and the acquisition of a hard insular ego structure. This means that man stands at the point of the greatest danger, yet of the greatest positive potential. For the physical body to be a true vehicle of the spirit, sacrifice of the small I to the true 'I' of spiritual power is necessary. Five is to do with the sacrifice at the centre of the cross, the point of pinning and yet of release.

The glyph of the number five is made of the cross of matter over the circle of spirit, as with the glyph of Saturn, but seen in its redemptive light it is the reverse, the cross of the power of Christ over the world. (See 'orb'.)

The five petals of the rose convey the same meaning – it is, formally speaking, perfection. But that bewitching beauty, along with its scent, lulls the spirit to sleep, and it is then the Rosa Mundi, the Rose of the World, or the maya of creation. But the blood of conscious sacrifice (the thorns) awakens the Christ in a man and the rose is then the Mystic Rose, the world in which all has been reassumed, purified – and in which the marriage between spirit and matter has been accomplished. Thus, the five petals represent in iconography the five wounds of Christ, as the red rose is often a symbol of Christ's sacrificed blood. (See 'rose'.) Similarly, the core of the apple forming the five-pointed star, and the apple itself (see 'Adam and Eve') signify both the danger and the glory of the world.

The stigmata in art are those five wounds imprinted upon the physical body, sometimes with a flow of blood, in certain saints and other holy people. The five-pointed star is discussed under the heading 'devil'.

FLAGELLATION

From Latin *flagellum*, 'a whip', diminutive of *flagrum*, 'whip, scourge'. Flagellation was a commonly used and accepted practice of the middle ages, on the principle that as the flesh sins, so it should be punished. In monastic discipline, at the daily confession in the chapter house, this was the punishment most meted out by the abbot. The offender was required, on his knees, to disrobe down to the girdle, and the punishment ceased when the abbot indicated: there were however, strict rules about how and by whom it should be given. Flagellation was a part of religious life in medieval times; it is known that many great saints and Church dignitaries had their own private scourges to do penance for their sins.

So great was the zeal in the 12th century that public shows of flagellation upon others and upon self, were a common sight. In a way, it took the place of penance. In the 14th century, there was renewed zeal by those who thought that the Black Death was a sign of God's wrath for man's wickedness.

FLEUR-DE-LIS

A French word, 'flower of the lily'. It was the royal insignia of France from 1147. Originally completely covered by these flowers, from the time of Charles IV the banner consisted of three fleurs-de-lis on a blue field. The symbol occurs in English armorial bearing due to early English claims on French territory, and was featured as quartering in the English royal arms until the rule of George IV.

In the Church, due to the beauty of the flower and perhaps to the biblical 'Consider the lilies how they grow … Solomon in all his glory was not arrayed like one of these', it was at an early time used in representations of the Annunciation and as a symbol of the Virgin Mary. (See 'lily'.) It is also seen as the termination of certain crosses, when it is either a cross-fleury or fleurée (a) or in diminutive, a cross fleurette (b).

FONT

Latin *fons*, 'fountain, source'. The word font is already used in Old and Middle English to denote the baptismal font, the carved stone or marble basin with lead lining used to contain the holy water for the sacrament of baptism. The part of the church where it stands is known as the baptistery. Fonts were of varying shapes in early Christianity, each symbolising some aspect of the meaning of baptism. In the 11th and 12th centuries the most common form was the tub without stem: it was only in the 12th and 13th centuries that the bowl was mounted on four legs, and only in the 14th that it had a single stem. These forms were related to the modifications that took place in the rite itself. In the earliest days of total immersion the rite took place in a space lower than ground level (symbolising also descent and re-birth), but when infant baptism began in the Middle Ages the font was raised for conven-

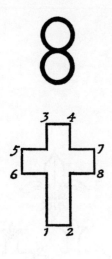

ience to ground level, and later, when sprinkling was substituted, it became smaller and was raised higher on a pedestal. In these times, the consecrated water of the font was often stolen because of its magical properties, and it was as protection against this that fonts began to be covered. Originally plain covers, they eventually gave rise to the many beautifully carved, hanging, wooden canopies found in English churches.

There are two aspects to the symbolism of the font – the water in the font itself, as the Immaculate Womb of all matter, and the pure fire of the Holy Spirit seen in the image of the dove (q.v.) often found above it. These two elements are inextricable – a man is spirit and matter, and it is the spirit in him which is able to transform the fallen matter. As the spirit is constantly active in creating such rebirths, the fonts are frequently octagonal in form. The number 8 is simply a glyph of one cycle or octave leading out to begin another. It represents the work of the spirit in the continuing cycles of progression towards a purified vehicle.

The font is always to be found at the western end of the church: this is the material end, as is equally the nave (Latin *navis* 'ship'), the ship that redeems man on the material sea of existence.

FOUR DOCTORS OF THE CHURCH

The four Doctors or Fathers of the Church are often shown together in iconography: they are St. Jerome, St. Ambrose, St. Augustine and St. Gregory. Together they established the Church and its doctrines, and from the 10th century onwards were regarded as divinely inspired and infallible. They are four in number because four is the number of stability, of the establishing of power on earth as with the Evangelists (q.v.) and such archetypal images as the four rivers in the Garden of Eden, the four points of the compass, and so on.

St. Jerome: born circa 342, ascetic and translator of the Old Testament and New Testament into Latin (The Vulgate), is seen either as a cardinal carrying a miniature church in his hand, or as an ascetic with wasted limbs and carrying a book and pen; also in the latter role sometimes with a lion in accordance with legend.

St. Ambrose: born 340, is seen with episcopal robes and with mitre and crozier, holding a book. A persuasive orator and advocate of asceticism, he is often seen with a bee-

84

hive, after the story that a swarm of bees alighted on his
mouth as a child and did him no harm. More frequently he
has a scourge, an emblem of the severe penances inflicted
by him upon sinners.

St. Augustine: born circa 354, was a great theologian
and author of a monastic rule which subsequently gave
rise to the order using his name. Above all, he made a
system out of the strands of Christianity. His greatest
work, and the first of its kind in literature, is 'The Con-
fessions'. He is dressed as a bishop carrying a book.

St. Gregory: born 540, known as Pope Gregory the Great,
was a reformer of Church liturgies and music, and a strong
advocate of celibacy. He is represented as being of dark
complexion and with the tiara of a pope and a dove near
his shoulder.

FRANCISCANS

One of the four main orders of friars (brothers depending on alms for support), known also as the Order of Friars
Minor. They were founded by, and named after, St. Fran-
cis of Assisi circa 1209, and reached England in 1224. They
were bound to poverty and gained respect for their scholarly achievements. Roger Bacon was a Franciscan.
Because of their grey habits, they were known as Grey
Friars.

FRATER, FRATRY, FRATERY, FRATERER

Old French *fraitur*, an abbreviation of Low Latin *refec-
torium*, 'refectory'. The dining room of a monastery, and
Fraterer the monk in charge of it. (See 'refectory'.)

FREEMASON

('Refer also to 'mason'.) Originally said to be a stone
cutter who used a chisel as opposed to one who could only
dress stone with cruder implements, or simply build walls.
Thus the word is said to be a contraction of freestone-
mason. (Freestone is stone that may be cut with relative
freedom into blocks and then worked by chisel.) Due to the
special skill of masons – those nameless artists responsible
for beautiful windows and sculpture, and moreover the
custodians of spiritual truths through their work – privileges were conferred upon them, for instance freedom of
movement from country to country. In this sense the guild

of masons enjoyed a liberty not entertained by other guilds.

Moreover the mason, both in his external trade and symbolically, was always the shaper of matter, and held a special place in the occult traditions of ancient civilisations. His secrets concerning structure were very much the same as those of the spirit of man within the structure of the physical body. Thus the idea of 'free' occurs on various levels. It should be remembered too that the medieval cathedrals were built wholly on the sites: it was only after the plague at the end of the 13th century that the work of masons began to be done in 'shops', places distant from the building itself, as in the Wye Valley, and that work was transported from there to the site. This was just one of the many factors in the decline of medieval tradition, which culminated in the Reformation, the Dissolution of the Monasteries and the inner meaning of the masonic tradition itself. (See 'mason').

FRESCO

Italian *fresco*, 'fresh', from the Old High German *frisc*. Painting on walls of churches during the medieval period was done with watercolour whilst the plaster was still wet – hence the term. This accounts for the durability of the colour so embodied.

FRIAR

French *frère*, Latin *frater*, 'brother'. A name given to a brother in one of the four mendicant orders – that is those orders depending on alms for their existence – the Dominicans, Augustinians, Franciscans and Carmelites. (See under each heading.) The original sincerity of such a dependence is demonstrated by the fact that certain of the orders were not allowed to receive money. All came to Britain at the beginning of the 13th century.

FRITHSTOOL or FREEDSTOLL

Anglo Saxon *frith* or *frid*, 'peace', plus 'stool'. A plain stone seat that used to stand in the sanctuary of certain churches affording sanctuary to criminals who reached it: the privilege was endowed by King Athelstan in 900 and not abolished until 1623. A sanctuary church boundary was determined by crosses outside the town. Once inside the church and seated on the frithstool, the criminal could not be seized. In the churches where the privilege applied, a priest was on watch and the well known sanctuary knockers (as the one at Durham) were used to gain entrance. The period of freedom varied between thirty and forty days, after which serious offenders were obliged to leave the country. The records of Beverley Minster name hundreds of such sanctuary seekers, and it was the abuse of the privilege that finally led to its annulment.

FYLFOT

A word said to be a rendering of 'fill the foot'. It is used from medieval times to denote the swastika cross, the turning cross of great antiquity (q.v.). But in this context it denotes merely an ornament of classical antiquity in the form of the swastika which was used as an ornament for embroidery and sometimes in window decoration, thus filling the foot of cloth or window.

G

GALILEE PORCH

In medieval churches a porch at the west end so named was used as a chapel for penitents and those excommunicated from the Church. The name is said to derive from Latin *galeria*, 'a long porch'; but the many images of water belonging to the west end of a church (stoup, font, nave, porch) suggest that this name was probably used with reference to the Sea of Galilee and to the faith required to walk again upon the surface of the waters. Equally as Galilee was distant from Jerusalem, so the porch was at the furthest point possible from the sanctuary, the privileges of which were being sought.

GALLERY

After the Restoration in 1660, it became common to erect galleries at the west end of a church to make room for growing congregations, and also to house a small orchestra and/or choir. Previously, some 'lead' singers would have sung along with the congregation. The band, consisted, according to availability, of violin, cello, flute, clarinet, hautboy and bassoon; this situation pertained until the advent of the organ in the 19th century.

GARGOYLE

Old French *gargouille*, 'throat', Latin *gurgulio*, 'gullet' or 'windpipe'. Thus the connection with the waterspouts spewing out rain from the gutters; and also, symbolically, by the aid of the grotesque animal or human heads, spewing out forces of evil from the house of God. Equally they can be seen as sentinels against evil forces attempting to gain entry. In many cases, though the mouths of the creatures are open, the water is conveyed through a lead spout above or below the figure.

GARDEN OF EDEN

Old High German *gart*, 'enclosure' and Eden, a Hebrew word meaning 'delight', signifying the innocence of man in his angelic state as body of light (de-light), before his involvement in the time process in the material world. Innocence means without harm (Latin *nocere*, 'hurt, harm'), and the light here implied is a different one to that of the diurnal light and dark.

The Garden is enclosed or guarded, and the expulsion from it is a deprivation of that protection through a misuse of the will, and an exposure to the physical world involving the division of the senses and the 'fall' described in Genesis. (The story in Genesis is an allegory of physical birth.) The involvement is at the same time a saving grace, a means of a man refinding his will, without which his error would have gone unchecked, assuming devilish proportions. The intuitive awareness, the unfallen state, is described as the Tree of Life, and the externalised awareness as the Tree of Knowledge from which Eve took the apple. Both these trees are depicted in church iconography.

The apple represents the whole world and the fulfilling of its purpose, in which case it is the golden apple of Greek mythology; it is also, negatively, the suffering incurred by man in becoming involved in the process – i.e. eating it when offered it by the serpent. Latin *malum* can mean 'apple' and 'bad', depending on pronunciation.

Also depicted in iconography is the quartering of the Garden of Eden by the four rivers described in Genesis. These rivers symbolise the archetypal division of energy from the one source. The lower planes are born of, and are

88

constantly fertilised by, the higher, and appear first as the elements, fire, air, water and earth.

Pison – signifies joining and encompassing – the function of pure spirit: it is associated with a place where gold is found.

Gebon – signifies bursting into life.

Hiddekel – signifies light fluid movement.

Euphrates – signifies power which is fruitful.

On the subtle plane in the human being, the divisions are into: pure spirit (fire), etheric or life body, connected with laws of growth and with thought (air), astral or desire body connected with feelings and animal desire (water), and the physical body, subject to laws of the mineral world (earth). On the strictly physical plane, these become the nervous system (fire), the breathing system (air), the circulatory system (water) and the digestive system (earth).

(The symbolism is continued under 'Adam and Eve'.)

GENEVA BIBLE

See under 'Breeches Bible'.

GILBERTINES

An English monastic order founded by St. Gilbert of Sempringham, the monks following the rules of the Augustinians and the nuns (it was generally a mixed house) following the rules of the Benedictines. At the Suppression there were 26 houses in this country.

GLORY and CHRIST IN GLORY

Latin *gloria*, 'fame, renoun', from a base meaning 'to cry out, to sing', from which the Latin *gallus*, 'cock', really 'the singer'. It is the cock that heralds the day. And it is singing out, i.e. sound, that produces the world: Son is the same word as *son* (French) 'sound'. Sound and creation are one and the same: what has been created has been sung out. Thus in its present context it is both a singing out in the joy of creation and the radiant light of divinity.

A glory is the name for the light radiating from behind God or Christ in iconography, embracing both the nimbus around the head and the aureole surrounding the body. It represents the perfectly functioning inner bodies of a man,

89

purified of the opaqueness and distortions found in the unregenerated. It is used in representations of the supernatural events in Christ's life – the Transfiguration, the Risen Christ, the Ascension and the Day of Judgement. The clearly outlined elliptical shape is more specifically known as a 'mandorla' (q.v.). In sculpture, a 'Christ in Glory' is often found from the 13th century in the tympanum above the west door.

GOSPELS

Old English *godspell*, from *god*, 'good' and *spell*, 'tidings', Low German *spellen*, 'to say'. For Christianity, the good tidings are the story of Christ as given by the four Evangelists, Matthew, Mark, Luke and John. They constitute the first four books of the New Testament. (See 'Evangelist'.)

GOTHIC

Latin *Gothus*, Greek *Gothos*, 'Goth' – a member of an ancient Germanic tribe who in the 5th century overran the greater part of the Roman Empire. The term as applied to architecture has nothing to do with that tribe, but has come to be used to denote the usurping of Roman style by an alien style. Vasari, 16th century painter and architect, was the first to use the term to describe buildings of the Dark Ages since they were the result of the Gothic invasions and therefore barbarous. Sir Christopher Wren used the term Gothic to denote the later 'vandalising' of the classical purity of his buildings. But broadly speaking the term is now used to denote medieval architecture over the period from the 12th to the 16th centuries.

The architecture of this period, of course, reveals a spiritual strength diametrically opposed to the associations of the word itself. The driving force behind it all was a sense of aspiration, for it would seem that the spirit could not fly high enough in its endeavour to reach heaven, and this is embodied in the external fact, the form of the cathedral. Architecturally the change was from a rounded heaviness to a soaring height. Key concepts were elasticity and balance, refinement and tension. A mason would tap a pillar to hear its tone, to assess the correctness of its stress and strain. A cathedral was in this sense a highly-strung balance of downward weight and upward thrust, a phenomenon reflecting the finely balanced earthiness and spirituality of the period. Thus the problem of vaulting, and the phenomenon of the buttress. Stone was used in a completely new way and all apparent immobility and heaviness due to gravity was somehow transcended. The ribs of arches and the vaulting caused early writers to use the image of the avenues in a forest, and to see the whole as a flowering of the Tree of Life.

Gothic architectural style is for convenience divided into three periods, but styles overlap as in all such attempts at nomenclature; for instance, the end of the Early English and the beginning of the Decorated is not clearly definable. The following table gives two random interpretations, showing the problem:

EARLY ENGLISH	1189–1272	1189–1307
DECORATED	1272–1350	1307–1377
PERPENDICULAR	1350–1500	1377–1458

Overlapping of styles is best seen in the study of window tracery in its correspondence with the above periods. (See 'window'.)

GRANGE

From Medieval Latin *granea*, 'barn for grain' from *granum*, 'grain'. Thus, a collection of such buildings, domestic buildings, and land constituting a farmed unit, owned by a particular monastery, and managed by lay-brothers (q.v.). The number of granges increased in a spectacular manner in the second half of the 12th and beginning of the 13th centuries, due to gifts of land from benefactors.

The monastic granges however were not found upon grain but upon sheep-farming, which was the greatest national source of revenue in the middle ages. Cistercian houses especially, situated in remote places, owed the increase in their wealth to their astuteness in the business of sheep-farming.

GRAVEYARD

Grave is from Anglo-Saxon and Old High German *graf*, from Gothic *graba*, 'cave, trench, grave'. It now signifies an excavation made to receive a dead person or a monument marking a dead person. Gothic *graban* also means 'to carve' in the sense of engraving a stone, thus the modern meaning of incising or engraving.

Gravestones in parish churches are not found before the 16th century. Monuments for the wealthy were erected within the church and the poor had no monument. When it became necessary to extend monuments outside the church, there was obvious differentiation between rich and poor. Larger copies of the altar were called 'altar tombs', and those with sides open 'table tombs'. A simple slab on the ground is called a 'ledger'. It was mainly in the 18th century that there was imitation of classical themes – urns, sarcophagi and so on.

Due to the general symbolism of the points of the compass where the north is death both to the human spirit and in nature, it was a custom in medieval times to bury the bodies of suicides, reprobates and unbaptised children in the north side of the churchyard. (See 'cemetery'.)

GREGORIAN CHANT

See under 'plain-song'.

GRIFFIN

Latin *gryphus*, Greek *grupos*, 'curved, hook-beaked'. As a classical mythological beast, the griffin, with head, wings and talons of an eagle, and ears and body of a lion, is a symbol of vigilance. It has a combination of vigilant eye and courageous heart. In medieval times in the church, the negative aspects of the two creatures of prey made it the epitomisation of carnal appetites and evil.

GRISAILLE

French *gris*, 'grey', from a Germanic origin, plus *aille*, a Latin adjectival suffix. The name is given to a type of stained glass used in the 13th century which had a grey-green tinge, the object of which was to allow through a greater amount of light than the deeply stained windows permitted. The designs on these windows, as in the one at York Minster, consist of simple geometric patterns which became more complex and later incorporated foliage motifs.

GROINED VAULTING

Vaulting where the individual vaults cross each other at right angles: groining was used by the Romans and, when used by the Normans, simple ribs were added.

GUILDS or CRAFT GUILDS

Middle English *gilde* (from an Old Norwegian root), 'payment' or 'guild'. The word guild in the sense of a fraternity derives from the idea of payment for membership. Such fraternities, the fore-runners of Trade Unions, protected the interests of workmen against unjust masters, or the interests of masters against poor workmen. The guilds of the different crafts, already found in the 11th, and flourishing in the 13th and 14th centuries, were deeply involved in the business of erecting churches, and often advertised themselves in medallions in the windows of side-aisles or ambulatories. The religious guilds themselves – that is, fraternities devoted to the well-being of church members – met their end at the Dissolution of the Monasteries.

H

HAGIOSCOPE

Greek *hagios*, 'sacred', and *skopen*, 'to see'. See under 'squint'.

HALO

Latin *halos*, 'halo', Greek *halōs*, 'threshing floor'. Oxen moved round in a circular manner on the threshing floor and thus the often suggested connection between this and the disc of golden light surrounding the head of a divinity. It is also known as an aureole, glory or nimbus, but of these, the first two are used in error (q.v.).

It is hardly likely that this particular cyclic movement should have been adopted arbitrarily. As the bull is an embodiment of sexual power (in the zodiacal sign it is connected with glandular secretion), the halo may be seen as the radiant light of transmuted sexual energy which envelopes the head on the subtle plane.

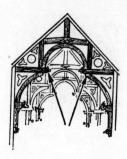

HAMMER-BEAM

A beam which began to be used towards the end of the 14th century in a Gothic-style roof to strengthen it by diminishing the pressure falling upon the walls. Its characteristic is that it does not go straight across the width of the roof. The ends of the beams are often decorated with carvings, especially with angels bearing shields.

HAND

See 'Dextera Dei' and 'blessing'.

HATCHMENT

In heraldry, an abbreviation of 'atcheament', which is an early modern English word for 'achievement'. 'Achieve' is from a French word *achever* meaning 'to accomplish', from French *à chef venir*, and earlier Low Latin *caput venir*, meaning 'to come to a head.' Thus the word is to do with personal achievement and, heraldically, social classification through this. A hatchment is an escutcheon or shield painted on a square panel, at one time hung – with the points facing N, S, E, and W – on the front of the house of a land-owner to indicate death. It was later to be hung in the church with which that particular family was associated.

HEART BRASS, SHRINE AND COFFIN

Some 15th and 16th century church brasses show a heart, either alone or held in hands. It was not uncommon in those days for the hearts of men killed in battle abroad to be sent back for interment, and such an interment was recorded on the walls of churches by the 'heart brass'.

Also, in monastic times, it was customary for parts of the body (viz. viscera, heart and body) of a much revered person, to be buried in different places; this was in the belief that the soul of the deceased would benefit by prayers offered by a number of congregations. Hearts buried separately had either special shrines, in some way suggesting the form of the heart, or coffins shaped to receive it.

HERALDRY

Middle English *herald*, Old French *heralt*, and derived from Old High German *harēs*, 'to proclaim': the second part of the word is from Old High German *waltan*, 'to govern'. Thus the meaning is the proclaiming of rights of government, as in the expression 'to herald' when a high official is announced. It only later signified the proclaiming of hierarchical precedence by means of emblems.

Heraldry began as signs or devices on the accoutrements of knights, especially shields, designating a particular family – a system developed in western Europe early in the 12th century, though emblems had been used nationally and personally in all civilisations. A means of being recognised in battle, pageantry, individual prowess, status in feudal life – all contributed to making an exact science of heraldry by the middle of the 13th century. All lords and many ordinary knights bore arms by this time. Combining of arms in one shield was originally caused through the union of two or more lordships or a wife's need to be distinguished from her husband.

By the 14th and 15th centuries, the needs of war had given way to the needs of family genealogies, and decorative tombs in churches show several generations of intermarrying by quartering a sheild and subdividing the quarters. Saints too acquired arms and emblems which often took the place of pictorial representation in the windows. Though symbolism was carried down in the emblems, much punning of names and other devices at this time began to make up the pictorial images.

| 1154 – 1340 | 1340 – 1405 | 1405 – 1603 | 1603 – 1714 | 19th century |

The Royal shield of England truly established itself between 1154 and 1340 with three lions 'passant' (walking with one paw raised): this covered the reigns of Henry II, Richard I, John, Henry II and the three Edwards. These lions have withstood all change and exist in the present English shield: they are also referred to as leopards, since the French accepted the name lion only when it was 'rampant' (standing erect in fighting posture on its hind legs).

From 1340, during Edward III's reign, quartering of the shield began, and from then until 1603 the French fleur-de-lis took precedence over the English lion, filling the 1st and 4th quarters. From the dating point of view, there are two periods – the first, between 1340 and 1405, has fleur-de-lis filling the whole space, but in the second, until 1603, there are only three in each quarter (known as 'France Ancient' and 'France Modern' respectively).

With the Stuarts, 1603 onwards, the previous arms were used, but, in the 2nd and 3rd quarters, the arms of Scotland and Ireland were added. Also at this time the 'supporters' of the shield became the familiar lion and unicorn, the unicorn taken from the Scottish shield. From the Restoration in 1660, it was made compulsory to display the Royal Arms in churches and the subsequent variations are often found there. Only in 1801 was the French fleur-de-lis removed from the English shield, giving the present lion passant, the Scottish lion rampant and the Irish harp.

There are two mottoes found along with the arms: 'Honi soit qui mal y pense' (also the motto of the Order of the Garter), and 'Dieu et mon droit'. The first is usually associated with an anecdote in Edward III's life, but can be generally read as 'Evil be to him who thinks evilly on a thing' or 'Evil will come to him who thinks evilly'; and the second, the parole of Richard I before a certain battle, is literally 'God and my right', signifying God first and then his kingship, his individual will dependent upon God alone.

The study of heraldry is highly complex, but explanations of some basic terms – 'field', 'charge', 'blazon', 'escutcheon', 'hatchment', 'supporters' – will be found under their respective headings.

HERSE or HEARSE

Middle English *herse*, 'a moveable frame' over a tomb for holding candles or to take the cloth cover or pall. From Old French *herce*, 'harrow', the frame resembling the harrow in form. Such a wooden frame was part of the church furnishings and old ones have perished: however a few metal frames still exist on tombs.

HIBERNO-SAXON

'Hiberno' is from Latin *Hibernia*, 'Ireland'. The term refers to the admixture of the early Irish crude monastic style and the indigenous style of the Saxons, which took place during the influx of Irish missionaries during the 7th century in Britain.

HIGH CROSS

The purely sepulchral slabs and monuments with a simple cross or monogram of Christ, which were found in large numbers in Ireland, died out in the 10th and 11th centuries, and in their place, vertical crosses, so called high crosses, began to be erected. The best examples belong to the 10th and 11th centuries and are the final flowering of that great period of Irish religion, learning, and art, which started in the 6th century. They are covered in elaborate sculpture showing scenes from the scriptures.

Whereas sepulchral monuments marked the resting place of the dead, the high crosses proclaimed the doctrines of the Church, giving a feeling of awe to the sacred ground where they stood. Most of the high crosses are in Ireland, but the Celtic influence is found in a few in Northern Ireland and especially in the Scottish standing stones and crosses which have a great delicacy in their ornamentation. Crosses in Wales and Cornwall do not have the same artistic merit.

Ireland, circa 900

Wales, circa 1000

HOG-BACKED STONE

A monumental stone placed horizontally over a gravestone which, because of its central ridge and sloping sides, gave the impression of a hog's back. They were usually about six feet long, carved with runes and designs typical of the period and had beasts' heads at one or both ends. Such stones are few in number and are found in Scotland and Northern England; they belong to the 8th and 9th centuries, the period of the commingling of Saxon and Irish cultures.

HOLY WATER

See under 'stoup'.

HOOD-MOULDING

Old English *hod*, from a Germanic base *had*, 'to protect', giving the word 'hat'. The stone moulding over a window or door acting to channel off the rain: it is also known as a 'dripstone'.

97

A Latin word – 'hospitality', from a root meaning 'guest'. *Hospitium* is the word used for the guest-houses in a monastery. The receiving of guests was an important and revered part of monastic life, based on St. Benedict's rule that 'all guests should be welcome as Christ Himself'. As accommodation was free and monasteries were 'stopping places' of the middle ages, the resources of certain houses were often severely stretched. The monk in charge is called variously Guest-master, Hosteller, or Hostilarius.

HOST

Latin *hostia*, 'sacrificial victim'. The Host is the consecrated wafer or bread which represents the sacrificed body of Christ, partaken by celebrants at the Eucharist. Partaking of it is also a symbol of the sacrifice of man's individual will to the corporate body of regenerate Man. (See 'Mass' and 'blessing'.)

HOUSELING BENCHES

Saxon *husel*, 'Eucharist, sacred bread'; Gothic *hunsl*, 'sacrifice', and other words associated with the meaning of holy. A houseling bench is a moveable wooden bench used before the introduction of altar rails. In pre-Reformation days it was placed before the communicants receiving sacrament and covered with a houseling cloth, the purpose of which was to prevent crumbs from falling to the floor.

I

ICON

Latin from Greek *eikon*, 'image, likeness, statue'. In the Church, specifically the Greek Church, it means a portrait of a saint or of Christ with the face of coloured enamel showing through a metal cover or superstructure. It is more generally any sacred likeness in the form of a statue or painting. Actual representations of Christ are not found until the 3rd century, the divinity of Christ being considered beyond representation. Early symbolic images of Christ as Orpheus soon gave way to the Shepherd, the

Sacred Monogram and the Fish. Early representations of gems and lamps show Christ as a young man of classical beauty; it is only later in the 4th century that he was portrayed as an older figure, a kingly ruler with a halo, and in Byzantine art with a beard. His image was still however non-humanised, rather solemn and spiritual in feeling.

The Cross as the place of Christ's suffering did not appear in art until the 5th century, and Christ's body is always shown fully clothed until the 11th century. From the 12th century, the bearded Christ is universal. It was only with the Gothic period that he was portrayed as man suffering, naked and twisted, and only later, when man became the measure of all things that this suffering was sentimentalised in order to bring each individual into a relationship of suffering with him.

I.H.S.

See under 'monogram'.

ILLUMINATED MANUSCRIPTS

A translation from the Latin would be literally 'lit-up writing by hand'; illuminated manuscripts are the equivalent of stained glass in the books of the monks of the medieval period, and have derived their name from the radiant effect of the gold used. As an art form it came from a natural need to decorate and give free rein to the imagination. The original overspill into the margins finally lead to the fine miniature paintings which were one of the finest achievements of medieval art.

The religious zeal of the 6th and 7th centuries in Ireland produced much beautiful illumination, notable for the use of geometric design. Typically Celtic animal shapes, elongated and intertwined, were called 'lacertines' or lizards. The best known example of this period is the Book of Kells (8th century), also called the Book of Columcille because it was found in a monastery founded by that saint. Following this, in Northumberland, is the Lindisfarne Gospels or Book of St. Cuthbert, which had Byzantine suggestions in the figures due to the missionary flow between Britain and Rome after the time of St. Augustine. Ravages from attacking Danes ensued, destroying the Northern tradition, and King Alfred's stand against these invasions caused the art of illumination to flourish in Winchester, the ancient capital of Wessex. Here the famous Benedictional of St. Athelwold (end of the 10th century) was written: it had many departures from the Celtic and Celtic-Saxon style due to the influence of Carolingian art (the period beginning with and following the reign of Charlemagne, circa 770–900, where there was a return to the strictly Roman classical model).

From the Conquest until 1300, illumination, influenced by French work, continued in Canterbury, Bury St. Edmunds and at Peterborough. During the 13th century the demand for smaller copies of the bible increased due to the teaching friars, and as it did, so did the need for minuteness in the work. At the end of the 13th century, however, Paris had become the capital of miniature painting and remained so for a long time; but a change had come about. Hitherto it had been the monk who, labouring only for love, had spent much of his life illuminating his manuscripts, but now the lay-miniaturist, working for profit, had come into being. For instance, in Britain, in the well known Queen Mary's Psalter (14th century), the sacred themes have scenes in the margins of contemporary life, suggesting the work of a lay artist. There was now a profession of scribes and illuminators.

The 15th century was the apogee of miniature painting. Many secular works were done under patronage; but by the 16th century the work had become too elaborate, and the powerfully felt simplicity of the earlier centuries was gone. Also painting on canvas was now at its height and superseded the work of the illuminator.

IMPOST

Latin *impositum*, past participle of *imponere*, 'to place upon'; thus the horizontal moulding on the capitals on top of a pillar, pier or corbel upon which an arch is placed.

INCENSE

From Latin *incensum*, 'something burnt', 'incense'. Originally in the Old Testament the term implies 'frankincense', the sweet gum of the frankincense tree. Mixed spices were later used in New Testament times.

The use of incense in religious ritual has always been a symbolic act of purification. Any odour of decay (the lower fallen nature of man) is permeated and purified by its sweet scent (perfect Love of the higher planes). The swinging of the censer in the Mass at the altar and over the communicants is in the interests of such purification. It is in the Mass, above all, where purity is demanded in every detail.

INDULGENCE

Latin *indulgentia*, 'gentleness, remission', *indulgere*, 'the act of indulging, the privilege of remission granted as a favour'. In the Church, the remission was of the pains of purgatory; that is, the punishments due for certain sins: they were granted in return for payments towards the upkeep and rebuilding of the cathedrals. Such indulgences were the source of revenue for many of the rebuilding operations after disasters to structure, whether by war or from natural causes.

In the Middle Ages, 'pardoners' or 'questors' were men authorised by Rome to give indulgences in return for money – the abuse of which Chaucer makes mock in the Canterbury Tales. Indulgences were also offered to those about to fight in the service of Christ – as for example, the Pope's plenary (full) indulgence in 1095 to those who undertook the first Crusade.

INFIRMARY

In and Latin *firmus*, 'strong, robust'; thus 'not strong'. In a monastery, a room used to house the sickly, usually located near the east end of the church and on the south side. The infirmary has the long form of the church, with the aisles containing cubicles for the sick: often the west end was the infirmary itself, with the east end forming the chancel with its altar. In larger institutions the chapel was a separate building along with kitchen and other rooms. The infirmary is not solely a place for the sick; those monks who had professed for 50 years were allowed to 'retire' there, for a less rigorous existence.

The monk in charge was the *infirmarius*, sometimes called the *magister infirmorum*, 'master of the infirm'. An abbreviated term used for the infirmary is *farmery*.

INTERDICT

From Latin *inter*, 'between' and *dictum*, 'something spoken, a command'. In ecclesiastical terms, a decree that excludes people from Church rites. In England, the refusal of King John to accept Stephen Langton as Archbishop of Canterbury, resulted in an interdict upon the whole country between the years 1208 and 1214. The result was that churches were closed, no bells were sounded, the people were deprived of Mass, there were no sacraments except for infants and the dying, bodies were buried in unconsecrated ground, sermons were preached in the churchyard and marriages took place in the porch.

The Pope did much to appease the petitions of the Cistercians in remote places, and certain concessions were made; but during this time, King John robbed the Church mercilessly, especially the wealthy Cistercian houses, demanding such fines that many of the poorer houses had to sell religious vessels, and monks themselves were obliged to disband. For the common people it was a terrible and unprecedented deprivation. The only parallel was an interdict upon the city of Norwich due to violent conflict between people and monks, between the years 1272 and 1275.

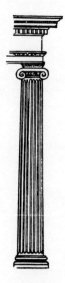

IONIC (COLUMN)

From *Ionia* – part of ancient Greece having its own particular architectural style. The columns are of slender proportions: the capitals are decorated with volutes and the shaft is fluted. Contrary to the Doric, this column has a base. The column was based on the elegance of the female form as opposed to the rugged simplicity of the Doric. Often in Greece it was transformed into a Caryatid, a virgin bearing the burden of the pediment. The Ionic is the polar opposite of the Doric. Correspondingly, all the philosophers of the Ionic school (Thales, Anaximenes, Anaxagorus, Heraclitus) stress the material universe, aiming to establish that created things come from a universal physical source – water, air, atoms and fire.

I.N.R.I.

See under 'monogram'.

IRIS

See under 'lily'.

J

JACK-IN-THE-GREEN or THE GREEN MAN

A figure or face partially hidden in foliage, widely used in ornamental carvings in the medieval church. This was a representation of the beneficent spirit of vegetation or the tree-spirit, whose return to life was celebrated on May Day by the decking of a chimney sweep in a wicker framework covered with leaves and flowers.

On a boss

JACOBEAN

A term referring to work in the history of art produced between 1603 and 1625 during the reign of James I, whence the name arises. 'James' is a version of 'Jacob' (Jacob, Hebrew 'the supplanter'). Late Latin has *'Jacomus'*, a version of Jacobus, which through many variants became James. The period also loosely extends beyond 1625, covering a style of heavy oak furniture, which characteristically has bulbous legs. Examples of Jacobean woodwork can be seen in many British churches.

JAMB

French *jambe*, 'leg', from Low Latin *gamba*, 'hoof'. The side post of a door or a window.

JESSE TREE or THE TREE OF JESSE

The tree of this name is found in medieval stained glass windows and illuminated manuscripts and is shown growing from the loins of a reclining figure. Jesse, the shepherd, was the father of David through whose line was descended Joseph, the father of Jesus, and the Jesse Tree shows this lineage with the progenitors before the Babylonian captivity depicted as kings and those after it as patriarchs. Each progenitor is labelled by name at the termination of a branch of the tree and the Virgin Mary is at the summit with the Christ child in her arms. Symbolically, the stem does not touch the child, an indication of his divine incarnation. The tree depicted is usually a vine (q.v.) – the mystic vine, a symbol of spiritual fruitfulness. (There are examples of the tree with Christ crucified at the summit.) A Jesse Window is the name applied to a window containing this imagery.

The name Jesse denotes the affirmation of pure being (Latin *esse*), and in this sense the tree is the Tree of Life. The implication is that through the continuous spiritual striving of many ancestors, a being arises worthy to become the father of the man Jesus, which is the Christ. The further implication is that though man's spiritual power has been reversed and now lies in his loins, that is in the form of sexual power used in a prone position, nevertheless it can undergo regeneration and recover its original function. Ths is the Christ state, potentially within all men, and the attainment of which is the aim of all religions.

JOHN THE BAPTIST

John the Baptist is frequently found in iconography in connection with the baptism of Christ. Distinguishable by his hairy apparel, John is the first of the three Johns in the New Testament – three aspects of love (*Johanan*, Hebrew 'grace of God'). He represents the working of the Holy Spirit within the physical body (hair), and the need to reverse its distorted values. John the 'beloved' disciple of Christ represents the devotion necessary in the feelings, the cleaving of the soul to what it knows to be Wisdom. John, the Evangelist, represents the potential break-out from the small logical mind, the yoke of cosmic forces and time itself, into a new dimension, and therefore has the symbol of the all-seeing eagle.

John the Baptist affirms the process of regeneration, proclaiming the birth of Christ as man on earth, and the potential birth of Christ in each man, a process which can only come about through dipping or washing in the Jordan to give a new order of life.

K

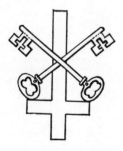

KEY

The etymology of the word is said to be unknown. However its meaning is bound up with the nature of the sound of the letter 'k': this is formed by the locking of the tongue to the roof of the mouth before release. The symbol of the key, though associated with several saints, belongs specifically to St. Peter, through the words in St. Matthew,

'And I will give unto thee the keys of the kingdom of heaven'; thus the key has come to represent the power vested in Peter and subsequently in the Church itself.

But this statement contains the paradox of the key, for it has the power to lock and unlock, two aspects that are represented by the crossed keys of Peter. They are silver and gold, the symbolic colours of moon and sun, or matter and spirit: the power of God may have become locked in the physical world, but it may also be unlocked. Individual man, full of error, and locked in a physical body, via the fall, is given the means to rediscover freedom through the formally structured Church; but a formal, locked system is a danger – Greek *petros* 'stone', may be a corner-stone, but it is also rigid. The secrets of life and death are bound in the physical world – in time and space: Peter holds the keys. But it is in the inner temple, through the unfolding of the Christ within, that the true key to release from its tyranny lives. Thus the symbol of Peter is often of crossed keys over an inverted cross, indicating the need to reverse power involved in and directed to the physical world.

The locking and unlocking is seen most clearly in the field of music. Music is written on clefs (French *clef*, 'key') and has its own particular key. This is because matter is in effect condensed vibrations – all that lives vibrates at its own frequency. Sound, in fact, is nothing but creative power. But it is only necessary to resonate a given form by an outside stimulus of the same frequency – i.e. a musical note – to be able to destroy that form. Thus the locking of music in musical notation and its power to reach back behind the physical appearance are aspects of each other. Such power in music was understood and used in the early Church. (See 'organ' and 'choir)

KNIGHTS HOSPITALLERS (or KNIGHTS OF ST. JOHN)

The Knights Hospitallers were originally concerned with caring for pilgrims at the Holy Sepulchre in Jerusalem. Their name derives from the hospices they maintained – 'hospice' is from Low Latin *hospitium*, 'hospitality' or 'inn'. The alternative name derives from St. John the Almoner, Patriarch of Alexandria in the 7th century, who aided Christians after the fall of Jerusalem into Saracen hands. For various reasons, the revenues of the community increased after the First Crusade in 1099 and the then head of the community offered to fight against the

Mohammedans. Thus the order was divided into three classes: knights of noble birth who were to be soldiers, priests who were to remain in the Church, and serving brethren who were to be ordinary soldiers.

Originally they wore a black robe with a white linen cross on the left breast, but later it was decreed that whilst on military duties they should wear over this a red military greatcoat with a white cross.

The order came into Britain early in the 12th century.

KNIGHTS TEMPLARS

An order of monks based upon using force of arms in the protection of Christian pilgrims during the period of the Crusades. it was founded in Jerusalem in A.D. 1118 and declined in importance upon the evacuation of Palestine in 1291. The name Templars is derived from the fact that the house in which the order originated was near the Dome of the Rock, the mosque built upon the site of the Temple of Solomon.

In the beginning the Templars dedicated themselves to a life of extreme hardship and purity, but later they wielded much power through property (9,000 castles in Europe in the 13th century): their hierarchy ranged from the knight down to the craftsman. The order came to Britain in the 12th century, their church in London still remaining. Many of the churches were round in form, others polygonal. (See 'church'.)

L

LADY CHAPEL

A chapel dedicated to the Blessed Virgin in cathedrals and churches, usually found at the extreme east end behind the high altar but sometimes projecting from the main building. (See 'Virgin Mary' for symbolism.)

LAMB

15ᵗʰ century window, All Saints: York

German *lamn*, connected with Greek *lambda*, (the letter L λ) and Hebrew *lamed* (the 12th letter of the Hebrew alphabet).

The image of the lamb figures frequently in Christian art, on missals, tympani, capitals, and so on. It represents

Christ as 'the lamb sacrificed from the foundations of the world'. This sacrifice is that of the innocent white victim – God limiting himself through manifestation – the sacrifice of the one for the many. Manifestation is in the natural world, which can only perpetuate itself through a process of mutual eating, through one life being sacrificed to another: in this sense all things are mutually dependent. The ultimate sacrifice is God's sacrifice of Himself as Jesus Christ the man, so that all men may feed on Him; this is the essential message of the Eucharist where it is said that a man's sins are 'washed away by the blood of the Lamb'.

The idea of sacrifice is expressed in the Greek *lambda* λ which, when super-imposed over *gamma* γ (letter G), gives the six-pointed star, the wheel of Being, the Logos. In the illustration, John the Baptist holds the book with the lamb upon it, a double image of the Spoken Word and the sacrificed Son of God.

The Hebrew connection is through the letter *lamed* which contains the idea of sacrifice in its symbolism, for in its corresponding 12th card of the Tarot, the image is of a man hanging upside down. Conscious sacrifice is a hanging upside down of all worldly values; for when man is born into a physical body his power is inverted. The lamb is also seen in the sacrifices of the Paschal Lamb of the Hebrews, Easter being the celebration of the delivery of the Israelites from the Egyptians (symbolically spirit from the bondage of matter) by the smearing of the blood of the lamb on their door posts.

In iconography, prior to 683, the lamb is a symbol of Christ, often bearing the chi-rho monogram or a cross upon its forehead. The representation of Christ as a man was only allowed after the year 683, when the Council of Constantinople decreed 'We pronounce that the form of Him who taketh away the sins of the world, the Lamb of Christ our Lord, be set up in human shape, or images, henceforth, instead of the formerly used Lamb.'

LANCET WINDOW

Latin *lancea*, 'a light spear'; thus a narrow pointed window especially associated with the Early English period.

The one at the east end of the church behind the altar symbolises the male spirit, raised out of the material world – the west of the church. It should properly have upon it an image of the risen Christ rather than Christ crucified. (See 'east end' and 'Crucifixion'.)

LANTERN

Latin *lanterna*, 'lantern', Greek *lamptēr*, 'light, torch'. The lantern is the open structure at the top of a tower in a church; in a cathedral it is the central tower over the crossing which allows the centre of the church to be illuminated (See 'crossing' and 'transept' for symbolism.)

LAST JUDGEMENT

The Last Judgement is a common theme in medieval art. In it the 'wicked', those who have continued in a direction of error, are shown being consigned by Christ to the fires of Hell on his left, and the 'righteous', those who have taken the road of spiritual re-birth, are shown being drawn into Heaven on his right. An angel holding a sword sometimes separates the two or St. Michael may be seen weighing souls in the scales.

Due to the literal interpretation of 'a thousand years', in Revelation, there was among early Christians an expectation of the Second Coming, the Last Day when all would be held to account; but though this had not materialised by the end of the first millenium, the dread of the Final Judgement continued, and representations of it found their way into prominent places in the church building, as in the tympanum of the medieval cathedral, particularly in France. Such a message over the main west portal was a reminder of the destiny of all men. In the centre of the representation is Christ as judge in a mandorla (q.v.). The imagery was carried through into the parish church in the 'doom' (q.v.), often painted in pre-Reformation times in the filled-in space between chancel and rood-screen.

Christ as judge is prefigured in the Egyptian Osiris, and both cull the harvest of the work of man on earth. The idea of a process unfolding and folding back upon itself is inherent in the Alpha and Omega glyphs (q.v.). The idea of judgement is contained in the book, the Book of Life, which Christ often holds upon his left knee, and from which nothing is left unrecorded. This judgement shows the ultimate triumph of good over evil where all error is consumed by the fire of the spirit, and a New Jerusalem is established. As far as an individual man is concerned, however, though he is said to be judged, it is his *own* record that is laid bare before his own gaze.

Such a judgement recurs constantly in man's earthly incarnations, for through the fascination of the world, the maya of existence, he is blind to his state in the spiritual worlds. He regains that eye of self-knowledge upon death only, when each element in him goes to its own place. In this sense he constantly judges his error and accumulates the fruit of his work in each life in readiness for the final liberating of his real Self. But despite the forces of the world, the real Self lives eternally in every moment of time, capable of separating truth from falsity: it is an eye of Truth, not of moral judgement. In this sense a man's work is to recover this eye, this awareness, so that his life is a constant rehearsal for death – a separation of his own sheep and goats.

LAST SUPPER

The word 'supper' is from Old Norwegian *supa*, 'to drink, sup'; compare with Sanskrit *supas*, 'broth'. The word 'sop' (the sop handed by Christ to Judas) is related to sup, and is simply the cake of bread soaked in the communal dish, the custom of the East.

Representations of the Last Supper are second only in number to the Crucifixion. The passing on of Christ's power through the shared bread and wine, and the subsequent shared meals of the early Christians (the *agapē*, Greek 'love') was to become the Lord's Supper, the sacrament of the Holy Eucharist (Greek *eukharistia*, 'thankfulness' from *eu*, 'good' and *kharis*, 'grace'). It is represented, in this light, on the altar-piece or reredos in the church – a scene of awe-ful solemnity; whereas elsewhere in art the treatment is more dramatised, with the stress on Judas' betrayal. No representation of the Supper is known in art before circa A.D. 800, and those to which we are now accustomed are misleading on a factual level, for the Jewish custom of the time was for meals to be taken in a reclining position upon the floor, resting on couches around the three sides of a low table. The Latin name for the couches, of which the central one was the seat of honour, is *triclinium*.

The significance of twelve apostles is treated under the heading 'apostle'. The significance of the mystical supper is discussed in part under 'Mass'. The bread and wine are basically the substantial body of God, the whole universe, and the life force that animates it: and, in that universe, life can only continue by a ruthless process of mutual eating. In man, microcosm of that universe, the blood is the medium of the life force, the mediator between spirit and body, and acts in either of two ways. Either it surges in anger, producing a state of disease, or it flows evenly and harmoniously, giving a state of health. The first is the state of fallen man, full of hate and bestiality, and the second is that of the regenerate man, who through sacrifice has surrendered his lower self, and who through love relates himself again to the whole world – to the *whole* Man. Jesus Christ is the perfect Being, human and divine, and his sacrificial act of shedding blood, foreshadowed in the Supper, allows his power in a sense to be eaten. He is the God who is being eaten by humanity in order that the earth should be re-spiritualised. He has made something available. Thus, the taking of bread and wine at the Sacrament is essentially an individual man's act of self-remembering, a joining of his separate self to the whole. Christ's gift is only available at the place where a man has made his own sacrifice, that is internally, in his heart, before he reaches the external altar of the church. To make this sacrifice is each man's own private drama, and the three central figures in the Lord's Supper correspond to parts of himself, for the apostles, through their respective natures, each fulfilled a special and conscious role. They are John, Peter, and Judas John is portrayed on one side of Christ, intimately close to him, with Peter on the other side, whilst Judas is portrayed on the near side of the table or moving out of the picture having received the sop. Of these three only John is not found wanting.

The reason is that love, always associated with John (John, Hebrew *Johanan* means 'Jah is gracious') is the only total way by which that Christ power may be received. Utter selfless devotion brings about the wisdom of the Logos. (For this aspect of John see also under the heading 'Evangelists'.) Peter (Greek *petros*, 'a rock, stone') on the other hand represents the hard knowledge in us, the seeing without feeling. Such clear-sightedness and dedication may set up the Church, but it can soon deteriorate into the hair-splitting wars over dogma. Judas (Hebrew, strangely meaning 'praise') represents the vulnerable part in man – the capacity to betray what the

110

spirit knows as truth for the smallest selfish gain. Moreover, Judah, the same name, is the land of the Jews from which the word Jew derives, and it was they who rejected the inner message of universal love offered by Christ because their hope of a temporal and a personal King had not been fulfilled. Thus, psychologically and historically Peter and Judas are dangers. Christ knew he was to be apprehended, and could have been found at any time. The role of Judas was the most difficult to play: Christ's instructions to him are unequivocal, and the offering of the sop (such a gesture coming at a crucial point in the ancient 'mysteries') underlined the bitter acceptance of his role. He was to take the scorn of men of the spirit, as Christ took the scorn of the ignorant.

LAVATORY or LAVATORIUM

Latin *lavare*, 'to wash'. In a monastery, a lavatory is usually a long stone trough at the entrance to the refectory where monks washed their hands before eating. There are also examples of small octagonal buildings in a corner of the cloister near the refectory.

LAY BROTHERS or CONVERSI or FRATRES CONVERSI

'Lay' is from Old French *lai*, Latin *laicus*, Greek *laikos* 'belonging to the people' (*laos*, 'people'). A member of a monastic house under the same vows of poverty, chastity and obedience, but who was exempt from the rigid offices of the choir monks. Being 'of the people', lay-brothers were unable to read or write, and devoted themselves to the practical running of the monastery, whilst the function of the choir monks was to fulfil the Opus Dei, 'the Work of God', in the seven daily offices. They were alternatively called *conversi*, i.e. those 'of the people' who having been converted put themselves under monastic rule.

When monastic houses acquired land, and sheep farming became the practice, lay-brothers ran the farms or *granges*, reciting prayers in the fields at canonical hours. The lay-brother system was largely due to the ideals of the Cistercian order. Whereas in other orders seculars were brought in to do manual labour, the Cistercians, in remote places, saw the brotherhood as a working community. Due to various social and economic reasons, however, the most obvious of which was the Black Death, (1359), the lay-brother system gradually ceased to exist, and after this their buildings were adapted for other purposes.

These buildings were always built at the west (material) end of the monastery, as opposed to the east (spiritual) end. The number of lay-brothers exceeded that of choir monks by two or three to one.

LECTERN

Middle English, from French *lettrum*, from Low Latin *lectrum*, 'reading-desk'. The lectern is the desk upon which the Bible rests and from which the lessons are read. Over it frequently presides the figure of an eagle (q.v.), which by its soaring flights and powers of sight symbolises the Logos, the Word and Intelligence in which all things are simultaneously embraced.

Thus the lectern is on the south side (heraldically the left) as opposed to the minister in the pulpit, God's mouthpiece, on the north side (heraldically right). The Word is manifest in the form of the Bible, and is specifically associated with St. John because, of all the gospels, his is the spirit that transmutes the written letter and touches the new dimension of the Higher Intelligence.

The eagle in relation to the four symbolic animals of the four Evangelists is discussed under 'Evangelist'. In a monastery, a lectern is often corbelled out of a wall in the refectory, and it was customary for readings to be made while the monks were eating.

LEY-LINE

A word from the same source as Old English lea, lee, leigh, meaning 'Pasture' or 'clearing'; thus the connection with a track or line of subtle energy lying in low open spaces. Recent research has shown that ancient sacred monuments were aligned upon such field forces present in the earth – the same forces that determine mass movements of the animal kingdom. It is demonstrable that cathedrals and smaller churches were sited upon such tracks, including dowsable water tracks that moved up the nave to a confluence of lines to blind springs at the place of the altar.

Thus, though the general alignment of churches was east–west, these lines of force account for the many inexplicable anomalies in church buildings, in which for example, chancels are on the skew from the nave either to the north or to the south, or there is a bend in the nave itself. It also explains why Christian edifices were built on already existing sacred sites, chosen at a time when men's sensitivity to such forces was more active.

LIERNE VAULTING

French *lien*, 'tie, bond'. In vaulting of the 14th century, a short cross-rib – i.e. one that does not spring from the wall but crosses from rib to rib. This produces intricate patterns known as 'stellar vaulting'.

LIGHT

Old High German *licht*, connected with Latin *lucere*, 'to shine'. The actual apertures in a wall through which light passes, as opposed to the whole concept of a window itself. Thus a window may consist of three or any number of lights.

LILY

Latin *lilium*, Greek *leirion*, 'lily', connected with Greek *leiros*, 'pale, delicate'. In Christian art the lily is a symbol of the chastity and purity attributed to the Virgin Mary: the Angel Gabriel is represented holding a lily in his hands at the Annunciation. In the crown of King Solomon, the lily denotes kingly and perfect love. In this sense, it is connected with the *Lila* of Hindu philosophy where the word signifies the play or game of God – a play which is the other aspect of the groaning struggle of man on earth. Where the lily is found, there is always the meaning of love shown from higher to lower, as with the Angel Gabriel's role of divine messenger to man; also Greek *iris* (the flower, the iris, is often substituted for the lily) means 'rainbow', which was symbolically a sign of reconciliation between God and man, as in the story of the Flood.

Due to the association of the Crucifixion and the Annunciation – both being celebrated around the spring equinox – and since both are essentially acts of divine grace, there are a number of instances in wood-carving and window decoration showing Christ crucified over a lily plant. This is a peculiarly English device.

LION

Greek *leon*, probably from a Semitic origin – i.e. Hebrew *lābi*, 'lion'. In Christian art, the lion is the sign of the

Evangelist mark, who in his manner of writing exemplifies the qualities of Leo, the fixed fire sign of the zodiac. This archetypal image of the lion denotes energy establishing itself in a self-authoritative way, and on its highest level denotes courage, strength and love. It is these qualities that make the all-conquering Christ to be seen as the Lion of the Tribe of Judah in the Book of Revelation.

But the real inner power of the lion has given way to misused power – the animal passions in man have brought about the debased, devouring aspect of the lion within him. Energy has to be transformed and the true lion found so that ultimately, led by the Christ child, it can lie down together with the lamb, symbol of the innocent state of man. This is the divine state in man, when self-authority has been handed willingly into the hands of the Creator.

LLAN

The Welsh word for 'church', and prefixed to many Welsh place names. Originally it was a piece of ground – a sacred enclosure granted to a priest.

LYCHGATE or LICHGATE

A combination of 'gate' and Old English *lic*, Middle English *lich*, 'a body whether alive or dead'. The Old German counterpart and modern German *leiche* means 'corpse'. The lychgate is the gateway with a roof at the entrance to the churchyard where the coffin rests awaiting the arrival of the officiating clergyman prior to interment.

LOUVRE or LOUVER

Old French *lovier*, Medieval Latin *lodium*. The meaning was originally of a simple opening over a fireplace. The lantern or tower of medieval buildings was designed with sloping boards, called louvre boards, so as to let out the smoke, let in light and also keep out the rain. Thus the angles of the boards in a belfry window in churches are sloping to fulfil this function.

LOZENGE

French *losange*. A diamond-shaped figure used in heraldry and as a moulding in Norman architecture.

114

Latin *lux*, 'light', and *fer*, from *ferre*, 'to carry, bear'. In popular understanding, Lucifer is the epitomisation of evil, a spiritual being responsible for the fallof man, but his name means literally 'bringer of light'. He is both at one time, because fire and light are the pre-condition of creation, and creation itself is in a sense death, since power is locked into each specific life-form created. In this sense, Lucifer, the morning star (in fact, the planet Venus) is a cause of mourning, since not only does each day bring light and life, but it opens up the circus of painful existence once again. (See 'cock'.)

This duality, Lucifer's high estate and awe-inspiring fire of creation, and the prison of the world resulting from his intellectual pride, causes him to be represented as a being of deceptive beauty and as a hideous serpent. Satan, similarly, is in one sense a positive creative power, but he is also a negative limiting one, and this is seen in the planet Saturn's rings and the god Saturn's connection with time. Equally, the Devil is a negative aspect of God the Creator, for 'devilish' signifies that which is orientated to material inertias as opposed to the spirit from which they derive.

The serpent, associated with all three, crawls on its belly and is full of wile and evil intent; but it is at the same time the storehouse of that great power which awaits regeneration, seen in the symbolic casting of the skin and in yogic kundalini. Such dialectics abound everywhere.

LUNETTE

French word meaning 'little moon'. The word is applied to objects or designs having a small circular, semi-circular or crescent shape. Architecturally it refers to an opening in a vaulted roof, the purpose of which is to let in light.

M

MAJESTY or CHRIST IN MAJESTY

Majesty is from the same base as Latin *magnus*, 'great'. The name in Christian iconography refers to a sculptured figure or painting of Christ, seated enthroned, crowned, and in an act of benediction. He is often in the presence of the apostles and surrounded by a mandorla (q.v.). The apse dome and the tympanum over the west door were the two places in the church used most often for showing off such a powerful image.

MAGI

'Magi' is plural of Latin *magus*, from Greek *magos*, 'a Persian priest; a magician'. There are many legends about the three kings or wise men who, it is said, foretold the birth of Christ and followed the star to where it took place. They were in fact not numbered until Origen, and not named until after the 6th century. Such astrologer wise men would certainly know the connection between the heavenly bodies and momentous happenings on earth. But their significance lies in that they symbolise the three-fold nature of man as a reflection of the Trinity. It is three 'kings' who foretell the birth and pay homage, indicating that this is a happening destined to transform the three fallen parts of a man's being, re-installing the divine authority (the kings) in each. This can be seen either in terms of man's whole evolution, or in terms of one man's lifetime. Thus, the significance of the gifts they bring.

Balthasar (Persian 'war council'), shown dark-skinned, represents the physical body, his gift being myrrh, connected with embalming and the sacrifice of the body; *Caspar* (Persian 'treasure-master'), shown yellow-skinned, represents the soul, his gift being that which affects the life of the feelings or soul, frankincense; *Melchoir* (Persian 'king') shown white-skinned, whose gift is gold, represents the pure intelligence of the Logos. As kings and Gentiles, as opposed to the Jewish shepherds, they also mark the new dispensation – the fact that the birth was a gift to all men for all time.

MALTESE CROSS

The form of the cross was used originally by the Knights called the Hospitallers of St. John, whose work at the time of the Crusades was to tend sick pilgrims in Jerusalem. It is an eight-pointed cross said to symbolise the eight beatitudes in Matthew. It is thus essentially an emblem of love. Later the order had a more military role, and finally, expelled from Rhodes by the Turks, settled in Malta in the early 16th century, whence the name.

The cross is found over Norman doorways and some-

116

times in the tympanum. It is often miscalled a 'pattée cross' (q.v.), a cross whose arms have flat terminations.

MAN

Old High German *man*, and related to Sanskrit *manus*, 'human being'. The *ma* part of the word indicates that he is born of the matrix or womb of matter and the plural form 'men' indicates his involvement in the mental process of measuring and counting (Latin *mens*, 'mind, reason', also *mensis*, 'month', and *mensura*, 'measure' etc: also see under 'Amen'). Thus the duality implicit in his situation as a being who can see and reason about his own physical involvement in the world.

In Christian art, the head and the other animals of the fixed signs of the zodiac symbolise the four Evangelists (q.v.). The head, as in the diagram, corresponding to the fixed air sign Aquarius, is the symbol of Matthew. The sign is concerned with memory and assimilation of information for unification into a whole, for the ultimate goal of man is that he should see all diversity in the material world as having a common origin, so that he may be drawn together with his fellows into one whole Man. Thus the significance of the forthcoming Aquarian age.

MANDATUM or MAUNDY

The Latin word *mandatum*, means 'order, command'. *Maundy* is from Old French *mandé*, from the Latin. The command referred to is that given by Christ to his disciples in St. John 13 v.34 – 'I give you a new commandment – Love one another; love one another as I have loved you'. This is related to the washing of the disciples' feet prior to that command (v.14) – 'If I, the Master, have washed your feet, so ought you to wash one another's feet'. Thus the Mandatum has come to mean the washing of feet as a sign of humility and service – a token of that love.

In monastic life, the ritual had its own variations. In Cistercian houses, for example, the Mandatum took place each Saturday in the lavatorium, used for washing hands before eating. It was performed by the monk in charge of the kitchen that week. along with an assistant to dry the feet. In other houses, the Superior washed the feet of thirteen monks. symbolic of Christ and the twelve disciples.

The ritual was later seen in Maundy Thursday, a day

when the feet of thirteen poor people were washed not only by clergy but also by the reigning Monarch. This latter practice, however, ended after the reign of James II. Now all that remains is the diluted form of charity to the poor.

Not only is the washing of feet a sign of humility and love, but it is symbolic of the purifying of the natural man: it is through his feet on the earth that the direction of his inner intent is disclosed.

MANDORLA

The Italian word for *almond*. The mandorla is the almond-shaped line drawn around the full-length figure of Christ, usually with fine lines radiating outwards from the body, showing the perfected inner light of divinity. The treatment varies according to the medium, whether it is sculpture or painting. The mandorla is associated with Christ of the Last Judgement, and especially with Christ in Majesty, though later, in medieval times, it became common to depict the Virgin Mary in the same way. Another name for it is the 'mystic almond'.

The image of the almond is a reference to the fruit of the tree which by its form suggests the womb, thus the womb of the world from which all developed and within which the redemptive power of Christ operates. The almond tree is itself associated with purity of birth. In Arabic, the word means 'to waken' since it is the first tree to awaken in early spring with its white blossoms.

The mandorla is also known as the *vesica piscis* (Latin, 'bladder of the fish'), again an image of the waters of the womb of the world within which the Christ power radiates. In this sense Christ is the 'Great Fish' in the sea, having descended into that sea to redeem floundering humanity. (See under 'fish' for its symbolism.) Sometimes the mandorla is referred to as an *ichthus*, Greek, 'fish', and again simply as the 'aureole' (q.v.). It is exclusively the property of Christ and the Virgin.

MASON

Said to derive from a Germanic base *mak*, 'to make'. 'Make' can be taken on two levels, internal and external. The masonic teaching goes back to the earliest civilisations and has the basic idea of building an inner, regenerated body out of the fallen physical one. In this inner sense

118

the word 'mason' can be seen as 'son of ma', that is 'son of substance'. It denotes that a man can consciously shape or make the course of his life – that he is no longer shaped by the forces external to him. He is reborn out of his substance, by his own will.

These external forces under man's control are symbolised by him standing within the cube looking out onto its three pairs of faces – above-below (cosmic forces and the earth), before-behind (duality of future and past), right-left (the doubleness of rational thought, yes and no), all of which symbolise the limitations of the world. But, when the cube is unfolded so as to remain in one piece, it becomes the Latin cross of Christianity upon which man is transfixed. If the process is reversed, and these limitations are transcended on the cross through sacrifice, then the cross folds back into the cube and becomes a true cornerstone for a new edifice.

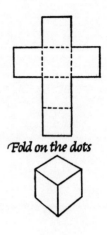

Fold on the dots

It is not surprising therefore that, on all counts, the Latin cross should have been used in the external work of the builder, and that the cathedral should have symbolised that inner work. Masons were the holders of inner and outer secrets, and the religious aspirations of medieval times came to a head in this co-joining of outer form and inner meaning.

Also, as men sensitive to the field forces of the earth, master builders aimed to increase the efficacy of their buildings as places of prayer by precise siting. Recent investigation has done much to confirm this aspect of the siting of most major religious buildings. (See under 'freemason', 'mystery play' and 'ley-line'.)

MASS

The celebration of the Holy Communion in the Western Church, from an early time, has been known by the name 'Missa', which supposedly became 'Mass'. It is said that the word 'Missa' came from 'Ite missa est', an injunction to catechumens, those being instructed in early Christianity, to go at a certain part of the service, the remainder of the service being for the initiated: and that it was later used for all the faithful at the end of the service. The words could mean 'Go, the assembly is sent away', or 'Go, the Mass is ended.'

The focal point of the Holy Communion however is the symbolic partaking of the body and the blood of Christ, and it is more likely that the significance of the words lies in the connection with Old English *maessa*, 'feast', and Italian *messa*, 'a course at table', both of which are connected with French *masse*, 'barley-cake', which in turn is from *massein*, 'to knead'. The link throughout is the basic one of eating, and in such a fundamental ritual it is likely that the inner meaning would find embodiment in the word.

The key to the Mass lies in the reciprocal feeding by which all levels of beings in the world subsist. From spiritual beings down to the microbe, life is possible only by eating and then being eaten by another form of life. This is apparent enough in nature. But psychologically too, human beings feed upon each other, the stronger absorbing the weaker and the weaker gaining strength from surrender to the stronger.

'As above, so below': the principle holds on all levels. On the level which concerns us, Christ's sacrifice is literally food for the whole race of Man – at this time in his evolution, a real spiritual food, the body and blood, has been made available, represented by the bread and wine in the sacrament of the Eucharist. But conversely, in his fallen state, man is poor food for a Higher Being: he impedes the harmonious working of the spirit world. To be of service, he must first clear his own error. In short, religion, or the process of 'binding back' (Latin *ligare*, 'to bind'), is a reciprocal relationship – he has to recommit his will, to offer himself for use by a power, which in its turn, seeks to make itself available. (See further under 'altar'.)

Historically, the Mass underwent many changes. Originally it was administered to the church members by the clergy, and this held in Britain until after the Norman Conquest. Medieval times however saw the separation of clergy from laity, the mystery in the sanctuary from the people, so that in the end, except on the death bed or on rare occasions, the Mass was celebrated vicariously, and focussed around the raising of the host for adoration. In 1546, Henry VIII commanded that the Mass should be a 'Communion' in which all should participate. Thus the dropping of the word 'Mass' in the Reformed Church, and the distinction between the chalice and the communion cup (q.v.).

The setting to music of the liturgy, which developed into the 'mass' as found in Palestrina and Byrd, and later into the 'Concert Mass', derived from five passages (the 'Ordinary' or 'Common' of the Mass) originally sung by the congregation in response to five passages of plainsong sung by the priest. These five passages gradually became more elaborately treated and were sung by chorus and soloists. They are:

KYRIE	Lord have mercy
GLORIA IN EXCELSIS	Glory be to God on high
CREDO	I believe
SANCTUS	Holy, Holy (the Benedictus is really part of the Sanctus, but is often treated separately)
AGNUS DEI	Lamb of God

In the later Protestant settings – of Bach, for example – these sections were subdivided to give the possibility of a more varied musical experience, and this later gave a Mass which was more of a vehicle for a composer's skill, rather than for devotion. Thus originated the 'Concert Mass', performed without the original liturgy from the priest. The sub-divided sections of Bach's B minor Mass (the first great example of such a Mass), are as follows:

KYRIE ELEISON	Lord have mercy
CHRISTE ELEISON	Christ have mercy
KYRIE ELEISON	Lord have mercy
LAUDAMUS TE	We praise thee
GRATIAS AGIMUS TIBI	We give Thee thanks
DOMINE DEUS	Lord God
QUI TOLLIS PECCATI MUNDI	Who takest away the sins of the world
QUE SEDES AD DEXTRAM PATRIS	Who sitteth at the right hand of the Father
CREDO IN UNUM DEUM	I believe in one God
PATREM OMNIPOTENTEM	Father Almighty
ET IN UNUM DOMINUM	And in one Lord
ET INCARNATUS EST	And was incarnate
CRUCIFIXUS	Was crucified
ET RESURREXIT	And rose again
ET IN SPIRITUM SANCTUM	And I believe in the Holy Spirit
CONFITEOR UNUM BAPTISMA	I confess one baptism

SANCTUS	Holy
HOSANNA IN EXCELSIS	Hosanna in the highest
BENEDICTUS QUI VENIT	Blessed is He that cometh
AGNUS DEI	Lamb of God
DONA NOBIS PACEM	Give us peace

MAUSOLEUM

Mausoleum, from Greek *Mausoleion*, a tomb erected by Queen Artemisia at Halicarnassus in Turkey in 353 B.C. to contain the body of her husband Mausolos. This tomb was one of the Seven Wonders of the World: thus the word is used to describe any great sepulchral monument.

MAZE

Middle English *masen*, 'to confuse, puzzle'. In some cathedrals, particularly on the Continent, a maze was designed on the floor of the nave – a symbol of the souls' entanglement in matter and the necessity and possibility of finding a way out of it. (The *ma* part of the word denotes matter, and the letter 'z' denotes the zealous buzzing about of the entrapped soul trying to free itself.) In some cases the mason's name was known to have been engraved upon them.

MENSA

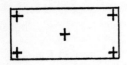

The upper slab of an altar. At the consecration of the church, five simple Greek crosses were engraved into the altar, a reflection of the symbolism of the 'five wounds of Christ' (q.v.). These may be seen in churches where the original slab has been preserved.

MICHAEL MOUNT or CHAPEL

The meaning of the name Michael is given under 'archangel'. In Cornwall, Wales and on the west coast of Ireland, hill-top chapels are found dedicated to St. Michael.

The tradition of St. Michael as saviour, judge of the dead and weigher of souls at the Last Judgement, current in the Middle Ages, comes from the story in Revelation of his overcoming the dragon. But it also sprang from more ancient roots, for in the Coptic period of Christianity in Egypt, the monks, continuing the indigenous worship of

Osiris as judge of the dead, identified him with the sun and built chapels to him high in their monasteries, from where the rising sun could be seen. Thus, with the infiltration of the monastic tradition into the Celtic areas of the British Isles, similar high places were built; and later the tradition was carried further in the dedication of a chapel or a room high in a church.

Angel Choir, Lincoln   *Michael with scales*

St. Michael is depicted with flaming winged feathers, symbolising his status of archangel and his association with the sun; he carries a sword representing his power over evil, or scales indicating his role of weigher of truth after death. His name, 'he who is like the Lord', indicates the deepest part of a human being, the Self, which has the power to cut through error – the dragon killed by the sword of truth. It is the Self that must come to the rescue at St. Michael's festival (the beginning of autumn), because it is at this time that man's spirit could die along with nature; he has to draw from his own resources, his true 'I', in order to realise the birth process of Christmas.

MINISCULE

French, from Latin *minisculus*, 'rather small', a diminutive of *minus*, 'less'. A small letter in ancient manuscripts and also found on monuments, as opposed to a majuscule or capital. The early Christian sepulchral monuments of Ireland contained Ogham writing or a debased form of Latin capitals, or both, but from the 7th century to Nor-

tanto melior angelif effectuf quanto

123

man times Latin capitals gave way to a form of writing consisting of few strokes but not yet cursive (that is, running together). About 300 examples of this miniscule writing on monuments occur in the British Isles, most of which are in Ireland and Wales. They often contain the words 'a prayer for' and the name of the deceased, and are decorated by Celtic spiral interlacing motifs.

MINISTER

Latin *minister*, 'servant', as opposed to *magister*, 'master'. Someone who carries out a superior's orders or ministers to someone's needs. In the church, one who does service for the Church.

MINSTER

Greek *monastés*, 'living alone'. (Refer to the heading 'monastery'.) The word was used in medieval times (Old English *mynster*) to designate only the church of an abbey or monastery, and now applies to churches that formerly filled that capacity. It is more loosely used to denote some of the larger cathedrals.

MISERICORD also loosely MISERERE

Latin *misericordia*, 'mercy, compassion', *misereri*, 'to have pity', *miser*, 'wretched', and *cor*, 'heart'. There are two uses of the word, both of which imply mercy by virtue of a relaxation of the monastic rule.

The most commonly understood meaning is that of the bracket or ledge on the underside of hinged seats in the choir of a cathedral, important since they represent the finest level of wood craftsmanship of the medieval period. (See under 'stalls'.) They are so called because they afforded the monks partial relief from standing during long services.

The second use is that of a room in a monastery which had some connection with the infirmary: its name varied a good deal. It was a room where indulgences were allowed, as for example the eating of meat – presumably for ill or elderly monks. (*See opposite*).

MISSAL

Ecclesiastical Latin *missale*, from *missa*, 'Mass'. A book containing the words sung and spoken in the Mass for a

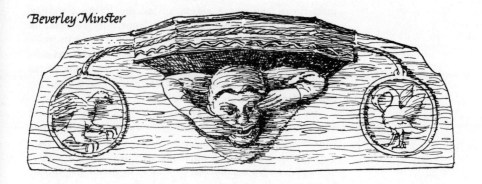

Beverley Minster

whole year and describing the ritual actions performed.
(See 'mass'.)

MITRE

Latin *mitra*, 'cap, turban', Greek *mitra*, 'belt, head-band,
fillet'. Its origin is obscure however and it is more possibly
connected with *Mithras*, 'god of light', from an Old Persian word. In this context, the mitre would be one of the
Mithraic vestments absorbed by Christianity in Rome, as
the Mithraic chief priest known as the Papa became the
Christian Pope. The mitre is the official head-dress of a
bishop, and starting out modestly with low sides it developed in the 13th century into a high conical cap divided
by a cleft, and having two fillets or threads hanging from
the back. It is likely that it assumed the shape of a fish-
head with reference to Christ who was known to early
Christians as the Great Fish (see 'fish'.)

By the 14th century the mitre had increased in size to a
foot or more, and was similarly more opulent. It is
recorded that one of the silver-gilt mitres from Fountains
Abbey, appropriated by Henry VIII, weighed 70 ounces.

MONASTERY

Latin *monasterium*, Greek *monasterion*, 'living alone'.
Greek *monazein* is 'to live alone'. The word monk is from
the same root.

The beginnings of monastic life go back to the 3rd and
4th centuries, to the wandering recluses, anchorites or
hermits of Egypt, as for example Ammon and Anthony.
Basil who lived in the 4th century first set up rules for the

125

purpose of the organisation of monks living together. When living together they became known as 'coenobites' (Greek *koino*, 'common' and *bios*, 'life'), and when in seclusion as 'eremites', a version of 'hermit' (Greek *erēmos*, 'solitary'). To the Church at Rome they were known as anchorites (Greek *anakhoreo*, 'I retire, withdraw'): having retired from life, they had no office.

The thread appears to go through Gaul to Britain with customs and buildings necessarily undergoing modification through climate. Monastic life is first found in Bangor. Wales it should be remembered was a Druidic centre of learning which absorbed this early form of Christianity because of the connection in kind. Thence it was carried to Ireland by Patrick. Ireland remained the centre of learning until Aidan was sent to Northumbria in 635 to evangelise England. Evidence still remains of the Irish monastics in the form of beehive settlements and oratories on the west coast, and their influence is clearly seen in the early buildings at Jarrow and Wiermouth. The great monasteries of Iona, Lindisfarne and Whitby all belong to this period.

There was always variance however between the disciplinary requirements of Rome and the individual Anglo-Saxon church with its Irish monastic infuence, and when Theodore was appointed to the see of Canterbury in 670 with the express purpose of introducing more conformity to rule, the spirit of monasticism in the early sense of the word could be said to have met its doom.

The Dark Ages followed, when almost all monastic buildings were destroyed by the invading Norsemen; and this was followed by the resurgence of monastic building after the Conquest in 1066. The intense religious zeal of the time produced the monastic houses of Durham, Canterbury, Norwich, Peterborough, and these, having the monopoly of learning, paved the way for the great period of cathedral building. The different monastic orders were the Benedictine, Cluniac, Cistercian, Augustinian, Premonstratensian, Carthusian, Knights Templars and Knights Hospitallers, along with the Friars and the Jesuits.

Architecturally, the church was the focus from which all sprang. The cloister adjoining in the south was surrounded by the most important buildings – refectory, chapter house, dormitory, along with the warming house, library and parlour. The infirmary and guest house and other lodgings were further removed.

MONK

Latin *monachus*, 'monk', Greek *monachos*, 'living alone'. Originally one living in solitude, performing religious exercises as in a cell or a desert. Only later did it come to imply a solitary life within a community, under vows and obeying rules of an order. (See 'monastery'.)

MONOGRAM (and other names of Christ)

Greek *monos*, 'alone, single', and *gramma*, 'something written, a letter'. Hence a joining of two or more letters to form a single significant device. The first two letters of the Greek word for Christ X and P form the monogram as in the diagram: it is sometimes called the chi-rho monogram, the sound in English of these two capitals, and this is universally used from the 4th century.

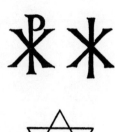

It has several variations, as the two in the diagram, sometimes being found as an X with an I (I being the initial letter of IHCOYC, Greek for Jesus). In each case, the monogram can be seen as a six-pointed star, signifying the Logos, or Wheel of Being, a glyph where the two interlaced triangles represent the Spoken Word. Here the male triangle, base uppermost, enters and works within the substantial world, base below.

Other common abbreviations of the name of Christ can be noted under this heading. In Greek art, the cross is accompanied by the inscription IC XC NIKA or simply IC XC. Greek C sounds 's': thus they are the first and last letters of 'IHCOYC XPICTOC' (Jesus Christ). NIKA means 'conquers' – thus 'Jesus Christ conquers'. This is sometimes abbreviated to XP NI 'Christ conquers'. In the Latin from the 12th century, Christ is designated by letters I.H.S. abbreviated from Jesus, Hominum Salvator, 'Jesus Saviour of men'. Or in the Greek again we find IHC abbreviated from IHCOYC, 'Jesus' or IHC with XPC, abbreviated from XPICTOC, 'Christ' – thus 'Jesus Christ'.

The scroll found over the crucifix bears the letters INRI, an abbreviation of Iesus Nazarenus Rex Iudeorum (Jesus of Nazareth King of the Jews), though an inner symbolism gives either of two alternatives: IN NOBIS REGNAT IESUS – 'within ourselves reigns Jesus', a reference to the quest for the Christ within, and IGNE NATURA RENOVATUR INTEGRA

127

– 'all nature is regenerated by fire', referring to the fire of the spirit, and its power to regenerate fallen man.

MONSTRANCE

Old French, from Low Latin *monstrantia*, from Latin *monstrare*, 'to show'. The monstrance is the receptacle in which the consecrated Host is exposed to the congregation for adoration. This was a late ritual – circa 1300. To be visible, the host was placed in crystal, and originally many different forms were used. After the 17th century the monstrance assumed the form of the sun radiating light. Symbolically, at the moment of showing, darkness and error have been dispelled by the intelligence and life-force of the sun, or Son.

MONUMENT

Latin *monumentum*, 'that which calls to mind', from *monere*, 'to remind, warn', both from the same base as Latin *mens*, 'mind, reason'. Thus a tablet or tombstone or construction to the memory of someone deceased.

After the Reformation, the simple religious symbols of the Catholic faith were supplanted in the church building by more worldly emblems. Large monuments showed the mourning families of the deceased, with emblems of death and the finity of human life – skulls, crossed bones, scythe and hour-glass: later in the 17th and 18th centuries, with classical influences, came the urn, sarcophagus and pyramid. All showed a self-satisfied assurance with the inevitable frailty of human life and the blissful life to come, represented by cherubim or angels playing trumpets. The inscriptions of these times stress human concerns rather than the mystery of the inner life, and extol piety and the philanthropic acts of the deceased.

Onwards from the end of the 18th century, a sentimental element enters the scene: Faith, Hope and Charity, for example, are represented with urns and dying flowers. This is the Neo-Classical style, faithfully copying classical models. In the 19th century, monumental work was largely consigned to the graveyard outside the church.

MOON

See under 'sun and moon'.

MOULDING

Old French *molle, modle*, Latin *modulus*, 'a small measure': 'model' is from this root. Reference is to the cavity into which a malleable material is poured, making a pattern of the same design for a moulding – that is the narrow decorated strip of stone or wood or plaster for cornices and panelling classically, and for the decorated arches and doorways of churches later. Two well known classical moulds are the 'dentil' and the 'egg and dart' (q.v.).

Early Norman moulding is crude, but, by 1150 or so, many were in use, such as the 'chevron', 'lozenge', 'billet', 'beak-head'. Later moulding became more varied and incorporated figures, beasts, birds and flowers.

MULLION or MUNNION

Old French *moignon*, 'stump of a tree'. A mullion is the upright stone dividing the lights (the panes of the windows) and screens in Gothic architecture. They are not found prior to Early English style – in Norman work the division of the window is a shaft too heavy to be called a mullion.

MUSIC

(See under 'organ'.)

MYSTERY PLAY

The medieval dramas performed at one time in the church or church-yard, and later in the towns, presented scenes from the Bible, and were so called because they dealt with the 'mysteries' of religion. But because they were enacted by different craft guilds, an etymological complication arose. Old French for trade is *mestier* (modern French *métier*), from Latin *minister*, 'servant', giving Middle English *mistere*, mistery, 'trade or occupation'. In this sense it is claimed the dramas are 'trade dramas', literally mystery plays. However, French *mystère* is used for such dramas, and this derives from Latin *mysterium*, Greek *mustērion*, to do with initiation into religious mysteries. This is also claimed to be the true origin of the word 'mystery' in mystery play, and much 'play' has been made over the two meanings.

Like so many words, however, the two meanings are not entirely unrelated, and in this instance attention is called to the true nature of craft. A craft involves the control of matter, and since matter is only the other face of spirit, such a control may lead into the secrets of spirit: the more a man searches into the laws of a given substance, the more he is rewarded by its inherent wisdom, and a craftsman's aim is to find them and hold them and himself in a fine balance. The condition of this balance, and of true art, is love for the material being used and the subjugation of the individual will: then those perfect laws may be of service. It is for this reason that in ancient civilisations master craftsmen were held in such esteem, that they were always associated with the temple, and that the guilds continued to be quasi-religious institutions in medieval times. All that was made then was made 'to the glory of God'.

The ultimate representative of this tradition is the mason shaping the temple itself, through control of material, which had become so sensitive as to produce the delicately balanced Gothic cathedral. On the inner level, every man is a mason, shaping his own substance so that its divine origin may reveal itself to him.

Historically, the mystery play gained a hold in this country during the 13th century, superseding the 'miracle plays', distinguished by being performed by professionals. As opposed to the individual miracle plays, mystery plays were written in groups or cycles embracing a number of themes from the Old and New Testaments. Performed as part of the observation of the feast of Corpus Christi instituted in 1264, they continued as an integral part of Church life for over two hundred years. Of the many cycles only those from Chester, Coventry, Wakefield and York remain in anything like a complete state. (See 'mason' and 'freemason').

N

NARTHEX

Greek *narthex*, 'the giant fennel' or 'small casket for unguents' from a Sanskrit root meaning 'reed'.

In the early basilica form of the early church the narthex was a long arcaded porch suggestive of the hollow stem of the plant, at the west end of the church. It was a place, like the 'galilee porch' of later years, for penitents, women or catechumens – that is those not admissible to the body of the church. Narthex is still used to denote the porch at the west end of the Catholic church containing the stoup of holy water.

Like so many other parts of the west end, the narthex has associations with the waters of life. See 'galilee', 'stoup', 'font', 'nave', 'west end'.

NATIVITY

Latin *nativitas*, 'birth'. The Nativity, or Birth of Christ, is the first major event in the Christian calendar, leading to the Death and Resurrection. Like the Crucifixion and the Last Supper, it is often represented in iconography. On the highest level the birth is that of God on earth at the darkest point in man's involution. It is a momentous event reconciling man to God through an act of Love, and with the message of sacrifice. Man's darkest point, his cross, is at the deepest concentration of his ego – his small self. It is this that he individually has to sacrifice to allow the birth of the Christ within. With the cosmic impetus already rooted in mankind, its effect is destined, by degrees, to transform the physical body, feeling, thinking, and the will.

Such a new birth is only possible after deep anguish and darkness of the soul. In the nativity myth, the darkness is represented by the birth taking place at the sun's lowest ebb, when it would appear that the light and life of the sun is disappearing for ever. In fact Christmas is celebrated on the 25th of December when it is indisputably clear that the sun is beginning to arise in the heavens again.

The humility required for the birth to take place is symbolised by the stable – both the ox and ass are beasts of burden. The birth of the child, the original Christmas present, is of a virgin, indicating that it can only take place within the purity of the soul. Again, it is simple shepherds who bear the good tidings; and all aspects of the story affirm the need to return to innocence. (See 'Magi' for further symbolism.)

NAVE

Latin *navis* 'ship'. The nave in the church is the place of the people, the place where the people are saved. The ship is the Church of Christ which upholds the souls of men above the storms of the waters of materiality.

On a larger scale, spiritual truths are protected in this ship or ark through periodic deluges. Truth may be submerged by ignorance, but the ark contains the seed of its future rebirth. The same ark is seen in the cradle which upheld Moses and saved him and the Jews from the forces of oppression symbolised by Pharoah. And in a way, each individual human being is born into the waters of life, where he is cut adrift at the *navel*, the source of physical succour, and where he must find his own salvation in the spiritual ship.

NIMBUS

Latin *nimbus* 'cloud, thunder-cloud'. The word in Christian art came to mean the bright vaporous light around the head of a divine being. It is of pagan origin, the Romans using it as an indication of the power of the sun around the head of celebrated mortals, but, in Christian art after the 11th century, it was reserved exclusively for saints, martyrs, apostles and for Christ himself. There are many variations of shape, including the ring, disc, triangle and square. Other names for the nimbus are 'halo' and inaccurately 'aureole' and 'glory' (q.v.). Latin *nimbus* however is a materialistic image, for the light is that inner radiance which comes of spiritual purity.

The cruciform nimbus, one of the most common in all Christian art, is exclusively reserved for Deity and especially for the Son, the Second Person of the Trinity, referring to Christ's sacrifice as man on the cross. Representations of Christ without it are rare. (See 'halo'.)

NINE ALTARS

In the retro-choir of some cathedrals is to be found the Chapel of the Nine Altars, connected with the nine orders of angels in Church doctrine. (See 'angel'.)

Symbolically it could be said that between God and man, or between man realising his own divinity, lie nine levels. 9 is the square of 3, the Trinity, representing the unfolding of these divine powers in body, heart and mind. It is a magical number, complete in the sense of non-changing – for instance 9 plus 9 equals 18, and the sum of the digits 1 and 8 make 9. Equally 9 times 9 is 81 and the sum of these digits makes 9. The end of the ninth month in

132

the womb gives way to a new birth, as the expiration of the ninth hour on the Cross rent the veil into the eternal plane. Nine is the number of *initiation* denoting the final recovery of all that a man once was – just as 9 itself turns back into itself as indicated.

NOAH

Noah is a Hebrew word meaning 'rest'. Noah and the ark riding the flood is one of the most commonly depicted themes in the Church. As a church is a ship of salvation in the waters of materiality (see under 'nave'), so the ark is a vessel, if we extend the imagery to cosmic cycles, which save Truth from being submerged by error. The allegory says that man's wickedness may bring about his own destruction, but each new cycle has in it the pure eternal seed that allows the renewed growth of the spirit and the fulfilling of man's ultimate purpose on earth. Thus Noah represents both the rest between such cycles and the Divine Intelligence, Greek *Nous*, that oversees this development.

His three sons represent the three parts of man's being, the three natural divisions of consciousness – head, heart and will. *Japhet* means 'the extender', a word used in connection with the northern portions of the world as then known (head); *Shem* means 'name, fame', in the sense of the 'name of God', God as love (heart); and *Ham* is a word originally meaning Egypt, derived from an Egyptian word *kem*, 'black' (will). The animals, clean and unclean, represent all that has gone before, external and internal to man's development, which is being carried through to the next cycle. God's grace and forgiveness – indicated in the story by the dove and the olive leaf, both symbols of love and reconciliation of heaven and earth – is also symbolised by the rainbow. The continuing overseership of the Divine Intelligence in the new cycle is symbolised by the high mountain Ararat where the ark finally comes to rest.

NONES or NONA HORA

From Latin *nonus*, 'ninth'. The ninth hour of the monastic day. Counting 6 a.m. as the first canonical hour (Prime), services were sung every three hours: thus nones was sung at about 3 p.m. The hours were variable however, according to the season. (See under 'Offices'). By the 14th century the Office of Nones had come to be sung

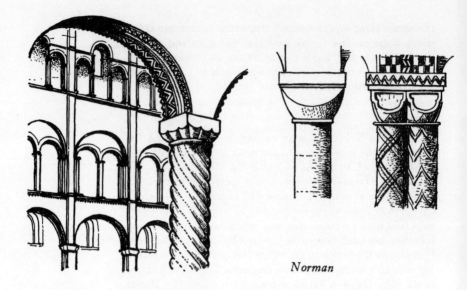

Norman

generally earlier – so much so that the present-day term 'noon' came to signify the middle of the day.

NORBERTINES

A monastic order. See under the alternative name 'Premonstratensian'.

NORMAN

Old French *Normant*, 'North-man', describing the Scandinavian race who conquered Normandy in the 10th century and settled there. This Norman/French race conquered England in 1066, bringing with them an unprecedented spate of building in which the churches of the religious orders and most parish churches were built. The Anglo-Saxon features were replaced by the apse, central tower, the three storeys of the basilica, and a western doorway. The cathedrals and abbey churches emphatically showed this Norman style, but it was not long before the indigenous English tradition reasserted itself. By the 13th century, most east ends were pulled down giving place to the square end and greater height. The central tower however remained the most distinctive feature of English cathedrals and abbeys. Among the

134

many features are arched windows and decorated arched doorways.

NUN

Middle English *nunne, nonne*, from Low Latin *nunna, nonna*, meaning 'old lady'. The meaning has come through Greek *nenna, nannē*, 'aunt and uncle': and all from Sanskrit *nanā*, 'mother'. In medieval times the word was used as a term of respect for a woman of age and experience, especially that of motherhood; in the same way an old man was respected in the term *nonnus*. Thus it is respect and veneration for experience that is found in the use of the word when it came to be applied to a woman belonging to a religious order.

O

OBEDIENDIARY

From Latin *obedientia* 'obedience'. The name is given to the monk in charge of a particular department of a monastery, referring to his obedience to the Rule. The important obedientaries, most of which had separate accounts, are as follows: – Precentor (music, books, services); Sacrist (church and its ornaments); Cellarer (general management, commodities); Infirmarian (care of the sick); Fraterer (care of the refectory); Chamberlain (dormitory and comforts); Almoner (care of the poor); Hosteller or Guest-master (provision for guests); Kitchener (culinary activities); Novice-master (care and teaching of novices).

OFFICES

From Latin *officium*, 'a service, duty'. The Offices are the seven daily monastic services sung at intervals throughout the day, based on the words in Psalm 119 'Seven times a day do I praise Thee', and which were made rule by St. Benedict circa. 525–550. The Offices were basically the singing of Psalms (along with lessons and readings), so that all 150 of them were sung within the space of a week. Counting 21 Psalms a day, three remained, to be added at some point.

In reality, the first service was an eighth sung during the night – originally 'Nocturns' or night-vigil, which later came to be called Matins ('what has to do with morning'). The first of the seven offices was *Lauds* (praise of daybreak); the second *Prime* (first hour of light, soon after Lauds; the third *Tierce* (3rd hour after Prime; the fourth was *Sext* (sixth hour after Prime); the fifth *Nones* (the ninth hour after Prime); the sixth *Vespers* (after Hesperus, the evening star Venus); and the seventh *Compline* (the completion of the day).

It has to be remembered however, that because of the seasons, with changing periods of light and dark, the time between the Offices would have been shortened or expanded accordingly.

The first hour, Prime, was fixed for convenience, to be at 6 a.m., as at that hour, at the equinoxes there is equal day and night. This gave the following fixed pattern around which modifications could take place – Prime 6 a.m. Tierce 9 a.m., Sext 12 mid-day, Nones 3 p.m.; Vespers 6 p.m., Compline 9 p.m.

Of the seven Offices, the most important are Lauds, called 'Earthly Rise' and Vespers, called 'Earthly Rest'. At the present day, the night service Matins is cancelled out by joining it to Lauds, in an early service, Lauds–Matins. The time of this varies according to the particular Order.

OGEE

Old French *augive*, meaning a 'double curved arch'. Further than that, the origin of the word is doubtful. In this form of arch, the line of each side is composed of a concave and a convex curve. The single line of such an arch also constitutes a form of moulding known as ogee.

OGHAM

Old Irish *ogum*, modified to *ogham*, from the name of the legendary Ogna. A Celtic system of writing (British and Irish) consisting of twenty letters formed by short strokes made at either side of a transverse line, usually at the angle of the tall stones upon which the writing is found. They are mostly sepulchral stones bearing the names of the deceased and his father, usually joined by a word equivalent to the Scottish 'mac'. The writing is often found along with debased capitals, and several have crosses showing the joining of Celtic and Christian cultures.

OIL

Latin *oleum*, Greek *elaion*, 'olive-oil'. Oil is symbolically 'love' – the power of compassion. Oil burns, illuminating error by light of Wisdom: externally and internally it is a lubricant and makes for the smooth inter-relating of parts, as its psychological counterpart, love, makes for unity between men. It is love that leads to Wisdom. (See in more detail, variously, under 'Christ', 'candle', 'unction'.)

ORATORY

From Latin *oratorium*, from *orator*, 'one who speaks or prays'. A chapel for private prayer. In current usage, the oratory is a building often attached to a church for private prayer, or a chapel for private or family worship in a stately home.

The name originated in the early Christian Church. In the 5th and 6th centuries, Irish monks inhabited beehive huts, the continuation of a pagan style, and performed devotions in an adjacent building called an oratory. The oratory differed from the hut simply in that it had a raised platform acting as an altar and a rectangular ground plan taking sloping walls to a roof angle.

Later Continental influence brought the chancel and the bell-tower. The mason's art developed; but stone roofs still restricted the size of the church, and this brought about the early practice of not enlarging a church but building other churches on the site. This continued up to medieval times and gives the typically Irish feature of a group of small churches around the original oratory of the founder saint.

ORB

Latin *orbis*, 'ring, circle'. In Christian art, an orb is a globe surmounted by a cross, frequently depicted held by Christ as a child, and also in images of God the Creator. The cross symbolises the power of Christ's Crucifixion over the orb or circle of confinement which is the world. (See 'cross' and 'five wounds'.)

ORDER

Middle English *ordre*, from Latin *ordo*, 'a regular series, or arrangement': also 'a class or rank', as in a monastic fraternity. The order in architecture refers to the styles in

Greek architecture, basically three in number – Doric, Ionian and Corinthian (q.v.) – though the Romans in resurrecting these orders added two others, Tuscan and Composite. The order embraces the whole base, shaft, capital and entablature. (See 'column' and 'capital'.)

ORGAN

Latin *organum*, 'instrument, tool', Greek *organon*, 'instrument, tool'; related to Greek *ergon*, 'work, energy'. Only in medieval times did the word come to be used specifically for the musical instrument, the organ.

It is strange how the word came into use. Clearly the musical 'organum' of medieval times, a system of singing in intervals of 4ths and 5ths, and the organ itself, are related, and that both are in some sense a tool. Music making, this suggests, is a tool in the hands of man – essentially an aspiring and yearning of the spirit. Organ and organum are both then instrumental in linking man with God.

The need for harmony in the soul is also implied; inner work is to do with achieving harmony. Harmony in music has a scientific basis, for the most pleasing and perfect intervals have the most simple mathematical ratios – e.g. the octave has 1-2, the fifth 2-3, the fourth 3-4 and so on: it was only these elementary intervals that organum originally employed. Spatial harmony was also understood by the master builders of the cathedrals; relationship of transept to the whole length of the church, length to width of transept and so on, are known to have been considered in the light of the most simple ratios. Thus there was a subtle resonance between the harmony of the music and the harmony of the space it filled.

Historically, portable machines of the organ family were used in Graeco-Roman times, mostly in places of entertainment. The Church may not have accepted the instrument at first because of its secular association – certainly there is little reference to the 'organ' in the first few centuries of Christianity. In the 10th century, however, there are references to organs in Britain, along with indications of their laborious size and the manpower needed to supply air to the bellows. Organs were not used in ordinary parish churches, and here, music was the responsibility of the wind and string instrumentalists, who prior to the Reformation played in the broad rood loft in

138

front of the chancel, and later in a gallery at the west end of the church. There is always evidence in the internal structure of a church of the difficulty found in accommodating the organ or harmonium when they began to supplant live musicians in the 19th century.

ORIEL WINDOW or ORIOLE

Medieval Latin *oriolum*, 'recess, gallery', probably from Latin *oratoriolum*, a diminutive of *oratorium*, 'place of prayer'. Originally it was part of a house set apart for prayer in medieval times. From such a place, the lord of the house could look down upon and participate in a domestic service. Any projecting room, private chamber or gallery came to be called an oriole, still with its religious function; and finally the term came to mean simply a projecting window, either corbelled high up on a wall or rising straight from ground level.

OVOLO

Lation *ovum*, 'egg'. A classical and Renaissance convex moulding, usually a quarter of a circle, and often decorated by an egg and dart motif.

P

PALIMPSEST

A Latin word from Greek *palimpsēston*, from *palin*, 'again'; 'in reverse direction' and *psaio*, 'rub, crumble away'. The term refers to parchment upon which two sets of writings are found superimposed, and also to church brasses where the brass has been used on the other side for engraving, or over-engraving by changing the existing design. It was a common occurrence in the days of early manuscripts to re-use old parchment from which the writing had been erased, and often an older and more valuable document has been uncovered by careful deciphering of the original.

PALL

Latin *pallium*, 'cloak', and *palla*, 'woman's outer garment'. Thus the idea of a covering in the current meanings of either a small square of linen laid over the chalice or the black-purple cloth covering a coffin.

The word pall has a deep significance: it is essentially the cover upon God's own power by the act of creation. Its blackness is the heaviness of gravity and the *maya* that ensnares man's spirit. The word 'pale' gives a similar image of loss of life, and the verb 'to pall' suggests becoming weary by excess, especially of sensual indulgence. The whole idea is reflected in the associated word 'fall', as in the sense of the fall of man. To be appalled is to be aware of the truth of the situation.

PANTRY

Medieval Latin *panetaria*, 'bread-shop' (*panis*, 'bread'). A room in a monastery in which the bread and table necessities were kept. The buttery or botellerie (French *bouteille*, 'bottle'), as distinct from the pantry, contained all wines, beer and drinking utensils.

PARADISE

See under 'parvis' and in the context of the Garden of Eden under that heading.

PARCLOSE

Old French *parclos*, past participle of *parclore*, 'to shut in' (*per* and *clore* 'to close'). A parclose is a screen or railing in a church which encloses a shrine or tomb or shuts off a side chapel from the main body of the church.

PARISH AND PARISH CHURCH

Latin *paroecia*, 'parish', Greek *paroikia*, 'land around a church' – *para*, 'beside' and *oiein*, 'to dwell'. Thus a parish is originally the smallest area in the jurisdiction of a rector or vicar, a division of a diocese.

Most parish churches in Britain had their origin in the Norman period and were of simple form, with or without transepts. With few exceptions they underwent many changes and present a confusing picture to the observer. The east end seems to be the first to have undergone enlargement. Later, as more accommodation was needed, aisles were added (most churches had none). Of the two aisles, the north aisle was added first due to the south side of the churchyard being preferred as a burial ground. In such an instance, the nave wall was often pierced leaving the upper part sustained by later pillars. Aisles were often added to both nave and chancel.

Later, aisles were again widened so that the aisle roof was brought level with the eaves of the nave roof, and in larger churches this meant the covering over of the clerestory; traces of this change can be seen on nave walls. At the chancel end, chantry chapels were often built on both north and south sides, so widening the whole church. Again, transepts would be widened to compensate for other changes. In the 14th century, a nave and chancel were seen more as a unit, and chancel arches were enlarged, but the overriding change was in the development of the rood-screen, which replaced the chancel arch, and became the characteristic of the medieval church. These in turn were in the main destroyed at the Reformation, causing visible structural changes. Thus many parish churches, in their architecture and fittings, represent almost a millenium of history, not counting a possible prior Saxon origin.

PARLOUR

Old French, *parleor*, from Latin *parlare*, 'to talk'. The parlour is a small room found in monasteries where talking was permitted, as for instance on the subject of trade, and private matters needing discussion. The room was only available on the consent of the prior or abbot. It was also known as a 'locutary'.

PARSON

Latin *persona*, 'human being, person' from the current medieval phrase *'ecclesiae persona'*, the person representing the church in a parish. The other meaning of Latin *persona* can be considered too – 'character, role', as on a stage, for the representative of the Church acts out man's spiritual drama in the rituals he performs.

PARVIS

Old French *parevis*, from Medieval Latin *paravisus*, from Latin *paradisus*, 'paradise'. (The basic meaning of 'paradise', deriving from Persian, is 'an enclosure or garden'.) The word was first used in medieval times to denote the actual courtyard in front of St. Peter's Church in

Rome, and only later came to mean the enclosed space in front of the western face of a cathedral or church. In the early Christian Church, such a forecourt had a fountain used for symbolic washing and for those not yet baptised.

The word is used loosely to denote the west porch of a church, and also a small room above the main west porch, looking out onto the forecourt. There is also obvious imagery in the fact that when the faithful enter the enclosure or the west porch of the church they are symbolically re-entering paradise.

PASSION

Latin *passio*, 'suffering, emotion'. The expression 'The Passion' refers to Christ's suffering on the cross and thus signifies the Crucifixion as described in the Gospels or as represented in art. The word 'passion' has two associations. One is the conscious suffering of Christ in his role as redeemer of man's sins by his death, an act of awful solemnity involving unthinkable *com-passion* (suffering with) for the human race. The other is the violent anger, the 'suffering' of the crowd at a wholly mechanical, uncontrolled level, which rejects Christ.

Thus in the imagery of the crucifixion, the element of reverential awe is side by side with the ignorant passion of the crowd: and in an individual man, the capacity for true suffering, for his own state and for others, is at war with his passion, his lower nature which mocks and destroys the other.

PASTORAL STAFF

'Pastoral' is from Latin *pastor*, 'shepherd'; staff is from Middle English *staf*, Old High German *stab*, 'staff, stick'. (See 'crozier'.)

PATEN

Old French *patens*, Latin *patena*, 'pan, shallow dish', from Greek *patanē*, 'pan'. A paten is a small shallow dish, usually of gold, silver or pewter, used to hold the wafer in the celebration of the Eucharist. It is made to match a particular chalice though most of the medieval patens preserved have become separated from their chalices. When preserved together it is often due to the tradition in the 13th and 14th centuries to inter them with the ecclesiastics who used them.

142

PATTEE or PATEE CROSS

French *patte* 'paw, foot'. In heraldry, a cross with the arms having a broad flat end. It is sometimes called a 'Maltese cross', but this is an error. (See 'Maltese cross'.)

PAUL

See under 'Peter and Paul'.

PAX

Latin *pax*, 'peace'. Originally, during the celebration of the Mass, the members of the congregation received the kiss of peace, the *osculum pacis*, from the priest. Later, for convenience, a small tablet of gold or silver, bearing an image of the Crucifixion, to which the priest had already given the kiss of peace, was passed around to be kissed by the congregation.

PECTORAL CROSS

Latin *pectus*, 'breast'. The cross is usually of solid gold or silver bejewelled and worn on the breast by bishops and abbots, and often contains a holy relic. In its position on the breast, the cross acts as a prism for forces flowing out through the bishop into the communicant.

PEDIMENT

The word is thought to be a form of 'periment', a version of pyramid. It originally denoted the triangular structure crowning the front of a Greek building, and then came to mean any such struture, triangular or rounded, over a portico or door. A more likely origin of the word, however, is from the Latin root *ped*, 'foot' which can be seen as a euphemism for sexual power.

This would point to the significance of the triangle in the Greek civilisation in relation to the unfolding of man's inner development. The foot or base of the triangle represents the material forces of gravity and the grounded energy, and the apex of the triangle the forces of light, of Apollonian order, mental clarification pulling upwards. The resulting isosceles triangle represents the potential equilibrium between the two.

The pediment was known to the Greek as the *aetos*, the 'eagle', and was considered a particular gift of the gods. The space in the triangle was called the *tympanum*, 'kettle-drum', suggesting the tension between the opposing forces, and was filled with sculpture – as that of Phidias on the Parthenon. It was considered the crown of the temple in the same way that the carving over the cathedral door was considered the consummation of all artistic effort. (See 'tympanum'.)

PELICAN

Greek *pelekinos*, from *pelekys*, 'axe': originally a Babylonian-Assyrian word *pillaqu*, 'axe'. The connection with axe is found in the related Greek word *pelekas*, 'woodpecker'.

The sacrifice or wounding theme is found in the fable of the pelican where the young were reputed to be fed by the disgorging of its own blood. Thus it came to symbolise the sacrificial act of Christ on the cross and was in early Christianity used as a symbol of Christ's life work. Examples are found carved on early lecterns in place of the now customary eagle; and the pelican is also found in heraldry. Though the feeding on the blood is now disproven, the large pouch from which food is disgorged remains an image of the nurturing of the young in spirit.

PENDANT

Latin *pendere*, 'to hang'. An ornament hanging from the ceiling, associated with the Perpendicular period, and especially found in stone vaultings, as in fan-vaulting where the fan spreads out from the pendant. They were often richly carved.

PENTAGRAM or PENTALPHA

Greek *penta*, 'five and *gramma*, 'something written or drawn': the five-pointed star is also called a 'pentalpha' because its form appears to be the consequence of five inter-locking 'a's (*alpha*, Greek 'a').

PERPENDICULAR

A period of English architecture following on from the Decorated, approximately 1377 to 1485, and broadly equated with the 15th century. It is typified by the upright lines of the bars of windows and of panelling. Larger windows necessitated transoms; that is, horizontal bars. Since the arcades of the nave and clerestory windows were

Perpendicular

heightened, the triforium was almost dispensed with. In the vaulting, complex ribs and panels give rise to the fan and pendant vaults. The style is also referred to as Rectilinear, with especial reference to window tracery.

PETER AND PAUL

St. Peter and St. Paul are both establishers of the Church in Rome, and in iconography stand next to the Evangelists in importance. They are commonly represented at either side of Christ enthroned, or at either side of the altar.

Peter (Greek *petros*, 'stone' – referring to his function of founder of the Church) – holds the two crossed keys, one gold one silver, the insignia of the papacy. (For symbolic aspects of the 'key', see under that heading.) Paul (Latin *paulus*, 'small') was so named after his conversion: before this he held the Hebrew name Saul. Clearly the name Paulus would have a spiritual significance, and the literal translation itself indicates smallness, in the sense of humility and unworthiness to receive the gift of revelation. In his own words he considered himself 'less than the least of

145

the Apostles'. Paul is represented with a sword, referring both to his martyrdom and to his warrior-like work in spreading the message of Christ. He also carries a book indicating the importance of his message, that it is a new dispensation not only for the Jews but for all men.

PEW

Old French *puie*, 'raised seat, balcony', from Latin *podium* and Greek *podion*. The word was originally applied to a raised place from which a preacher read, and later acquired the meaning of a compartment or stall or fixed bench for a congregation: the term 'pew' simply indicates that the construction was raised.

From the 14th century, the nave of larger churches had fixed seats of oak with carved ends at the aisles, sometimes with finials (called 'poppies'). The propertied families had their own high, enclosed pews, sometimes called stalls, and paid for the privilege of such pews according to their nearness to the altar: in fact, in smaller churches, there was little room for the common people. In cathedrals, families of distinction, the patrons of the establishment, erected pews immediately to right and left of the altar, and some of these edifices, made of stone, still remain. The nave however originally had no seating as such. Sometimes a stone bench is found along the inner walls for the use of the aged and infirm, and this gave rise to the expression 'the weakest go to the wall' or 'to go to the wall'.

In parish churches after the Commonwealth, long benches superseded the family pew system, expressing the emancipation of the people; indications of the old high pews can be seen in columns of the nave where pieces have been cut away. (See 'stalls'.)

PIER

Low Latin *pera*, through Greek *petra*, 'rock'. A mass of stone, as opposed to a column, supporting an arch or a roof. The word is, however, loosely used instead of 'pillar' in Norman and Gothic architecture, and even sometimes in place of 'column'. A pillar has more of an ornamental character, though fulfilling the same function as the pier.

PILASTER

From pillar (q.v.) and *aster* (a Latin suffix indicating diminution or inferiority). Thus a pilaster is a flat, rectangular column against a wall with a shaft, distinctive base and capital, but with the base projecting only about a third of its depth from the wall.

PILLAR

Latin *pila*, 'pillar', the etymology of which is said to be doubtful. A support, not necessarily of classical proportions, for an arch or roof. Whereas a column is round, a pillar may be clustered, composed of several smaller columns making a massive whole. Each period has its own particular form.

Symbolically the pillar is a sustaining power, a bridge between lower and higher levels, earth and spirit. In man the pillar is the vertical spine which raises him heavenwards out of the earth and around which lie subtle channels of energy connecting sex and head centres. A pillar of fire, in biblical reference, is the regenerated energy; a pillar of salt is the energy retained to the service of the lower self. The vertical pillar or column represents unified will, the force that aspires upwards against material inertias – something also seen in the form of the letter 'I', as used to denote the individual man.

In ancient symbolism, two pillars (as in the Temple of Solomon) indicate the polar opposites inherent in creation, and the need for them to be reconciled. In the Tarot cards the pillars signify the inevitability of negative and positive, the Law and the free spirit, and the balance that must be found between them. This is also suggested in most medieval cathedrals, for there are two towers, one at either side of the west door, which when opened leads the eye in a direct line via the single central tower, to the altar, the place of final reconciliation.

The hazardous nature of the journey through the dual gates is also suggested in comparing Latin *pila* with *pilare*, 'to rob, deprive of hair' (*pilus*, 'hair'). Deprived of power (hair is always symbolically a man's power) he has to erect his own unifying 'pillar'.

PILGRIM

Middle English *pelegrin*, Latin *peregrinus*, 'foreign'; *per*, 'beyond' and *ager*, 'territory'. Thus someone who voyages away from home; the main purpose of foreign travel, in the days in which the word originated, was to visit a religious shrine.

PILGRIMAGE OF GRACE

The original Latin name was *Itinerarium Gratiae*: the name of a considerable revolt against Henry VIII's suppression in 1536 of all monasteries (376 of them) that had an annual income of less than £200. It was based in the East Riding of Yorkshire where many houses had suffered. The revolt at one stage looked as it had achieved the King's compromise, but ended by the hanging of the ringleader Robert Aske and the abbots of Fountains, Rievaulx, and Jervaulx Abbeys, and the Prior of Bridlington. A lesser insurrection in Lin⌐ ⌐lnshire also failed.

PINNACLE

Low Latin *pinnaculum*; *pinna*, 'point' and *culus*, a diminutive suffix. In Gothic architecture, it is the slender turret-like point on buttresses, roofs or parapets, often decorated with foliage.

PISCINA, and DOUBLE-PISCINA

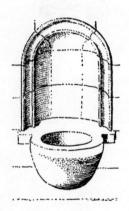

Latin *piscina*, 'fish-pond', from *piscis*, 'fish'. A piscina is a stone basin in a niche in the wall of a church near the altar, and sometimes in the ground near the altar and sometimes standing away from the wall near the altar, used by the priest for emptying the rinsings of the chalice and paten during the celebration of the mass. In this country it is usually found on the south wall. Two drains together constitutes a 'double-piscina', and these belong to the Decorated period (roughly 1272 to 1377). In the reign Edward I, it was directed that the priest should, in the interests of ritual purity, wash his hands after the offertory in the celebration of the mass, in a separate drain to the one used for the vessels. Later when the priest consumed what was left in the vessels, the practice was discontinued.

PITTANCE

From Latin *pietas*, 'piety, compassion'. An extra allowance of food given to monks above the normal quantity, on feast days or special occasions. Normally pittances were the gift of benefactors, or bequests upon anniversaries of benefactors, most probably as an encouragement to the monks to say prayers for their souls. The modern usage has a derivative association when it signifies smallness of quantity.

PLAINSONG (GREGORIAN CHANT)

The word plainsong was a rendering of the Latin *cantus planus*. It was first used at a time when, in the 14th and 15th centuries, musical experimentation was increasing and it was necessary to differentiate plain or unadorned song from *cantus figuratus*, song with a florid figure accompanying it. Plainsong is essentially free speech-song, set to the words of the Psalms, with natural inflexions at ends of breaths or verses – a prose rhythm rather than a fixed beat.

It has its origins in the Jewish synagogue, but even more so in the Greek modal system. As in all development, much error crept in, and the name of Ambrose (end of 4th century) and Pope Gregory (end of 6th century), are landmarks in its reform. Gregory added four more modes making eight in all, and his influence was such that plainsong and Gregorian chant became virtually synonymous. Church music developed harmonically, and the art of plainsong, partly due to inadequate notation,was debased or lost. Upon an attempt to re-form the art in the 19th century, the monks of Solesmes in France found upwards of a hundred different versions of one particular plainsong, an indication of its condition.

So much is this music bound up with the use of the voice, speaking or singing, that some of the early small glyphs indicating rises and falls, phrasings, poises, and so on. have been adapted and are seen in our present day punctuation as comma, semi-colon, question mark and the like.

PLINTH

Latin *plinthus*, 'plinth', Greek *plinthos*, 'brick'. The plinth is the lowest part of the base of a column, classically plain and square, but in Gothic columns subdivided and moulded.

POPPY-HEAD

Latin *puppis*, 'the poop of a ship'. (French *poupée*, 'doll', is so named from the carved poop). *Puppis* is connected with *papa*, 'father', both from a root meaning 'to swell'. A poppy-head is the raised and ornamented top of the ends of benches in a church, often cut in the form of a fleur-de-lis. Many can be seen in the choir stalls of cathedrals and some in the naves of parish churches. None exist prior to the 14th century, and they are associated mainly with the Perpendicular period. Another name for poppy-head is 'standard'.

PORTICO or PORCH

Latin *porticus*, 'a colonnade' or 'covered gallery', from *portus*, 'entrance, harbour'. In a large church the portico or porch is the covered entrance at the west front: it also refers to the projecting entrance in either the north or south walls.

The harbour image provides yet another instance of the 'water' symbolism associated with the west end of the church: the image is of the sea of life the soul enters at birth. Water is in the stoup and the font, and the nave is the ship on that sea (See 'west end', 'east end', 'nave' for symbolism.)

PREACHER

Old French *prechier*, from Latin *praedicare*, 'to proclaim, announce' (*prae* 'forwards' and *dicere*, 'to speak'). Thus one who speaks forth the gospel.

PRECENTOR

From Latin *prae*, 'before, in front', and *cantor*, 'singer'. The officer in charge in a monastery or cathedral who leads the singing. In monastic life, he had one of the most important roles. He was responsible for arranging Divine Offices, was keeper of music and all books, instructed and corrected monks in their reading of lessons, was responsible for organising processions, and was keeper of the mortuary roll. His assistant was called the Succentor.

PREDELLA

Italian, 'a foot-stool' or 'kneeling stool'. The origin of the word is not certain, but it is likely that the letter 'r' has intruded into the Latin root *ped*, 'foot'. It denotes a step or platform on which an altar rests; it also denotes a raised structure behind the altar itself. The raised dais for the altar is also referred to as a 'foot-pace'.

PREMONSTRATENSIANS or NORBERTINES

An Augustinian monastic order founded by St. Norbert in France in 1120. The name is from the place name Prémontré, which derives from French *pré* and *montré*, Latin *pratum monstratum*, 'the indicated meadow', because it was shown to him in a dream that he should erect his monastery at that particular place. This order was known by the name White Canons of Augustine. There were 35 houses extant in Britain at the Dissolution, of which Eastby Abbey in Yorkshire is one.

PRESBYTERY

Latin *presbyterium*, from Greek *presbutērion*, 'the place of the presbyters' (*presbuteros*, 'elder', from *presbus*, 'old').

The presbytery is thus in the eastern end of the church, in the sanctuary where the clergy perform their rituals: the term is often applied to the whole sanctuary but it is specifically the area east of the choir and before the altar. In a cathedral it is usually elevated one step above the choir and has the name 'gradus presbyterii'.

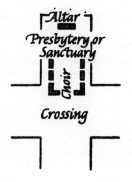

PRESBYTER

From the same root as 'presbytery'. Thus the meaning of an elder or leader in the early Church giving the word 'priest'. Later, in the Presbyterian Church, such a priest was called an 'elder'. The term 'presbyter' now also denotes a group of presbyters meeting in and representing a given district.

PRIEST

Middle English *prēst*, from Old High German *priester*, derived from the Latin *presbyter* through Greek *presbuteros*, 'elder' (*presbus*, 'old'). The original meaning from *presbus* is 'leader of a herd'; compare Latin *prae*, 'before' (Greek *para*, 'proceeding from') and Greek *bous*, 'ox'. The venerated leader of the animal kingdom became the leader in the world of the spirit.

PRIORY AND PRIOR

Old French *priorie*, from Latin *prioria*, 'former, better', from a base as in *primus* meaning 'first'. A branch monastery of nuns or monks subordinate to an abbey is called a priory. Priory is also used to denote an independent house of regular canons which was the seat of a bishop, as in the Augustinian Order. In the same way that an abbey derives its name from an abbot ('father'), the priory is so called from the prior, the first in rank under the abbot or bishop.

PULPIT

Latin *pulpitum*, 'platform, stage, scaffold'. The pulpit is the raised structure from which the minister addresses the congregation. Formerly such platforms, made of stone or wood, were attached to a wall or pillar in the nave for the address to the congregation. Very few pulpits remain of earlier date than the Perpendicular period, and these are polygonal in shape and often approached by a concealed stairway: they frequently have finely ornamented canopies. Pulpits were also erected in the refectories of monasteries for readings at meals.

In the sense that the priest is a vehicle for divine prophecy, a representative of the power of God, the pulpit is properly on his right side – to the left of the chancel as seen by the congregation. The lectern containing the Book, the formulated Word, is on the opposite side. (See 'right and left'.)

PULPITUM

(Same derivation as 'pulpit'.) The term 'pulpitum' is sometimes used instead of 'rood-loft' (see 'rood'), the screen with gallery above, supporting the great crucifix and separating the nave from the chancel in pre-Reformation times. It was also the high place from which readings were made. In cathedrals, such a stone screen with gallery, often housing the organ, is invariably a 'pulpitum'. It usually contains statues of saints or kings and intricate canopy work. This sculpture suffered much at the Reformation and was subject to much restoration later.

PURBECK MARBLE

A type of marble from Purbeck in Dorset used for columns in some of the early cathedrals, and giving a highly polished finish. In later centuries, the marble was much used for the making of memorials and tombs.

PUTLOG HOLE

On the outside and inside of the walls of ancient monuments are to be found small square holes. These were made by workmen during building operations for the erection of scaffolding. The cross pieces of scaffolding upon which floors were laid were the putlogs. The origin of the word is from Old English *pytt* 'well' or 'hole': thus the log in the hole.

Vitruvius, the Roman architect, calls them appropriately '*columbaria*', after their resemblance to pigeon holes. Today that is their chief function.

PYX

Latin *pyxis*, Greek *pyxis*, 'a box'. ('Greek *pyxos*, the 'box-tree, boxwood'). A pyx is a casket containing the Host (the wafer symbolising the sacrificed body of Christ). It is used in the blessing of the people in certain services, and also for carrying to the sick. In classical times, it was simply a box in which valuables were kept, but Christianity adopted it as a receptacle for relics and for the reserved sacrament. The pyx and the ciborium (q.v.) were both used for this purpose, but latterly the ciborium was a larger vessel for use on the altar, and the pyx, smaller, came to be used for administering the Host to the dying (the viaticum).

Q

QUARREL

Old French *quarrel*, from Medieval Latin *quadrellus*, diminutive of Latin *quadrus*, 'a square'. A small square diamond, or square-shaped pane of glass, fitted by lead into a window: also an opening of four leaves in tracery of the Perpendicular period.

QUATREFOIL

See under 'trefoil'.

QUIRE

See under 'choir'.

QUOIN

Old French *coign* and Modern French *coin*, 'corner', from Latin *cuneus*, 'wedge'. In Saxon architecture

153

especially, it denotes the angle of a church wall where the wall is of rough stonework and the corner or quoin is of dressed stone. The name is also used to denote the individual stones of which the whole quoin is built.

R

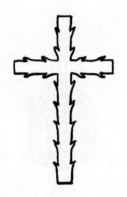

RAGULY CROSS

Middle English *ragge*, Old Norwegian *rogg*, 'tuft of fur or rough hair'. Thus a cross whose limbs are notched at equal distances on both sides.

REBUS

Latin *rebus*, the ablative plural of *res*, 'thing, object'. An enigmatical representation of a name, by pictures suggesting parts of the name, in the nature of a riddle. Such a device is found in coats-of-arms, quite apart from heraldry, and on monuments and tombs. Members of the clergy especially were subject to such treatment.

RECTOR

Latin *rector*, 'leader, rule', a word applied in Low Latin to a bishop, abbot or priest. In the English Church he was an incumbent, a parish priest who had the right to the greater tithes of corn, wood and hay, as well as to the lesser tithes. This privilege, as well as the freehold of the rectory, continues today despite the effects of the Dissolution of the Monasteries, when many rectorial tithes came to an end, some being sold to non-ecclesiastics who were called 'lay-rectors'. A vicar (q.v.) does not have this protection.

REFECTORY

Latin *refectio*, 'a re-making, re-freshment', from *reficere*, 'to re-make' – thus the general idea of restoring the body through food. The dining hall of a monastery was usually on the south side of the cloister. The terms FRATER, FRATERY, FRATRY, from an old French abbreviation *fraitur*, are also used. When erected over the vaulted cellars and above ground level, the refectory is indicated by the words FRATER OVER.

It was one of the most hallowed parts of the monastery, with rituals devised to recall and be an extension of the Last Supper (q.v.). The basic bread and wine apportioned to each monk was the same food as in the sacrament, and the accent (at variance with some aspects of monastic life) was on cleanliness. Tables and the bread thereon were covered by linen, the air was scented by herbs, mats and rushes were at the entrance, and the lavatorium for washing hands was provided outside the refectory.

The first substantial meal of the day was after sext (about 12 mid-day), and was eaten in silence except for the reading of holy works from the pulpit built into the wall of all refectories. (St. Benedict's Rule indicates that not all monks should act as readers, but only those with eloquence to inspire the brethren). Food not eaten could be sent to the gates for the poor; extra food on feast days had the name 'pittance' (q.v.); the meal ended by a return to the church to offer thanks. The original ideal of 'no flesh of four-footed beast' was much modified over the years along with other laxities in the Rule, until in the second half of the 15th century, general eating of meat, on certain days at least, was common.

The giving of thanks for food received was essentially to the Lord, the Provider, but the sacredness of eating returns to the idea of sacrifice, for in order for a man to live, lower forms of live have to be sacrificed. This is the way in which the Lord's universe is run; it is the core of life, physical and psychological. (see also under 'mass').

REFORMATION

Literally, a re-formation of the state of religion, a slow growth of dissatisfaction and protest (hence Protestantism) mainly against papal rule, spiritual and temporal. The leaders were Wycliffe (1324–84), Luther (1483–1546), Zwingli (1484–1531), Calvin (1509–64), and Knox (1513–72). Behind the English Reformation lay the attempt of Henry VIII to extend the power of the monarchy into all aspects of national life. The controversies of the early 16th century between King and Pope came to a head in the Suppression of the Monasteries (q.v.). The act of Supremacy under Queen Elizabeth in 1559 marked the final separation from Rome.

Church interiors suffered drastically from these

changes. Following upon the destruction of buildings and confiscation of property in the monasteries, came the 'Disendowment of the Parishes' under Edward VI with the appropriation of much wealth and property belonging to the parish churches. Finally the ruthless destruction of icons under Cromwell, saw the end of the parish church as it had been for hundreds of years. Wooden rood screens, wall paintings and iconography connected with the old order were virutally obliterated.

The Reformation was however an inevitable move away from medieval innocence to sophistication through knowledge, and the growth of a sense of individual importance. Such a change involved the throwing off of the yoke of the Roman Church, and this was encouraged by the spirit of the Renaissance which filtered into this country during the reign of Henry VIII. Medieval building and tradition was dying; enough churches had been produced in the medieval period and so it was not in new churches, but in the interiors of the old, that changes were henceforth made. There was now a deterioration in style – the humanity of the new grew into a visible complacency, most noticeable in the expressions of the wealthy donors on memorial monuments. On tombs, records of the worldly attainments of the deceased were preferred to sacred figures. Many factors were involved: Flemish craftsmen had already brought classical idioms into Henry's court, and the massacre of St. Bartholomew later gave rise to the influx of Huguenot craftsmen. Literature, printing, the introduction of a book of Common Prayer, and classical ideals – all contributed to this flowering of a new age.

REGULAR CLERGY

From Latin *regula*, 'a straight staff, a rule'. The inmates of a monastery are called 'regular clergy' because they live under the rule of a monastic Order. Ordinary clergy, in the world, are 'secular' clergy, from Latin *saecularis*. 'worldly, temporal, of an age'. This was the only meaning of the word 'regular' until the 16th century.

'Clergy' is from Old French *clergie*, from Latin *clericus*, which in the original Greek meant 'lot' or 'inheritance'. As it was first used in the Church, it implied that the clergy considered that the Lord was their entitled inheritance. Later, as in the word 'clerk', it signified a learned or scholarly person – the prerogative of the Church at that time.

RELIC AND RELIQUARY

Middle English *relyke* from Latin *reliquiae*, 'remains'. Thus, the body or some part of the body of a martyr or saint kept for religious veneration. Originally bones were the principal relics, but later the intimate possessions of a saint were kept for the same purpose. For example, in Ireland in the 5th and 6th centuries, the bible, bell and crozier (pastoral staff) belonging to the founder of a particular church were treasured as having magical properties, and each article had its own custodian. Metal covers called reliquaries or shrines were made to cover them, and these give us some of the finest Celtic art of the time.

The use of relics had its origin in the practice of saying mass over the tombstones of 1st century Christian martyrs in the catacombs in Rome: it was a reminder of a Universal Church founded upon their sacrifice. The idea was perpetuated in the 'altar stone' used at the celebration of mass, which still applies in the Catholic Church. This is a small consecrated stone on the altar, wrapped in wax cloth and containing pieces of the bones of saints.

In medieval times there was much competition between churches for superior relics, many of which were brought back from Rome to this country by diligent church men like St. Wilfrid, whose journeys to Rome helped to establish the Roman use here. Clearly much abuse developed in the trading of relics, some examples of which are:- bones of the Blessed Mary Magdalene, and her handkerchief (Ripon leper hospital), a phial containing the Virgin's milk (Walsingham), a bit of the true cross (Fountains Abbey). Such relics were kept in the crypt or protected part of the church for veneration by pilgrims. Chaucher makes play of their abuse in the Canterbury Tales.

The devotional care taken to preserve bodies of saints, and to make shrines worthy of pilgrimage finds example in St. Cuthbert (Durham), Thomas à Becket (Canterbury), St. Edmund (Bury St. Edmunds). Often, heads and bodies of saints were kept in different shrines.

In the consecration of a new church, relics were always used in remembrance of the early martyrs upon whom the Church was founded.

French, literally *re-naissance*, 're-birth': specifically the re-birth of ancient Greek ideals, art and literature during the 15th and 16th centuries in Europe. (The original Italian word was similarly *rinascita*, 're-birth'.) Formerly only describing a change in style, it was only in the 19th century that it came to signify a whole period. Exact dates are not easily definable. Petrarch in the 14th century had already started a return to classical Roman forms, and Florence artists developed this revival.

The transplanting of the Gothic spiritual aspiration, with its quality of primitive innocence, into the new growth of naturalism was an inevitable step in the individualising of man. The movement out into the world of scientific clarity was a move from the nameless work of Gothic craftsmen to the birth of an individual self-awareness which, whilst extolling the virtues of man, was destined to end in a stale imitation of the original.

The influence from Italy passed into northern Europe at different times, until finally no aspect of Western life, including thought, language, music, science and medicine, remained untouched by it. In England, though Henry VIII had employed Italian workmen earlier, it was only in the 17th century that Inigo Jones introduced the true Renaissance idiom. Prior to this so-called Tudor Gothic style, the heavy Jacobean style between 1600 and 1625 had already moved away from pure Gothic. Wren, in the 17th century, broke new ground in building his London churches, for there had been no previous model for churches classically designed, and his ingenuity produced many variants of roof, column and steeple. (See 'column' and 'order'.)

REREDORTER

Rere and *dorter*, from Old French *arere*, 'at the back', and *dorter*, an abbreviation of the word 'dormitory' (Latin *dormire*, 'to sleep'). Thus the reredorter in a monastery is the room at the back of the dormitory containing closets and having wooden seats, divided partitions, and a drain of flowing water below.

Other names of medieval times are all euphemisms, as Latin *dormitorium necessaria*, 'what is necessary to the dormitory' – sometimes simply *necessaria*; or *garderobe*, 'place for keeping clothes'. Other words in guide books range from *privy, closet, latrine,* to *gong* (Old English connection with 'go').

REREDOS

Old French, *arere* means 'at the back', and *dos* is from Latin *dorsum*, 'back'. The reredos is the screen at the back of the altar, often highly ornamented with carving. They vary in height – some, for example the one in Durham cathedral, rising almost to the roof.

RESPOND

Latin *respondere*, 'to reply'. Half of a pillar or a pier projecting from a wall to support an arch, as at the chancel: thus the idea of one part of the arch responding to, or meeting, the other.

RESURRECTION

Latin *resurrectionem*, 'rising from the dead', from the past participle *resurrectum* or *resurgere*, 'to rise again, resurge'. The actual Resurrection of Christ is not described in the Gospels, and representations of the rising from the tomb do not appear until the 13th century. Usually, the three Marys were shown at an empty sepulchre. Representations became increasingly literal and humanised, contributing to the erroneous thinking of the resurrected body as the ultimate and fixed state of man after death.

At death, all religions have the idea of consciousness passing through a period of purgation of the inner bodies (astral and mental), depending upon their prior record on earth, until the light of pure Spirit is attained. But this re-righting or purification of fallen energies towards spiritual perfection is a life process too – the end of all religions on earth. This is why, in Christianity, the conquest of forces of darkness by those of light, is associated with and illustrated by the resurrection of the sun at Easter, the vernal equinox – a cosmic enactment of the ever recurring possibility in man.

When the work is completed, a man is worthy of the name 'saint': his consciousness is light-filled in the middle of darkness. He lives in his true spiritual Self in the state we normally associate with death. He is, in this sense, in death when alive, as he will be alive when dead, so that for him the transition from life to death is imperceptible, with no need for an interim period of purgation.

RETABLE

Latin, *re*, 'back', and table. A shelf or ledge found behind and above the altar, holding the cross and other miscellaneous vases.

RETRO-CHOIR

Latin *retro*, 'at the back, behind', and choir: thus the part of the church behind the place where choir sits. It is usually in the form an of ambulatory or walking place behind the high altar.

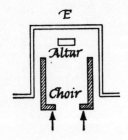

RETURNED STALLS

Stalls in the choir of a cathedral are so named when they turn transversely from their general east to west direction, at their western end. Such stalls are allotted to dignitaries, and many have intricate canopy work, one of the features of the cathedral. Many however suffered in the name of restoration.

RIB VAULTING

A projecting band which ornaments, or is part of the structure, of a ceiling. Plain ribs crossing at right-angles in Norman work gave way to intersecting ribs. In the English periods, groins have ribs (groins are the intersecting edges formed by vaults meeting), and intersecting ribs have bosses. During the latter part of the 14th and 15th centuries, the increase in the number of ribs brought about 'fan vaulting' where the ribs start individual drop points (pendentives) and become functional arches. (See 'lierne vaulting').

RIB AND PANEL VAULTING

This vaulting supplanted the Norman type where individual vaults crossed, forming groins (see the above entry). The ribs supported thin stone panels.

RIGHT AND LEFT

'Right' is from Old High German *reht*, cognate with Latin *rectus*, 'right, straight', and Greek *erektos*, 'erect'. 'Left' is from Middle English *lift* or *left*, originally meaning 'weak, infirm'. Old English is *lēf*, 'infirm, diseased', and derives from Latin *letum*, 'death'.

160

Right, and all its associated meanings, are to do with power and privilege, whilst the connotations of left are of loss and disease. References throughout the Bible are symbolic and denote an inherent difference of function in the two sides of a human being, stemming from laws operating on the highest spiritual level. The division in the God-head occurs when free uncommitted power becomes tied or limited in the act of creation: it is the decisive Will to act (Father) that is embodied in the right side, and that which has been given birth to, the formulated world, including the substance of which it is created (Son and Mother), that is embodied in the left side in a human being. This may be seen in physiognomy and in right and left handedness.

The right-left symbolism goes through Christian art: in a broad sense it is spirit, matter – good and evil. The sun and moon (q.v.), for instance, are respectively at right and left of Christ on the cross, (heraldically, not as seen by the spectator), and Christ sits at the right hand of God the Father. In representations of the Last Judgement, those who have elected to go the way of Christ are taken up to his right, whilst the condemned are consigned to hell on his left. The Book of Life, the world and its destiny, is held on the left knee, whilst the blessing is given by the right hand of power.

Markedly too, the head of Christ on the cross always falls to the right side, symbolising the surrender of self-will to the Will of the Father: equally it is Christ's left leg, the fallen left side of man, that is fixed and sometimes bent under the firm right leg, the Will, on the cross. In the story of the Garden of Eden, Eve is properly placed on Adam's left, for she represents the loss of power in the will to the feelings and the material world. Again in the church itself, the minister, as representative of God, is in the pulpit on the north side, and the lectern containing the Word (the Book again) is on the south. In effigies of the crusaders, the left leg is for a certain Period, crossed under the right, a mnemonic that the ego has been sacrificed to the Higher Will.

ROCOCO

Probably adapted from French *rocaille*, 'rock, work', since rock work features along with scroll and shell ornamentation as part of the florid and over-profuse style now

known as rococo. This followed on from, and is characteristic of, the fashion of the period of Louis XV. The name,
along with Baroque, tended to be used in a denigratory
manner, but is now more accepted as a period with its own
special value. Subject matter and treatment, in poetry and
architecture, were pastoral and delicate. The period is
between 1700 and 1750, and Watteau and Boucher are the
names most associated with it.

ROMAN CEMENT

The early 19th century was the grand period of restoration of the English cathedrals. The so-called 'Roman'
cement was often used indiscriminately, and was a compo-
sition of small fragments of stone, marble, brick and so on,
mixed up with lime.

ROMANESQUE

This term denotes architecture, based on Roman art,
which extended from A.D. 475 (the end of the Roman
Empire) to the end of the 13th century, when the Gothic
style took over.

During the 10th to the 12th centuries, there was a
change from the inert solidity of the Roman tradition to
problems of structural equilibrium, a delicate play of
thrust and counter-thrust found in the Gothic cathedrals
of the 13th century.

ROOD

Middle English *rod*, 'cross'; Saxon *roda*, 'cross'. The
rood is the large crucifix on the screen above the entrance
to the chancel showing Christ in mortal agony; it was the
focal point of the pre-Reformation church.

Early in the Middle Ages, two pulpits (ambos), one on
either side of the choir, were used for readings at the
Eucharist, but later this was superseded by the choir
screen (the 'pulpitum' of the cathedral) over which was a
loft, used in the same way, for readings and the chanting of
the Gospel. The loft supported a large wooden rood showing Christ crucified, usually with the Virgin Mary and St.
John on either side. This was the pattern in the parish
churches until the time of the Reformation when religious
intolerance, and then the Civil War, caused most of the
roods and screens to be destroyed.

Such screens and lofts differed in that those in cathedrals were of stone and had two staircases enabling the gospeller and the reader to move freely to and from their own side of the choir. Those in parish churches were of wood and had only one staircase, usually built in a pillar at one side: naturally it was these that were most vulnerable and suffered the most destruction.

Symbolically the rood is the Tree of Death, the tree of suffering: but a conscious sacrificial death is the condition and cause of a new life, and the second crucifix, upon the altar, representing that Tree of Life, is properly one that shows Christ crowned as King with radiating aureole. At the present time, a plain cross is usually found on the altar, but this misses an essential symbolism. The whole idea of the rood is connected with the 'rod' of authority, for through sacrifice, the root or rude power in man can ultimately be raised on the cross as regenerated spirit. (See the next entries, 'chancel' 'cross', 'Jesse tree'.)

ROOD-LOFT

A raised gallery over a rood-screen. The rood-screen is also called a rood-loft when it supports the large 'rood' or cross. The actual beam, which is sometimes above the loft supporting the cross, is in the medieval church a simple horizontal bar. The loft was reached by stairs in the wall

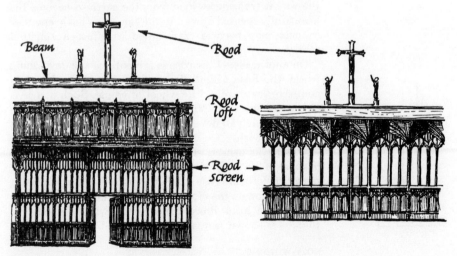

of the chancel or in a pillar, and prior to the Reformation was also used by musicians playing on festive occasions.

These stairs can be found in many parish churches, but the screens and lofts themselves were mutilated at the Reformation.

A rood-loft is also called a *jubé*, French, from Latin *jubere*, 'to command', the first word of the Latin prayer 'Jube domine benedicere', said before the reading of the Gospel from the rood-loft.

ROOD-SCREEN

'Screen' is from Middle English *scren*, 'screen'. The idea in the screen is that of protection and concealment. The rood-screen separates the nave from the chancel, the nave being the place of the people, and the chancel containing the sanctuary, the place of the priesthood, of the inner mysteries. (See 'rood' and 'chancel'.)

ROSE

Latin *rosa*, Greek *rhodon*, 'rose'. On one level, the rose is the Mystic Rose, that flower of the spirit attainable by man through sacrifice. This is the Christ level of being. The idea of sacrifice is seen in the thorn that readily draws blood, in guarding the prize, and in the five petals that represent the five senses that have to be overcome. The idea of development which the rose symbolises is seen in the way it transmutes food from the earth to become the beautifully scented flower: in the same way basic energies in man may become transmuted to effect a spiritual rebirth.

On another level the rose is symbolic of the developing world, the Rosa Mundi (Rose of the World), and is then connected with *rota*, 'the wheel of being'. Such a rose is connected with the Virgin Mary, the material sea, the womb in which all develops and out of which the Christ is ultimately born.

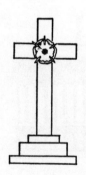

Whichever aspect, the rose denotes development, the purpose of life itself. It is used thus, and in all these senses, in the Rosicrucian rose where it is placed at the very point of transfixion on the cross. Its corresponding image in the East is the lotus flower (the womb) within which the Buddha is shown seated and enlightened.

ROSE WINDOW

A round window with tracery radiating out from a centre, found in many cathedrals in the wet façade,

164

especially in Europe. It often has twelve divisions corresponding to the twelve astrological types. Its symbolism is described under the headings 'east end', 'rose', and 'disciples'. At the west end is the nave – the ship that saves the souls of men on the sea of life: the rose is the symbol of development in that sea which has to take place before the mysteries of the sanctuary at the east end may be realised. The lancet window is male and the rose female – an extension of the line and circle which together give the number ten, the number of ordinal perfection, signifying in man the union of spirit and matter.

ROUND TOWERS

These towers, found in Irish monastic settlements, were built in the 8th and 9th and into the 10th centuries. They were essentially places of refuge, look-out towers, belfries and hiding places for valuables at the time of the Norse invasions. They are found in areas that suffered from such invasions. Composed of five or six storeys, the lowest one is inaccessible except by ladder, which points to their function as a place of refuge. Many stand in as perfect a condition as when they were built, a testimony to the immaculate masonry of the day.

ROYAL ARMS

When Henry VIII assumed Headship over the Church of England, Royal Arms began to appear in churches: it was not until the re-establishment of the Monarchy in 1660 however, that it became compulsory to display the arms of the reigning monarch in parish churches. The practice fell into disuse in the 19th century.

RUBRIC

Latin *rubrica*, 'red earth' or 'title of law written in red'. *Ruber*, 'red'. Hence also law. The rubric can mean either a heading, or a chapter in an illuminated manuscript, or a specific directive (usually emphasised by red writing) concerning a liturgy in the prayer book.

RUNES (RUNIC WRITING)

Old English *rūn*, 'mystery, secret', from Old High German *rūnēn*, 'to whisper'. An ancient system of writing, angular in style, belonging to the Anglo-Saxons, Scandinavian and ancient Germanic peoples. Derived from the Greek alphabet, it had added symbols and was adapted for incising into stone. The writing on the crosses and stones are of a memorial nature, as with ogham stones, containing the names of deceased and dedicator. Like ogham, the alphabet is divided into three groups, the number of letters varying with the period and known as Frey's family, Hagel's family and Tyr's family – from F, H, and T the first letters of each group. The first six letters, F U Th O R C, constitute the alternate name 'futhorc' by which the runic alphabet is known.

The writing has an early association with Christianity, being found on stone crosses and slabs – the Bewcastle and Rothwell crosses are particularly notable. Often Latin capitals are on the slabs, showing the merging of the two elements. The original meaning of the word clearly shows the use of runes in a magical context – for invocations and divination, for the evoking of beneficient and malevolent forces.

S

SACRAMENT

Latin *sacramentum*, 'oath, solemn obligation', *sacrare*, 'to set apart as sacred, dedicate', *sacer*, 'sacred'. Originally used as a Roman military oath not to desert post or standard, it was later used ecclesiastically as a translation of the Greek word *mystērion*, 'mystery', and meaning 'that which is kept sacred', a 'secret'. The origin of the Latin *sacer* is said to be doubtful, but see later in this entry.

Generally, 'sacrament' signifies one of the rites recognised and employed by the Church in which a visible outer agency is used to confer a spiritual grace upon man, with the aid of words of power. The two signs ordained by Christ himself, Baptism and the Eucharist, are basic to the Church ('necessary for salvation'), and of these the latter is the most momentous, simply called the Sacrament or the Blessed Sacrament. The Church of Rome, however, allows five other – Confirmation, Matrimony, Penance, Orders and Extreme Unction.

The idea behind a sacrament is of something effecting an involuntary link between God and man – an evidence of

His good will to man, regardless of man's good will to Him. It is a special impulse of power into life which is already, in all its manifestations, sacred. In the word *sacred*, *sa* is Sanskrit for 'spirit' or 'breath', and *cra* or *car* derives from Latin *creare* 'to create, cause to grow', from an Ayran base *ker, kor*, 'to grow'. All that is breathed out and developed from God the Father is sacred.

Conversely, man in his fallen condition has to understand this sacredness of all life – to grow in understanding in order to be a sensitive vehicle to receive the grace afforded in sacraments.

SACRARIUM

Latin *sacer*, 'sacred' – see in the above entry. The sacrarium is the part of the chancel within the altar rails, the most secret place, for Christ's grace is given here to all who are truly enacting their own sacrifice and atonement. In this place the hands open to give away 'self' and at the same time receive grace. All the spiritual force in the church is concentrated in the sacrarium. In man, the regenerated force is, by analogy, channelled into the head.

That this is to do with the transmutation of sexual energy into higher energy is suggested in the word 'sacrum', from the same root as *sacer*, the so-called sacred bone, triangular in shape and lying at the base of the spine. It was used anciently in sacrificial rituals with this knowledge. Thus too the division in the church – the symbolic rood screen (q.v.) protecting the sacred area from the nave, from being profaned by mixing with a lower level. (See 'chancel' 'east end', 'west end'.)

SACRISTY AND SACRIST

Latin *sacer*, 'holy'. The room adjoining a church where sacred vessels and garments are kept. The term applies only to cathedrals. The 'sacrist' of a cathedral or monastery was also the official keeper of books and music. (See 'vestry'.)

SAGGITARY

See under 'centaur'.

SAINT

Latin *sanctus*, 'holy'. The root *sa* in Sanskrit is 'spirit' or 'breath'. Pure spirit is essentially whole and unvitiated:

thus Latin *sanus*, 'sound, healthy'. A saint is one in whom the interests of self have been effaced and in whom the pure spirit operates without hindrance.

SALMON

Latin *salmo*, connected with *salire*, 'to jump': the *mon* part is connected with *mono*, 'alone'. The salmon has been used from early Christian times, because of its unique ability to struggle against the stream in its return to its spawning ground. This symbolises the spirit of man overcoming all obstacles in the attempt to return to the source from which he came.

SANCTUARY

Latin *sanctus*, 'holy': thus a holy place or shrine, but especially the most secret part of a place of worship. In the church it is that part of the church east of the nave – the place of the clergy. Its meaning is discussed under 'sacrarium' and 'presbytery'.

The word has come to denote generally a place of refuge because, under ecclesiastical law in this country, fugitives from justice in the Middle Ages could, upon reaching the holy place, take refuge and claim immunity for a certain length of time. This was called the 'right of sanctuary'. (See 'frith stool'.)

SANCTUARY KNOCKER

A heavy bronze knocker, often beautifully designed, on a door at the west end of some cathedrals – a reminder of the use of the privilege of sanctuary. (See 'frith stool' and 'sanctuary'.)

SANCTUARY LAMP

The sanctuary lamp hangs from the roof of the church, a little way in front of and central to the altar, and is always lit so long as the Sacrament (the consecrated bread and wine used at the Eucharist) is present. The permanently burning light denotes the ever present spirit of God.

SANCTUS BELL

Sanctus 'holy'. A bell used at solemn moments of the Mass, as when the Host is raised after consecration. A small handbell is now used, and was generally used prior to the Reformation. Often however the sanctus bell is housed in a turret on the outside of the church, between nave and chancel, and is rung from the inside.

SARCOPHAGUS

A Latin word from Greek *sarkophagos*, 'flesh-eating'. From *sarx*, 'flesh' and *phagein*, 'to eat'. Originally so-named because of a type of limestone, used by the Greeks in the making of coffins, which was said to allow the flesh to distintegrate quickly. The general meaning is now of a large stone coffin, or a structure erected above a grave of similar form, containing inscriptions relevant to the deceased.

SATAN

Latin, from Greek *Satanas*, Hebrew *Sātān*, 'the adversary, the accuser'. The arch-enemy of man, synonymous with the devil, having animal attributes and represented in Christian art as luring men into the pit of hell. The satanic forces are the accumulated errors of fallen man who has leaned his will towards the material world and to his own separate existence. Such an accumulation is a living reality, of monstrous proportions on the subtle planes, ready to lend its powers to those who offer themselves to it. On the other hand, separate existence, and the suffering attendant upon it, are the whetting stone for man's spiritual development. (See 'devil' and 'lucifer'.)

SAXON (CHURCHES)

Latin *saxo*, from west Germanic *seax*, 'knife', 'sword' – a weapon used by that tribe. The Saxons along with the Angles and Jutes migrated to Britain in the 5th and 6th centuries, and the term is loosely used in architecture to denote the period from then until the Norman invasion in the 11th century.

The churches of the Saxon period were built in the north under the influence of Irish missionaries, contrasting with the basilican-type churches of the south introduced by St. Augustine.They were modelled more on the hermit cell (the 'beehive') which gradually assumed a square shape – for instance in the oblong sanctuary and square west end tower. Monk Wiermouth (Sunderland) and St. Paul's (Jarrow) are two of the finest examples of churches, built by St.

Aidan circa 635, and modified later by Benedict Biscop and St. Wilfrid.

Up to the Danish invasions of the 9th century was also the age of inscribed and ornamental sepulchral stones. The pre-Christian Saxon erected mounds of earth and buried personal possessions with the body, but Christianity brought inscribed memorial stones, erect crosses, carved Hiberno-Saxon ornaments and runes on hog-back stones. Latin capitals and Saxon miniscules (q.v.) intermingled.

At the Synod of Whitby (664), a compromise was evolved between the basilica and Celtic forms; for instance the square presbytery was retained, but transepts and side entrances were added and the choir was separated from the nave. In the grafting of the Romanesque onto the Saxon buildings (these latter were largely made of wood), Saxon balusters, quoins and pilaster, (q.v.), suggesting the work of the carpenter, commingled with characteristic Roman brick work. Small windows in the west tower were a reminder of the Irish oratories. (q.v.)

From the purely religious point of view, at the Synod of Whitby, the Roman influence with its external dogmas and disciplines spelt the death of the Celtic monastic traditions. The former, through St. Paul, had remained in the Mediterranean area focusing on Rome, thus coming to southern England; the other had originated with the Desert Fathers focussing on Alexandria and, spreading to Ireland, had come to the Saxon north of England.

SCALLOP

Old French *escalope*, derived from the word *scale* which is from Old Higher German *skāla*, 'drinking cup' and Old Norwegian *skal*, 'shell' or 'husk'. Shell and skull are related words: both were anciently used as drinking cups. The scallop shell is a badge of the pilgrims who had been to the Holy Land, since it is said that these shells were found in abundance on the shores and were used as drinking cups and eating vessels. It also specifies, for the same reason, the emblem of the pilgrims to the shrine of St. James of Compostella in Spain. Architecturally, the scallop motif is found mostly in Norman capitals.

SCULPTURE

The characteristic of medieval church sculpture was its anonymity: moreover building and sculpture were not separable, and because all was the work of the mason, there was a homogeneity between the architecture and the figures adorning it. In the 13th century after a period of considerable heaviness, complete mastery was achieved over the material, and sculpture became the pride of the outer and inner faces of the church. In the 14th century, though the style was more decorative, work was still within the framework of the community of masons on the site. After the Black Death (14th century), figure sculpture ceased to be carried out on the site, the function of the mason changed, and work was carried out in quarry centres, as at Bristol and York. This incurred an inevitable division between the building and the work grafted onto the building.

SEDILIA

Latin, plural of *sedila*, 'seat, stool', from the root *sed*, 'sit'. The sedilia are a set of seats, made of stone and recessed into the south wall of the chancel. They are

usually three in number since they are intended for the use of priest, deacon and subdeacon during the Mass. Sometimes, however, there are only two or even one, an indication of the wealth of the church. Sedilia are often at different levels, and the canopies beautifully decorated.

SEE

Old French *se, sie*, from Latin *sedes*, 'seat'. Thus it is the geographical area over which a bishop presides or has his seat.

171

From the past participle of Latin *sepelire*, 'to bury'. A representation of the entombment of Christ was practised each Easter in the church, when a wooden imitation of a sepulchre was erected on the north of the chancel. These have not stood the test of time, but in some parish churches the original permanent construction of stone designed to contain the sepulchre can be found. The finest of these have the elaborate ornamentation of the Decorated Period.

SERPENT

Latin *serpent*, 'snake', from *serpere*, 'to crawl or creep', related to Greek *herpein*, 'to creep'. The serpent is symbolic of the powers of evil because it represents power that has been reduced to the level of the earth. On this level, man's will is divided – he is deluded by the duality inherent in the world of the senses and time. The subtlety of the serpent in Genesis is the trickery in that duality which leads him towards what is pleasurable and away from what is painful. In this sense he weighs up 'yes's and no's' with a subtle reason, represented by the forked tongue of the serpent.

The will is thus crucified in time and made impotent. This is symbolised by the serpent twined around the cross of limitation. (Note the connection between the senses and reason: Greek *pente* is 'five' and Latin *pensare*, 'to weigh out, think'.) The serpent is synonymous with Satan in the Christian myth and in Revelation is called 'the dragon, that old serpent called the Devil which deceiveth the world'. In iconography, St. George and St. Michael are represented in combat with it.

The serpent is fundamentally power or energy in a fallen state, usurped by the cunning ego and thus epitomising evil; yet by the re-directing of the will, it may be regenerated. Then, like the snake, it sheds old skins and acquires new ones, it becomes the healing force of the Greek god, Aesculapius, who took on the form of a serpent. It is also the raised, brazen serpent of Moses, which gave life to those who looked upon it, an image used by Christ of himself raised on the cross. Further it is the serpent force of Yogic teaching, Kundalini, which resurrected from its guise as sexual energy, is reinstated in its true seat of power, the head. In Byzantine work, Christ's body on the cross assumes a serpent-like undulation, showing that he has taken upon himself the old serpent and raised it up regenerated – the new Adam out of the old.

SEVEN LAMPS

In front of the altar of larger churches, seven lamps hang from the roof. This tradition derives from the words of the Apocalypse, 'And there were seven lamps of fire burning before the Throne which were the Seven Spirits of God'. 'Seven' can be seen as 's-even' or spirit-even or complete, for such a division of unity is found throughout the whole of nature.

The seven-branched candlestick, the seven churches of Asia, the seven days of creation, the seven colours of the rainbow, the seven tones of the musical scale, the seven major planets, the seven years in the fairy tale, are all part of this universal seven-fold structure. Each is a differentiation of the root power of God working in its own unique way. Seen from the point of view of the evolution of man, we have the seven races and the seven sub-races, and, on a smaller scale, a reflection of this in the seven year periods of a man's life, each of which is marked by some physiological and psychological change.

In Church doctrine there are the seven 'virtues' and their counterpart the 'deadly sins', and on the subtle plane (the seven churches of Asia in the Apocalypse can be interpreted this way), they are the vortices of power located along the spine and known in Yogic metaphysics as 'chakras'.

Upon seven stages being absorbed into one, that is, the process completed, a new octave begins. This is the eighth point. The glyph of the number eight represents the birth of a new cycle, and thus of eternity, because each end only gives way to a new beginning. (See 'font' and 'baptism'.)

SHAFT

Old High German *scaft*, 'shaft of an arrow, pole'; Latin *scapus*, 'shaft, stem', Greek *skēptein*, 'to support with a pole'. In architecture it is the main part of a column between the capital and base; but the term 'shafts' applies particularly to smaller columns clustered round pillars. In Early English work, for example, they are separate and of

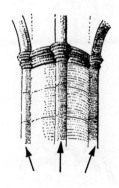

173

different material, often Purbeck marble. Such shafts vary in style according to the period.

SHRINE

Latin *scrinium*, 'case, box for papers, books and letters'. Connected with Latin *scribere*, 'to write'. A shrine in this sense is a cover for the bible of a saint, but it came to denote any case or covering for a venerated relic, as in the Irish Church where richly ornamented metal casings were made to protect the bible, bell and crozier.

A shrine has also come to mean that part of a church where such a relic is kept – and thus any place made sacred by holy events. The shrines of the saints in the cathedrals were places of pilgrimage, originally crypts where bones were preserved. It was only later that they were brought into the body of the church, where, due to the immense quantity of wealth deposited near them, careful guard had to be kept. The elevated watch-rooms through which the shrine could be observed can be seen in many English cathedrals. (See 'relic'.)

SLYPE

From Old English *slupan*, 'to move, glide'. It came to signify a narrow and covered passage-way: in monastic terms, a passage either between the chapter-house and transept, or connecting the church to chapter-house. Its uses are said to be various – a parlour for carrying out business transactions, a sacristy, or a treasury.

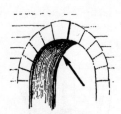

SOFFIT or SUFFIT

Italian *soffita*, 'ceiling', meaning 'fastened under' (Latin, past participle *suffixum* of *suffigere*, 'to fasten under'.) A soffit or suffit refers to the underside of an arch, or of any part of a building where an underface is in evidence, as in the ceiling of a vault, the underside of a cornice, or the transom of a window or door.

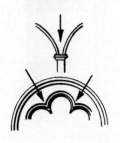

SOLAR or SOLARIUM

From Latin *solaris*, 'pertaining to the sun'. The Latin *solarium* is a balcony exposed to the sun. In medieval buildings it signifies a living room on an upper level, as for example with the abbot's house of some monasteries.

SPANDREL

Old French *espandre* from Latin *expandere*, 'to spread out, unfold'. A spandrel is the triangular space between arches. The word is also used to denote an irregular, uncommitted surface, as between the arch and cusp of a window, or between the ribs of a vault.

SPIRE

Old English and Middle English *spir*, 'spire', from Old Norwegian *spira*, 'point' or 'ear of corn'. Thus through the image, the prolongation of a tower tapering to a point. There are obvious connections with Latin *spira*, from Greek *speira*, 'coil, twist'; also with Latin *spirare*, 'to breath', giving the word spirit. All have some connection with the essentially 'aspiring' spire which is a visible expression of the spiritual zeal that gave rise to the Gothic cathedrals.

The placing of the spire in the cathedrals and churches is over the central tower, at the place of the crossing, in a sense the crux of the church form. (See 'lantern tower' and 'transepts' for symbolism.)

SPLAY

Middle English *splayen*, 'to spread outwards'; splay is an abbreviated form of display. It means the sloping, bevelled jambs of a window, spreading out to make a larger opening on the inside wall of a building. (See under 'window'.)

SPRINGER

The bottom stone of an arch which lies immediately upon and springs from the impost (the horizontal stone on top of a pillar), and seen for example in the bottom stones in the arches of vaulting. It may also mean the lowest stone in the coping stone of a gable.

SQUINT

Middle English *asquint*, from Old Frisian *schün*, 'oblique'. A hole cut obliquely in the wall of a medieval church, for instance in the transepts or side chapels, allowing the high altar to be seen from where it would otherwise not be visible. Squints vary in width and style in different parts of the country. They also bear the name 'hagioscope', a word which indicates their function more clearly – *hagios*,

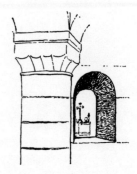

175

Greek, 'holy, pertaining to saints', and *skopos*, Greek, 'watcher, spy'.

STAINED GLASS

Until about the middle of the 12th century, images were painted upon walls and vaults in churches. From the cells of the hermits to the later monastic buildings, there had been little window space. But as the balance changed in favour of light, the use of coloured glass began to flourish. The first known instance is in the west front of Chartres Cathedral (middle 12th century), though presumably the technique had been known prior to this time. Scenes from the Old Testament and the lives of the saints were depicted, replacing the wall paintings. The effect of brilliant light in the colours was the result of using thick pot glass, full of bubbles, irregularities and chemical impurities.

Early windows, such as Canterbury and York, were made of small pieces of glass leaded together and were of rich ruby, blue, maroon and green. They were largely single figures of medallion form, and in the aisles so they could be studied by the people. After 1170 a technique called 'grisaille' (q.v.) was introduced; it was a grey-green type of glass with simple geometric patterns and only a little coloured glass. After 1280 new techniques were developed – a technique of silver stain was discovered, and larger pieces of glass were used with windows made of three or five lights. The imagination was gradually set free. But tracery in the windows forced the glass artist to adopt his figures to the forms presented, giving awkward shapes. By the Perpendicular Period (middle of the 14th century), the glaziers' work began to assume such an importance that it is evident that stonework tracery was designed before building to fit the needs of the glazier, especially in relation to canopied figures. This period saw an increased use of heraldry and a personalising of the people and themes presented.

The decline of the art of stained glass was due primarily to the influence of painting – the attempt to paint on glass, an influence from Flanders, caused the tracery to be seen as an obstacle in the way of the painter's conception. The 16th century was the time of the decline of glass and the rise of painting.

176

STALLS

Old English *steall*, 'stall, stable', Old High German *stall*, 'stable'. The meaning is a division or compartment in a stable; thus a similar division or recess in the form of a seat in a church. The stalls for the choir in a cathedral may be allotted to particular church dignitaries; the bishop especially has his own stall or 'throne', distinguished by its particularly fine carving.

The choir stalls contain some of the finest examples of medieval woodwork, and are known for their misericords, the secondary under-seats of each stall carved with mythological animals and contemporary scenes. (See 'misericord'.) The term was more generally applied to the wooden divisions erected in parish churches for the more privileged families of the congregation. (See 'pew'.)

STANCHION

Latin *stare*, 'to stand'. A vertical iron bar between the stone mullions in a window. The term is sometimes used for the mullion itself.

STAR OF DAVID

The interlacing to two triangles gives a six-pointed star often found in church iconography, a reference to the lineage of Christ through King David, described in the Old Testament. To the Hebrews it symbolised the triune God (Father, Mother and Son) reflected in His own creation.

The triangle with its base below, called the Macroprosupus, 'great countenance', is the divine triangle, light, and a symbol of fire, indicating energy raying downwards, encompassing and sustaining all below. The triangle with its base upper-most, called the Microprosupus. 'small countenance', is the dark triangle of man and nature, in which man aspires upwards from the insecure particularised point to embrace infinity. He can only achieve stability however, by attuning his three-fold nature (will, heart, head) to the Higher Trinity: the interlaced triangles represent God reflected in his creation, reciprocally, man's desire to return to his creator.

When the glyph has a dot in the centre, it is known as Solomon's Seal, the seventh point, or seal of completion in a man – a perfect balance in a marriage of polar opposites.

The Star of David has of course many aspects, but they

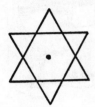

are all to do with the union of opposites – of spirit and matter, God and man, male and female, divisions inherent in the very act of Creation. For this reason it has always been a symbol of the Logos or the Spoken Word. The number six itself denotes this division – (its origin is in the word *sex*, 'six', the six points of the united triangles). The triangle of the Holy Trinity adopted in early Christianity has the base line uppermost, showing the support of the higher power for the lower. Here the Holy Spirit, the point of the triangle, points to the earth, egressing equally from Father and Son. (See 'Trinity'.)

STATIONS OF THE CROSS

The fourteen 'stations of the cross' belong mainly to the Roman Church. Originally varying in number, they are also called 'Via Calvaris', or 'Via crucis', and their purpose is to represent by painting, in fresco, or on canvas on the walls of the church, Christ's progression from the Judgement Hall to Calvary. They are as follows:

1 he is condemned to death
2 he is forced to carry his own cross
3 he falls under the cross
4 he meets his mother
5 Simon the Cyrenean helps him to carry his cross
6 Veronica wipes his face
7 he falls under the cross again
8 he speaks to the daughters of Jerusalem
9 he falls a third time under the cross
10 he is stripped of his garments
11 he is nailed to the cross
12 he yields up the Holy Ghost
13 he is taken down from the cross
14 he is placed in the sepulchre

Originally these points were actually in Jerusalem and used by pilgrims. Later, when the Franciscans were granted custody of the Holy Sepulchre, they erected images of these events (called 'stations') in their European churches so that pilgrimages could be done in spirit. The Dissolution of the Monasteries saw the destruction of most of the paintings of these stations that were an integral part of the pre-Reformation church.

STOUP

The stoup (Old Norwegian *staup*, Old English *stēap*, 'flagon') is a small stone vessel or basin set in the wall at the western entrance, now mainly used in a Catholic church. They were built in all pre-Reformation churches, but most have fallen into decay or have been removed entirely.

The stoup contains holy water (sometimes a fountain) which has been blessed against the force of evil. The self-crossing with holy water upon entering the church was a re-enactment of the baptism by which a member, received into the Body of the Church, was vouchsafed regeneration.

The holy water in the stoup and in the baptismal font has a two-fold consecration. First the water itself, clean but not distilled, is consecrated to banish impurities, and secondly, the essential ingredient, salt, is also consecrated. Salt is the principle of contraction, the hardening of the free energy of fire in the form of condensed earth – thus the expression 'pillar of salt'. But paradoxically, the psychological contraction, the ego, has within it the greatest potential – man's real Ego or Self. The negative symbol now becomes positive, as in the expression the 'salt of the earth' and in the food we eat, for without salt, food is tasteless. Thus the priest banishes one aspect of salt to give life to the other. Such a dialectic is seen under 'cross', 'tree', 'Lucifer' and so on.

Similarly, if water is seen in this way, the waters of materiality in which man flounders are his enemy; and yet at the same time water is the most powerful of cleansers (as for that matter is salt). Again we have two faces of one symbol.

STRINGCOURSE

A thin horizontal line of moulding projecting from the wall of a building.

SUN AND MOON

The sun and moon are frequently found in representations of the Crucifixion, especially in the medieval period: the sun is to the right of the head of Christ and the moon to the left. As in all other cases where it occurs, 'right' symbolises power and good, and 'left' the forces of deprivation and evil. The symbolism occurs in the most ancient of religions.

The sun and the moon are polar opposites. The sun is an embodiment of the Intelligence of the Logos – the Son in the Trinity. 'Sun' and 'son' are by meaning deeply connected in the sense that *sonare* (Latin, 'sound'), signifies the sounding out of the Word, the Logos, the intelligent ordering force in the universe. The sun is both the light of intelligence and the heat of life. The moon, on the contrary, is an embodiment of all that is to do with inertia, with the mechanical forces of nature. In most languages 'moon' means 'month' and derives from the root *me*, 'to measure'. The moon symbolises the whole material world, the death of free energy, and all forms of opposition to the will of man.

Sun and moon are aspects of each other – the power and intelligence of the sun works in and through the moon process, the counting process of the world. When at the term of the evolutionary process the physical world is re-spiritualised, the sun and moon will be seen to have been aspects of each other and such a duality will be no more. Thus the statement in Revelation:

> And the city had no need of the sun, neither of the moon, to shine on it: for the Glory of God did lighten it, and the Lamb is the light thereof–

and also the reason why they are found at either side of the head of Christ, for since he is the sacrificial Lamb and the agent of the re-spiritualising process, the city will be illumined by his light.

In extension of this, the moon in Christian art is significantly a crescent moon, the beginning of that new birth,

180

and the rest of the sphere is only partially, that is potentially, illumined. Equally significantly, on a purely scientific level, the sun and moon, as seen by man on earth, are
of identical dimension, a fact that corroborates what has
been said about their polar opposition.

SUPPORTER IN HERALDRY

The human or animal figures at either side of a shield
apparently supporting it. Such figures encouraged the
creation of an array of mythical beasts distinct from those
on the shields. They are not in evidence before the last
quarter of the 14th century.

SUPPRESSION OF THE MONASTERIES

The ruined state of the abbeys and the monasteries in
Britain is almost wholly due to the event known as the
Suppression of the Monasteries. The monasteries in the
course of 400 years had lost their original spiritual zeal:
their life had reached its term because of wealth and
general laxity in monastic rule. The original plan of Wol-
sey in 1528 to suppress certain smaller houses, in order to
endow the 'Cardinal College' at Oxford, was symptomatic
of the inevitable breakdown. This and other closures had
the sanction of the Pope, though the relationship between
the Pope and English monarchy was deteriorating. In
1535, however, Parliament, on the suggestion of Thomas
Cromwell, adviser to Henry VIII, ordered a 'visitation' – a
report on the monasteries. Eighty-eight were visited and
the result came to be known as the Black Book. Parliament, on the strength of this report, ordered the suppression of all monasteries with an income of less than £200,
and, of course, the confiscation of their property. 376
houses in the country were suppressed.

Two risings took place in opposition to this action: one
in Lincolnshire and one in Yorkshire. The Yorkshire one
assumed considerable proportions and was called the 'Pilgrimage of Grace'. It was finally put down and the abbots
of Fountains, Rievaulx and Jervaulx were hanged and
their monasteries given over to the king. During 1538–9,
150 other monasteries were taken over by the king in
devious ways and by 1540 all extant monasteries had been
suppressed and their wealth used on public welfare, as for
example in the founding of grammar schools or colleges,
or given to the courtiers who were favourites of the king.

The church or part of the church building of some of the houses, contrived to be retained as parish churches, and some took their place among the already existing cathedrals.

It should be pointed out that compliant abbots were given quite generous pensions, and the monks, whose numbers had dropped, on average, to 20 or less, received small pensions, and were often absorbed into the secular church.

SURPLICE

Medieval Latin *superpelliceum* (*super*, 'over' and *pelliceum*, 'tunic of skins' – *pelis*, 'skin'). The surplice is now simply a long loose robe worn by a priest not celebrating Eucharist, and also by the choir.

SWASTIKA

Sanskrit *svastis*, 'welfare', from *su*, 'well', and *asti*, 'being', which has the same source as the Greek and Latin verbs for 'to be'. The well-being implied in the symbol is that of the being of the universe or uni-verse (one turn), the wheel of life, within which lie a complexity of systems turning within each other.

Essentially a cross, the tails of the swastika depict the pattern of fire in rotation, the image of the turning Catherine-wheel. Though a universal symbol of great antiquity, it was also a Christian symbol by virtue of the fire of the sun, representing the spiritual fire of Christ. It moves in a clockwise direction, the apparent direction of the sun, but when reversed, the direction becomes 'widdershins', that is the contrary to the apparent motion of the sun and thus a force of evil: thus it was the emblem, for instance, of Nazi Germany. In Europe, the swastika was anciently known as Thor's hammer, an agent for shaping the soul through the hard blows given by the whirling tails.

It is sometimes called a *fylfot* – which is generally supposed to mean 'fill the foot'. Such a motif was used as decoration in windows or in embroidery. (See 'fylfot'.)

SWAN

Old English and Saxon both have the same, *swan*. The root of the word if Latin *sonare*, 'to sound', coming from a Sanskrit root meaning 'sound' – thus the connection of the name with the myth that the swan sings (swan-song) before it dies.

But the swan makes no such death song. The sound indicated in the myth is the original sound, French *son*, or Son of the Trinity: it is the Logos or Spoken Word, of which the lowest manifestation is the sound of the senses, a pale reflection. Thus, the original Sound, the essence of purity, dies at the birth of the physical world, giving way to an earthly sound, described in the myth as a death-song. This is of course another version of the fall into the physical plane of existence. Also since the Word follows upon the Will of the Father (number 1), the glyph of the number 2 assumes the form of the swan, as the number 3, with its three points completes the Trinity (q.v.).

The swan, as a bird, denotes Intelligence; as a white bird, Pure Intelligence, the Logos; it glides regally upon, and makes it mark upon the unformed waters. When it appears in myth or heraldry, especially in certain stories about the locating of sites of monasteries by saints, activity of the Intelligence of the Logos is always indicated.

T

TABERNACLE

Latin *tabernaculum*, 'tent', from *taberna*, 'hut, booth, dwelling'. (Note English, 'tavern'.) The basic meaning is of a portable tent used as a temple by the Israelites during their wanderings in the wilderness.

Hence the word came to mean something in which a precious or holy thing was deposited, especially, in the western Church, the ornamental receptacle for the pyx in which the consecrated Host (wafer) for use in the Eucharist is preserved. This at first hung over the altar but was later on the altar itself. 'Tabernacle' is also used for the niche behind the altar, where the Host is alternatively kept. A light hangs over the altar so long as the Host is so preserved. 'Tabernacle' has also been extended to denote the niches in inner or outer walls of a church containing statues or tombs of saints. Such recesses have ornamental canopies or arches of the period, ranging from the simple shallow and square ones of the Norman period to the

Decorated' period

deeply inset, highly ornamented ones of the Perpendicular period. The intricate carving is often called 'tabernacle-work'.

TAPESTRY

French *tapis*, 'carpet, tapestry', Latin *tapete*, 'carpet'. Tapestry is loom work and is to be distinguished from the smaller proportions of embroidery, which derives from *broder*, or *border*, 'to work the edge of'.

Tapestry was much used in the decoration of churches – for walls, and especially for the decoration of altars – from an early time. The town of Arras in Artois, France, was the first centre of manufacturing, giving the name of a type of tapestry called 'arras', woven in patterns rather like wallpaper. In the 15th century, manufacturers made religious and mythological pictures; the taste for tapestry flourished and 'hangings' were an important acquisition in the houses of the nobility. In 1607 the factory was established in Paris which later became known as the Gobelins, giving rise to the highest achievements in tapestry work.

Tapestry, like all weaving and spinning, is esentially a female activity, since it is associated with the weaving of the web of the material world, of the spell of illusion, the Hindu *maya* or cosmic spider. The Great Mother (see 'Virgin Mary') spins the world out of her own being. Thus tapestry work is associated with the principle of purity and maternity, and belongs traditionally to the Virgin Mary.

TAU CROSS or ST. ANTHONY'S CROSS

See 'cross' for the symbolism of the cross. The Tau cross, originally the Egyptian cross of life, became associated with the 4th century desert hermit St. Anthony, who was of Egyptian origin, and could be said to be the founder of the monastic system.

TEMPLE

Certain churches have the name 'temple', some through Protestant connections and some through association with the Knights Templars.

'Temple' is from Latin *templum*, 'a place or space in the sky ringed out for observation by priests or augurs in ancient Rome'. Augury was the art of divining through a

184

study of the flight of birds in that marked out place. The Latin word is from Greek *temeos*, 'a sacred place' from *temnein*, 'to cut'. Thus the general meaning later of any consecrated place set apart for worship.

There is also the connection with Latin *tempus*, 'time', said to be of doubtful etymology. The connection between the two is in the space ringed and cut off. As in augury, where the proscribed area contains eternal truths to be interpreted on the time level, so time itself is cut away from the eternal level, marking itself by the repetitive cycles of nature. In this ring men are enthralled. Yet eternity lives within time, and though the temple is a marked out institution, it embodies eternal truths which may be uncovered.

In this sense, stone circles are temples, for within the confined circle the mysteries of the cosmos were reflected and re-enacted: sacred dances, too, now reflected in children's games, had this function. Man is said to be his own temple in that all his experiences in time, properly used, can lead to his break-back into eternity.

The connection with the Knights Templars is through the Temple of Solomon at Jerusalem, circa 1000 B.C. This was destroyed and built over several times, but the knights who devoted themselves to the protection of pilgrims used the site for their headquarters – thus acquiring their name.

TESTER

French *téte*, Latin *testa*, 'shell, skull'. A flat canopy over a pulpit or tomb or, domestically, over a bed.

TIE-BEAM

A simple beam crossing from one side of the roof to the other, tying them together by supporting the king-posts and other timber work. It was used mostly in the Norman period but continued in medieval times when the beam was often slightly curved upwards towards the centre.

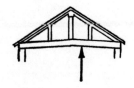

TOMB

Latin *tumba*, 'a grave for burying the dead'; the word is related to *tumulus*, 'heap of earth, mound', used as a burial place: both denote confinement to earth.

The physical body is also such a tomb, for the spirit falls

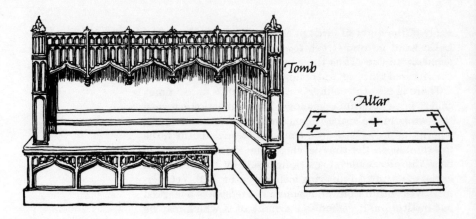

Tomb

Altar

into it and is held captive. This is the idea behind French *tomber*, 'to fall', as well as the fact of the body falling into the earth at death. The tomb as commonly understood is a stone block in the form of an altar – altar because it is here that material values are transformed into spiritual ones. Likewise the material body falls into the earth, is entombed at death, but only for the spirit to be resurrected into eternal life. In the Eastern Church there is a clear use of this symbolism for the altar is seen as both the tomb of Christ and the throne of God.

Early in Christianity in Britain, saints were interred in the crypts of cathedrals, but later, relics were brought to ground level to become the elaborate tombs or shrines which were the objects of veneration for pilgrims.

TONSURE

From Latin *tonsura*, 'clipping'. The shaving of the head arose in early monastic times as a sign of dedication to the service of God and of contrition for the fallen lower nature. In mythology the hair has always been seen as a symbol of power, as in the archetypal story of Samson. Hair, indigenous to the animal kingdom, is a relic in man of that primal power. Its sacrifice is another aspect of the aim to re-direct energy to spiritual and non-personal ends, and is a process which nature ensures in a man's wiser old age. The circular ring of the tonsure is said to be a mnemonic of Christ's crown of thorns.

From a historical viewpoint, it is interesting to note that at the Synod of Whitby in 664, there was violent controversy over the style of the tonsure, the indigenous

British Church favouring all hair being shorn at the front as far back as the ears. The Roman tonsure, as we know it, won the day.

TOWER

Old French *tour*, Latin *turris*, 'a high tower for defence purposes'. In English cathedrals the most imposing feature is the central tower above the crossing. It raises itself in the form of a spire. The tower is also known as the 'lantern tower' since it lets light in onto the crossing. (See 'crossing' and 'transept'.)

Due to structural problems because of the weight of the central tower, it often fell down, which accounts for the many awkward modifications and divergencies of style in later rebuilding.

TRACERY

Middle English *trācen*, through Old French, from Low Latin *tractiare* and *trabere*, 'to draw'. Thus in the tracery – that is the decorative stonework in the upper part of a window – the impression is of a regular pattern drawn upon the window. The use of tracery refers specifically to the windows of Gothic churches, the several names corresponding to some extent to the recognised periods, though overlapping makes exact dating impossible.

(a) *Plate tracery*: in the first half of the 13th century, when two lancet windows were made in one arch, the space remaining above was filled by a circle or quatrefoil.

(b) *Bar tracery*: about the middle of the 13th century increased piercing of stone caused a feeling that bars were creating a pattern. Thus the naming 'bar tracery' and the alternative name 'geometric'.

(c) *Flowing tracery*: about the beginning of the 14th century sinuous lines developed, with some irregularity of pattern. Heads of lights took the ogee form.

(d) *Perpendicular tracery*: soon after the middle of the 14th century, vertical bars were apparent throughout the window. The amount of the stone surface was reduced until at the end of the 14th century all curved lines had disappeared. All patterns were within vertical lines – a common feature due to the size of the window in the 'transom' or cross-bar. This remained until the end of the 15th century.

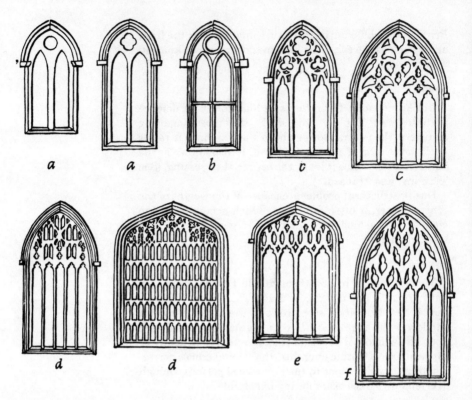

a   a   b   c   c

d   d   e   f

(e) *Reticulated tracery*: is the name given to the device of a repetitive pattern, and this overlaps geometric and flowing tracery.

(f) *Flamboyant tracery*: French *flambeau*, 'torch', denotes the flame-like style current in France during the Perpendicular Period in England. Though not indigenous to Britain, there was later imitation.

TRANSEPT

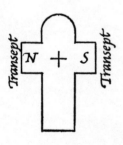

Latin *trans*, 'across' and *septum*, 'a hedge or enclosure'. The transept is the north-south extention that cuts across the church at right-angles before the sanctuary, giving it its cruciform shape. Such a form may be traced through modifications to the Roman basilica, but it arose, as do all forms, out of a correspondence with its essential function and meaning – in Christianity, the cross.

The cross has always signified the transfixing of spirit in matter, of eternity in time, and, as Christ's life shows, of divinity in humanity. The sacrifice of the human part to the divine is every man's inner work, and the crucial (cross) moment is the change of heart which allows this to happen.

The human body can be equated roughly with the cross and the form of the church. Symbolically, the place of the crossing is the place of the heart, above which is the 'lantern' or central tower letting in the light of understanding. Beyond this lie the mysteries of the sanctuary where, for those in whom a change has taken place, ultimate enlightenment is received in 'the place of the skull' – the literal translation of Golgotha.

TRANSITION

The term applied to the transition from the Norman to the Gothic styles, sometimes called 'the battle of the styles', between circa 1150 and 1200. It is seen as a movement towards refinement and delicacy, especially in the shaping of windows and arches, and in more slender columns, though in this period old and new often appear together. The pointed arch is said to have come from the Mohammedans in the Middle East, having been introduced via Sicily into France. It is found in use by the Cistercians, the first to adopt it, in 1150. The change to the pointed arch was also linked with the changing architectural problems, especially of vaulting: it also reflected the spirit of religious aspiration of that time.

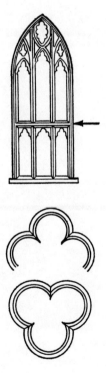

TRANSOM

Latin *transtrum*, 'a beam that runs from side to side in a ship'. The term now denotes the cross-beam of stone or wood across a doorway or window; it is used frequently to denote a bar or bars that cut across the middle of a window, and as such it is characteristic of the Perpendicular period.

TREE OF JESSE

(See 'Jesse Tree'.) For general symbolism of the tree, see 'Adam and Eve', 'Garden of Eden', 'cross', 'rood', 'Crucifixion'.

TREFOIL

Latin *tre*, 'three', and *foil*, Middle English 'leaf' from Latin *folium*, 'leaf'. A design, in arches and in window tracery, of three leaves. Already used in Saxon churches, the possibility is that it was of Saracen origin, as with the pointed arch and interlacing Norman arches. It became a symbol, in Christian art, of the Holy Trinity. Windows with four and five leaves respectively are known as quatre-foil and cinquefoil.

TRIFORIUM

Latin *tri*, 'three' and *foris*, 'door', or 'opening'. The term denotes the gallery of openings, found only in larger churches, immediately above the main arcades in the walls of the nave and transepts. Because it occupies a position where the roof slopes over the aisles, the gallery has no light and is often called the 'blind storey'.

The *tri* originally referred to the arcades of some Norman churches in this position, where there were three openings: later the term was applied to any gallery in this position. (See 'bay'.)

TRINITY

Latin *trinus*, 'three-fold'. It was not until the 2nd century that the word came to be used. The Christian Trinity is, as with all other trinities, a division of Absolute power: its three aspects, functionally different, yet mutually dependent, make one whole. Thus the expression 'three-in-one' – God the Father, pure generative energy; God the Son, the Word or Logos, the idea-world ordering and conditioning that power; and God the Holy Ghost, the force reconciling the first two and giving that flow which is life itself, and which on man's level, is the grace between God and himself. (Ghost is from Old High German *gest*, 'life, spirit'.) The glyph that incorporates these elements and which is found frequently in Church iconography is given here. Deus, God at the centre, has three aspects – Pater, Filius, Spiritus – clearly shown belonging to the centre but not to each other.

The three-in-one is also seen in the three-branched candle-stick, and in the glyph of the number 3 itself, for if the semi-circles are folded towards each other, the hitherto three separate points make a complete circle.

Generally in Christian art, God the Father was only represented by a hand, his creative power, or by an eye, his all-seeing power, emerging out of clouds. Only after the 12th century was God the Father shown as a head and

190

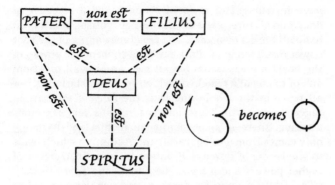

later as a whole body. When this occurs, he bears the orb, denoting power over the world. God the Son, more easily represented through the incarnations as Jesus Christ, is seen early in art, as a lamb, fish or vine, but mostly simply as the cross, since the cross of sacrifice denoted the uncommitted power of God transfixed by the Word. It was only in the 5th century that the crucified Christ and his suffering on the cross was represented; moreover, until the 11th century Christ was always portrayed clothed.

The Holy Spirit was always represented by a dove – the fiery dove of Pentecost, sign of reconciliation between God and man. As the embodiment of innocence and love, it rays forth its power at the baptism of Christ, at the Annunciation, and at the creation of the world, whilst in the church building it is found over the baptismal font and over the altar. When the Holy Spirit was represented anthropomorphically, a scroll was held in the hand, denoting the Book of Life, the destiny of man, though such representation was forbidden as sacrilegious by a papal edict early in the 17th century. The Holy Spirit was also represented, by biblical reference, as cloven tongues of fire.

The three aspects of the Trinity are found throughout nature. In the archetypal tree (tri), for instance, there is an interflow between the three parts – root, trunk and leaves. Energy drawn in through the root rises up the trunk in the form of the sap, and nourishes the flower and leaves. Correspondingly, man consists of will, feeling and thinking and ideally is a perfect reflection of the Holy Trinity, but he has been made imperfect by the fall and abuses his powers. The root power is biased towards sexuality, the heart is directed towards self-love, the head has become a

191

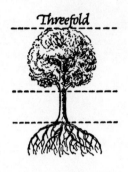

Threefold

mere instrument of rational thought and a recorder of data, and all three are at the behest of egotism, man's need to do all for his own gain. The true functioning of the root power results in immediate action of tremendous power; of the heart a compassion for all men and for all creation; and of the head a true logic which sees the relationship of all parts in the whole and thus the folly of separation. Since a man's will, heart, and head have a complex inter-working, there is much confusion in him and harmony only comes from a re-appraisal and retraining which leads to singleness of intent – an intent to be an instrument of higher powers and a true reflection of the Three in One. ('Thy Will be done in Earth as it is in Heaven'.) The blessing (q.v.) made by the thumb and two fingers is a symbol of the Trinity, and represents such a connection between God and man.

TRIPTYCH

Greek *triptykhos*, literally, 'three-folds', *tri*, 'three' and *ptykhē*, 'layer, fold'. A carving or painting done on three panels, especially meant to serve as a reredos and thus found immediately behind the altar. It is sometimes called an 'altar-piece'. Its three-foldness symbolises the Holy Trinity.

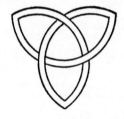

TRIQUETRA

Latin feminine of *triquetrus* (*tri*, 'three' and *quetrus*, 'sharp, pointed'). It is an ornament found on very early northern monuments, as in Celtic crosses, formed of three interlacing almond shapes and symbolising the Trinity.

TRUMPET

Middle English *trumpe*, French *trompe*, derived from Latin *triumphus*, 'triumph' and Greek *thriambos*, 'procession to Bacchus'.

In Church iconography, angels are often seen blowing trumpets (seemingly inapposite instruments compared to the gentler harp with which they also associated). This is because the sound of the trumpet symbolises the ruthlessness of the Day of Judgement and the final triumph of good over evil. It is 'the last trump'; and as in the card game where the trump card is left face upwards for all to see, all will be revealed and each being consigned to his own place according to his works. Thus the words in Matthew, 'and he shall send his angels with a trumpet and a great voice, and they shall gather his elect ...'

The seven trumpet calls in the Apocalypse (q.v.) announce the stages of liberation from the lower forces in the unveiling process, and indicate the importance of sound in the higher worlds.

TUDOR PERIOD

The period following on the Perpendicular and roughly equated with the first half of the 16th century – 1485 to 1558. The style was a continuation of the Perpendicular, plus the revived classical forms which had spread through French in the spirit of the Renaissance. The craftsmen of the Gothic tradition worked under the guidance of classically trained and orientated artists. Much of this style is to be found in domestic architecture but ecclesiastical tombs and monuments have clear indications of the grafting process.

TYMPANUM

Latin from Greek *tympanon*, 'kettle-drum', from *typtein*, 'to strike'. In Greek archtecture, a tympanum is the area of the triangular recessed face of a pediment at the end of a building: in medieval cathedrals it is the space between the lintel and the arch over doorways. In whichever period, there is the image of the tension of the skin of the drum, an image that has passed also into the naming of the membrane of the ear. In Greece, the tension was between

Greece

Ely, circa 1140

the opposing forces of energy and reason, of earth (base of triangle) and sun forces pulling upwards (point of triangle): in temples the space was covered with richly decorated sculpture and was recognised as the crowning achievement of the building. In the medieval cathedral, the tension was between the inertia of the earth and the aspiring spirit, a characteristic of the cathedral as a whole (see 'cathedral'). It is also a characteristic of any true religious process, where the aim of the free spirit is to become reconciled to the physical cage by which it is constrained. On the Continent, the main west door of cathedrals has a tympanum, invariably with the theme of the Last Judgement, the summing up of the work done, and here, as in Greece, the sculpture was the pride of the cathedral. Though tympani are found in small churches, with one or two exceptions they are not a feature of English cathedrals. (See 'pediment'.)

U

UNCIAL

Latin *uncialis*, 'to do with an ounce or an inch'. St. Jerome referred to very large letters of ancient biblical scripts by the words 'litterae unciales': the term refers now to such capitals, though not necessarily an inch high, used by the Greeks for inscriptions and sacred writings of importance. They are different in character from normal capitals and are found in biblical texts of the 4th to the 9th centuries. It was only in the 9th century that a smaller 'cursive' script (cursive means 'running together') was used in the writing of texts.

UNCTION

Latin *unctio*, 'anointing with oil'; consecrated olive oil used in certain rites for the healing of maladies, physical or spiritual; and in the Roman and Orthodox Churches, 'extreme unction' is the applying of oil to the physical body of the dying – eyes, ears, nose, mouth, hands, feet and thighs (seven in all, the first five being the organs of the senses).

The power of oil is inherent in the term 'Christ'. Its function is a healing one, since on the material plane it is the counterpart of love. Everywhere it eliminates friction and its application is an act of love and reconciliation between God and man. The ritual of anointing consecrates or makes holy, as in the consecration of a new church: its symbolism is universal, and still pertains today in the Coronation ceremony.

UNDERCROFT

Croft is from Old High German *chruft*, which is from Latin *crupta, crypta*, whence 'crypt'. Thus the same meaning as crypt – a vaulted room under a church.

UNICORN

Latin *unus*, 'one' and *cornus*, 'animal horn'; the one-horned mythical beast represented in medieval Christian art. It is traditionally said to lay itself down at the feet of a virgin, and in art the unicorn and the virgin are frequently seen together. This is because it is a symbol, through the horn that screws itself into a single point, of the pure undivided will from which the duality of the world has been expunged. As the world was born of the Virgin Mary, (literally the pure sea, the sea of substance) and Christ was born of the Virgin Mary, so the Christ-state in all men is attained through the purification of the body – that is a reversal of values normally committed to the senses. Only after such a birth can the will become single in its submission to the Will of God.

In heraldry, the lion and unicorn are the well known supporters of the English shield, but the unicorn was only introduced in 1603. At this date, James VI of Scotland caused one of the two unicorns which were the supporters of the Scottish shield, to supplant the Red Dragon of Wales.

URN

Latin *urna*, 'pitcher'. It is a vessel which contained the ashes of the dead in Roman times. The urn was re-introduced in art at the Renaissance and is often found in church monuments.

USE

Latin *usus*, 'custom, usage'. A 'use' is ecclesiastically a particular liturgy established in early Christianity in this country. Upon Augustine arriving in England and finding the country already Christianised, the conflict arose as to whether to adopt the prevailing liturgy or to impose his own Roman use. Pope Gregory's response indicated compromise in the words – 'instil this [the compromise] into the minds of the Angels for their use'.

Thus the term 'Augustine's new use' is basically the British liturgy. Later bishops attempted to re-affirm the Roman liturgy, each according to his preference. Thus, the Use of York, Exeter, Lincoln, etc. The Sarum Use, formulated in 1085 at Salisbury, replaced many of the original ones, and in 1549 the Book of Common Prayer affirmed only one 'use' in the whole realm.

V

VAULT

Low Latin *vulta* or *voluta*, from past participle of Latin *volvere*, 'to roll'. Thus the image of an arch or a series of arches as in a vaulted ceiling; and also the image of the vault as a leap which has the same arched form. The other vault with an arched roof found in churches is the underground chamber containing coffins.

VESTRY

Latin *vestiarium*, 'cupboard for clothes, chest', from *vestis*, 'garment, clothing', from Greek and Sanskrit roots. A room attached to a church where the vestments of the clergy and liturgical vestments are put on: it is also used for conducting Church business. In a cathedral it is called a sacristy (q.v.).

VICAR

Latin *vicarius*, 'a deputy, substitute'. This term was brought about at the Dissolution of the Monasteries when many of the tithes, customarily the right of the rector, were sold off. The vicar of a parish is technically one who has been appointed in place of a rector and who has no right to the payment of these tithes. Presently, the term vicar is loosely used to mean the incumbent of a parish, or any man in holy orders.

VINE

Vinum, 'vine', from a root *vī*, 'to bend, twine', as in *viere*, 'to bend or twist'. The symbol of the vine and the vine leaf is found frequently in Christian art, because of Christ's words 'I am the true vine ...'.

The vine, in the ramification of its branches, is the archetype of the Tree of Life. The blood system and nervous system of the human body, and the image of the ancestral tree, are all similar ramifications. When wine is drunk to represent the sacrificed blood of Christ at the Eucharist, each isolated man is re-affirmed as a branch of the whole spiritual tree. And the true significance of wine is also indicated.

Wine has the power to totally disorientate the mechanism of the physical body, a fact normally regarded in a negative light. In so doing, however, it also relaxes the empirical ego and reaches the essential level of a human being. Since wine has this power, it is analogous to the pure-spirit which penetrates errors of the soul to do with separativity, and reclaims him as part of the whole vine. Then he may be said to be drunk with the spirit. On both levels, without prior preparation, undiluted spirit is dangerous. it is not surprising on this account that wine is associated with the 'blood' of the Eucharist, for, on a subtle level, the blood mediates between spirit and body in a man. (See 'blessing'.)

VOLUTE

Latin *voluta*, past participle of *volvere*, 'to roll'. Thus the spiral scroll motif which figures principally in Ionic and also Corinthian capitals. It is retained in Norman capitals but was later supplanted by Early English foliage.

VIRGIN MARY

As the mother of Christ, the Virgin Mary figures prominently in Church iconography; but she is essentially the Great Mother of all mythologies. *Mary* is from Latin *mare*, 'sea', and signifies the sea or matrix from which all matter sprang.

The given etymology of the word 'virgin' is not satisfactory: Latin *virago*, 'a man-like woman', gives a clue to the real meaning of the word. Male *vir* 'man' and *gin* (Greek *gunē*, 'woman', from which genesis, begin, etc) indicate a state of oneness in the Godhead, with male and female aspects still undivided. The Virgin Mary, at this level, is the Bride of God, immaculate, unstained. But upon the male Spirit moving upon the face of the waters and the Word being made flesh, virginity in its true sense is lost. The unformed sea became substantial and formulated.

On the physical plane, this division is represented in man and woman with their physiological and psychological differences – but also having a shadow of the opposite pole in them, indicating their original androgynous (Greek 'man-woman') nature. In the ordinary meaning of the word, a virgin, either male or female, is one who has not surrendered to the external need to re-unite with the other half. The Virgin Mary of Christianity is a being untainted in this way, and thus a reflexion of the higher Mother principle (prior to creation), and a fitting vehicle for the 'descent' of God as man. This has been a condition of the birth of other divine beings, as Krishna and the Buddha. That immaculate (literally 'without stain') nature of the virgin is represented in iconography by the purity and clarity of her light blue vestments.

In the sense that all life is possible only through her, Mary, and all mothers, aim to give birth to a Christ child, for each physical body given birth contains a spirit whose end is to realise Christhood through terrestrial experience. This is why, next to Christ, the Virgin Mary is the most frequently depicted figure and regarded with the greatest reverence.

VOUSSOIR

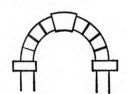

French word akin to *voute*, 'vault', and through this connection, meaning any of the wedge-shaped stones forming an arch, as above a door. The stone above the centre of the arch is called the 'key-stone'.

W

WALL PAINTING

From Norman times, much colour was used in the decorating of church walls. Norman doorways, arches and piers were all coloured in patterns similar to the pattern of the mouldings. What traces remain suggest that walls may have been covered by figures and geometric designs giving a display of colour which is hard to imagine when viewing the restored interiors of today. In the 15th century, wall paintings depicted scenes in the lives of saints and martyrs, a way of teaching a congregation unable to understand the Latin bible. After the 15th century, the primitive quality of the work, so full of feeling, disappeared under the hand of the accurate professional, a change that colours the whole of art history. White-washing, and the general destruction attendant upon the Suppression and the Commonwealth virtually destroyed all medieval wall painting. There are however notable attempts today to return, in part at least, to the original medieval colours. In restoration work, ribs and bosses, though not so much walls, have been brightly coloured to good effect.

WARMING-HOUSE or CALEFACTORY

In the claustral buildings of a monastery, the so-called warming-house was the only room where fires were permitted, though only from November until Easter. The warming house was something akin to a common-room where everyday activities could be carried out, such as tonsuring, mending of clothes, cleaning of boots, and in some cases the four times yearly blood-letting. In severe winter months, monks needed some refuge, as gardening and manual work would then be impossible. It was often situated under the dormitory.

WEATHER COCK

The weather-vane on the church spire indicates the changeableness of nature, and the cock symbolises the necessity for the spirit to keep a watchful eye, so that physical man is not blown hither and thither by every wind.

The changes in the winds are a part of the process of nature. The earth sacrifices itself in spring and summer to nourish the fruit and the flower, after which point, in autumn and winter, the created forms are sacrificed back into the earth. Thus the associations of development in the east and south winds (spring and summer) and of dying in the west and north winds (autumn and winter). (See 'cock' for its symbolism.)

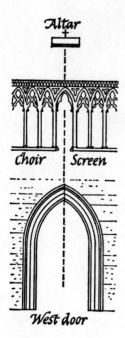

Altar

Choir | Screen

West door

WEST END

'West' is from a Germanic stem *we*, 'down', which gives Latin *vesper*, 'evening' and Greek *hesperos*, 'evening'. The orientation of the church is discussed under East. The West is a symbol of materiality, worldly values, the waters of life, as opposed to the spiritual sun of the East. It is connected with the general meaning of the word 'down', for man begins his life in the waters of the womb and then progresses to the realisation of the spirit from the experience the waters of life offer him. At the west end of the church are the stoup and font, both containing water, and the nave, the ship on the waters, whilst at the east end is the window allowing in the light of the rising sun. Thus the two poles in man, female and male, matter and spirit, are embodied in the form of the church. The journey between these poles is also symbolised in the great west door of the cathedral, which, when opened, aligns through the small gateway of the choir screen to the altar in the sanctuary. (See 'East'.)

WHEEL-WINDOW

A name for the rose-window (q.v.) usually found on the west face of a cathedral and so called because of the spokes raying from the centre. The image of the wheel affirms the significance of the rose as a symbol of development: it is the wheel of life which moves men round inexorably, in order that the truth of the spirit (the East) may dawn in them. Generally, wheels in sculpture and painting in medieval times are such wheels of Fortune, pointing out the vicissitudes of human life.

WINDOW

Middle English *windowe*, from Old Norwegian *vindauga* (*vind*, 'wind' and *auga*, 'eye'). The original function of the glassless window was to keep out the elements and to let in light, as the two parts of the word indicate. Thus the thick windows of early churches were splayed so as to allow in as much light as possible. Because of this, in monastic settlements and Norman churches, religious images or decorations were perforce on the walls. It could be said that the inner light of the hermit had no need of the outer light of the world, and that conversely, as worship became more externalised, the external light penetrated

200

the darkness until in the great cathedrals the interior was filled with the light from an expanse of multi-coloured windows. (See 'stained glass'.)

In the cathedrals, the transition from the simple openings of the late 12th century to the great spaces of the middle 16th century is reflected in the different styles of tracery (q.v.) which correspond broadly to different architectural periods. The following names are used to describe this tracery:

Lancet style with 'plate tracery' – circa 1190–1245
Geometric style with 'perfect tracery' – circa 1245–1315
Curvilinear style with 'flowing tracery' – circa 1315–1360
Rectilinear style with 'perpendicular tracery' – circa 1360–1550.

The last three of these are all forms of 'bar' tracery as opposed to plate tracery. (See 'tracery' for an explanation of this and for illustrations.)

In the first three there is considerable overlapping. Lancet, Geometric and Rectilinear do not exactly correspond with Early English and Decorated in architectural style. But the last, the 'perpendicular' tracery, is common to our parish churches and is accepted to span from the middle of the 14th to the 16th centuries. The most perfect tracery belongs to the geometric style with its simple circles and trefoils: here space and bar line are equally balanced.

WINE

See 'vine'.

WISDOM

From 'wis' and 'dom'. Middle English *wis*, from Old High German *wis*, 'wise', from an Aryan base 'to see': *dom* is an abbreviation of *dominus* 'Lord'. Thus, 'the wisdom or insight of the Lord'. In man, wisdom is the transcending of personal knowledge, the true end of religion, when the vision of man has become one with that of God.

WOOD-CARVING

Wood-carving in medieval churches did not assert its individual qualities until towards the end of the 14th century. The early work that has survived has no character and merely copies the stone mason's work in the tracery of windows. Decorations, with feeling for wood itself, developed in the 13th century with beautifully worked stalls, screens, bench ends, font-covers, pulpits and so on. Whereas the 13th and 14th centuries were the domain of the stone worker, the 15th was the domain of the wood-carver. At the same time, carpentry in the construction of roofs reached a peak in the 15th century with the arch brace, the beam and the hammer, whilst panelled roofs had beautifully carved bosses. Such excellence of wood-craft can be seen especially in the north of Britain, as at York, Beverley and Ripon, executed during the years 1490–1520, and equally in churches over the whole of Devon.

Carved screenwork and rood-lofts holding the cross all suffered irrevocably throughout the country at the time of the Suppression.

WYVERN or WIVERN

Middle English *wivers*, 'serpent', Latin *vipera*, 'viper'. A fabulous animal used heraldically, usually shown with wings, head and tail of a scorpion, and two legs.

Y

YEW

Old English *ēow*, from Old High German *iwa*, 'yew'. The Latin for yew, *taxus*, is related to Greek *toxon*, 'bow', because the yew was the finest wood for bow-making. It is also related to *toxicon*, 'poison', because the arrows of the primitive Greeks were tipped with poison.

The yew is traditionally the tree of death, and is found growing in churchyards – yet the sound of the word and nature of the tree itself (the affirmative 'y' and the length of life of the tree) suggest the opposite. It is an evergreen and lives to a longer age than the oak, some in Britain reputedly being between two and three thousand years old. Also, when polished, the wood has a capacity for resisting natural processes of decay. Thus in European legend, though it is the tree of death, there is also the aspect of immortality. As in all symbols, opposite faces are seen together, and to the Druids the yews near their temples denoted eternal life following physical death.

Z

ZIG-ZAG

A type of moulding of zig-zag pattern used particularly in Norman architecture. (See 'chevron'.)